Sexual Visions

Science and Literature

A series edited by George Levine

Sexual Visions

Images of Gender in Science and Medicine
between the Eighteenth and Twentieth Centuries

LUDMILLA JORDANOVA

The University of Wisconsin Press

The University of Wisconsin Press
114 North Murray Street
Madison, Wisconsin 53715

Printed in Great Britain

ISBN 0-299-12290-5

For Karl, with love.

Infinite Nature, where can I grasp you? How?
Where are you breasts, those fountains that maintain
all life throughout the Universe,
at which the parched soul slakes its thirst?
You flow and gush: why do I thirst in vain?

Goethe, *Faust*, Part I

Man seeks in woman the Other of Nature and as his fellow
being. But we know what ambivalent feelings Nature inspires in
man.

de Beauvoir, *The Second Sex*

Contents

Plates

Preface and Acknowledgements

On the surface, academic life appears profoundly individualistic; indeed, powerful institutional and psychic structures work to reinforce this. Yet I am continually struck by the necessarily collective endeavour in which we are engaged. The notion that ideas are private property has always seemed strange to me, especially since the most enjoyable aspects of intellectual work are those that are social – teaching, learning, and talking to colleagues and friends. This fact has one unfortunate consequence: it is impossible to either name or remember all the people who have shaped a particular piece of work. By way of compensation, however, there is the pleasure gained from offering thanks, even if it is directed in a less than focused way to 'all who have helped'. I know that my students, and those who have patiently listened and responded to seminars and lectures, have, like my colleagues, family and friends, given me help and encouragement beyond my capacity to describe. For the sheer pleasure I have received from those in whose company it has been possible to think, I am deeply grateful.

I owe a special debt to my colleagues in the Department of Art History and Theory at the University of Essex, who have supplied me with numerous references and answered my questions with unfailing kindness. In addition, I am indebted to a small number of friends for their fellowship, advice and support over a number of years, in particular Joyce Appleby, Gillian Beer, Catherine Belsey, Leonore Davidoff, Marcia Pointon, Roger Smith and Marilyn Strathern. I have also received generous assistance in the preparation of this book from Michael Bevan, John Christie, Simon Collier, George Custen, Elaine Jordan, Ornella Moscucci, Lee Quinby, Sally Shuttleworth and Ellen Todd. Some of these people commented on an earlier draft of the book: their comments and criticisms have been extremely valuable to me.

This book owes its existence to Edward Elgar, and I thank him for his friendly insistence. The current staff at Harvester Wheatsheaf, especially Farrell Burnett, have been more than helpful; their enthusiasm has made the last stages of completing it an enjoyable experience.

I have relied heavily on the library of the Wellcome Institute for the History of Medicine, London, and the library at the University of Essex, especially the Inter-library Loan Department. I wish to record my thanks to the staff at both these institutions. I am also grateful to the staff of the Special Collections Department, Tompkins-McCaw Library at the Virginia Commonwealth University, the State Archives and the Richmond Historical Society, all of Richmond, Virginia, and of the Prints and Photographs Department, National Library of Medicine, Bethesda, Maryland, for their courtesy and generosity. The research carried out in the United States was supported by a travel grant from the Wellcome Trust and by a research grant from the Royal Society. I thank both these organizations most warmly. Support from the Nuffield Foundation for a related project on the eighteenth-century family has assisted in the work for *Sexual Visions*, so my gratitude also goes to this agency.

Chapters 2 and 6 are revised versions of essays that have appeared in print previously. I appreciate the willingness of both Cambridge University Press and Free Association Books to give their permission to use them here. The full details of the earlier publications are cited elsewhere. All the other chapters have been given as seminar papers or lectures either in Britain or the United States and have therefore benefited from comments and discussion on those occasions. Gavin Ewart gave his kind permission for me to quote from one of his poems; the full citation is in the appropriate footnote.

I am well aware that authors cannot determine readers' responses; none the less, I would like to explain how I hope the book will be read. It is not intended to be a monograph for specialists but an accessible exploration of a set of closely related themes. Each chapter approaches these themes from a different perspective and hence has its own distinctive characteristics. Although the chapters are loosely in chronological order, and refer to one another, it is possible to read them as separate essays if desired. I have put the footnotes together at the back, but hope that the text can stand alone, without demanding constant movement to the notes. Full references are given in the Bibliography, an abbreviated system of reference being used in the Notes.

I also wish to record my thanks to the staff of the day nursery at the University of Essex, and especially to Linda Piercy and also to the following friends whose contributions to the well-being of myself and my family have been considerable: Joan Busfield, Jenny Newman, Michael and Rosemary Bevan, Lindsay and Paul Spendlove. Finally, I dedicate this book to Karl Figlio, with a vivid sense of my inability to put into words all he is to me.

Ludmilla Jordanova
Colchester, Essex

1

Introduction

Ivan Turgenev's masterpiece *Fathers and Sons* (1861) concerns the scientifically and medically gifted Bazarov. He is a nihilist who is enthused by German science, fond of dissection and destined for a life as a country doctor. Committed above all to rational enquiry, he has the misfortune to fall in love. The cold man of science is confronted by feminine warmth. His initial response to the woman in question summarizes his world-view: "'What a magnificent body!" Barazov pursued. "Shouldn't I like to see it on the dissecting-table!"'[1] What are the social and cultural preconditions of such a statement? What allows readers to grasp his point about the encounter between a man thirsty for knowledge of nature and a desirable woman? *Sexual Visions* is an attempt to answer such questions. The constellation of ideas that the novel gives voice to was not peculiar to Turgenev's time; it has a long history and enjoys continued vitality. It reaches deep into the scientific enterprise and into Western culture; it invites our serious attention.

This book is concerned with the biological and medical sciences between the eighteenth and the twentieth centuries. It focuses not on scientific research, nor on professionalization or theory formation, but on the cultural presence of these fields with respect to a particular theme: gender. The basic subject-matter of my work is twofold; first, the extensive writings about and depictions of the differences between men and women, and of sexuality, in scientific and medical contexts; and second, the assumptions such writings contain about the gendered character of natural knowledge.

I concentrate here on the culture of science, since the themes just mentioned manifest themselves in imagery of all kinds – traditionally the province of the cultural historian – and also, they slip continually between literature, political theory, art, natural history, medicine, law, social commentary and so on. These key themes may properly be described as cultural because they were not exclusive to one domain; they were resources, generally available as images and clusters of ideas. We are now more fully aware of the social dimensions of cultural phenomena. The social context that produces and sustains beliefs, ideas and art forms is central, yet to do justice to the full complexity and depth of imagery, methods are required that give primacy to the task of drawing out the implications, ramifications and resonances of dense concepts, such as nature and gender, and to the analysis of visual artefacts. The goal of a rich cultural history must be to extend the understanding we derive from social history in order to come to terms with the power of images.

Inevitably there are numerous assumptions behind my project, many of which cannot be fully articulated. However, I endeavour to make explicit as many of them as possible. A central tenet of my research has long been the belief that scientific and medical ideas can be understood as mediations. By this I mean that they speak to and contain implications about matters beyond their explicit content. Although it is customary to use the term 'ideology' in this context, I find this somewhat unsatisfactory, largely because it has strong pejorative connotations which are hard to purge, and because its recent overuse by historians has usually suggested the articulation, in a veiled form, of the interests of well-defined social groupings. I use 'mediation' as a general, flexible term which is intended to carry no moral or political overlay but rather to draw attention to the intricate transformations and multiple meanings of fundamental ideas in our cultural traditions. Just as we now recognize natural philosophy in the seventeenth century to have mediated religious and political conflict, so did the biomedical sciences of the eighteenth and nineteenth centuries mediate sex roles, gender differences and social stability.[2]

All discourses have the property of being mediatiors, although the precise resonances and meanings, like the domains mediated, are always historically specific. It does not follow from this approach that science and medicine are determined by economic-cum-social forces. There is no attempt here to 'reduce' one kind of historical phenomenon to another, or to impose a rigid hierarchy upon different categories of historical materials. Although I believe that some elements in social and cultural life are more fundamental than others from a psychic point of view, such elements cannot be placed in a sequence from which causal or explanatory priorities are derived. It seems worthwhile to leave such questions open, to think in terms of distinct levels or registers, yet to avoid placing these in an ordered sequence, which gives explanatory priority to pre-assigned categories.

An interest in the mediating properties of science and medicine gives rise to a related preoccupation with levels. I use the term 'levels' to signal that ideas, institutions, classes, and so on, have distinctive characteristics, whilst being at the same time related to one another. It is now readily recognized that conceptual systems and material conditions are different types of entities, that they change at different paces and function in different ways. To say this does not imply that either is autonomous, it merely indicates an appreciation of their particular characteristics. This enables historical work to become more subtle and it discourages us from conflating phenomena that are recognizably distinct.

Along with this recognition of 'level' as a helpful term, must go the realization that there are some aspects of human life that touch people more deeply than others, because these vary in the extent to which they inform social relations. Gender is one of these profound dimensions, since for all children, as for all societies, it is constitutive of basic identity. I see no way in which such a claim can be 'proved'; rather, it is an indispensable starting-point for the historical study of femininity and masculinity. Anthropologists have stressed the cross-cultural diversity with respect to sexual difference in theory and in practice; historians, similarly, can show how a recurrent preoccupation with an issue takes on a myriad of forms.[3]

The use of gender to mean social and cultural (as opposed to biological) sexual identity and the development of analyses of the dialectical manner in which sex roles and sexuality work, are relatively recent. The word 'gender' implies that masculine and feminine attributes are always defined in relation to each other, although its precise value for feminist scholarship is currently the subject of debate. None the less, it admirably fulfils a long-felt need for a term that always refuses a simple biological or essentialist understanding of male and female. Men and women may be born with different reproductive organs, but societies make femininity and masculinity along with the norms that determine who meets the criteria of womanhood and manhood at any particular time and place and for a specific social group. By the same token, sexuality is socially constructed.[4] We can never take terms like 'sexual', 'masculine' or 'feminine' as either stable or self-evident. The job of the historian is precisely to recover the fragile and fleeting significances they take on. At the same time, however, there are striking historical continuities, held in place partly through the language of myth, literature and art, as well as of law, politics and kinship. To say that something is socially constructed does not make it inherently evanescent, it merely signals that we are speaking not of a (natural) given but of a (human) construct. Determining the terms under which artefacts are constructed is a vital part of understanding them. Continuity and change are equally central to this task.

Gender is, of course, one such construct. Like the whole constellation of 'keywords' around it, gender is a composite idea. These terms have an almost organic existence, changing layers of meaning in the same way as geological strata are newly deposited, broken up and destroyed.[5] They are also composites because there can be no pure, contained definition of them, for this is only possible in the case of highly arcane terms in restricted use, not of those whose boundaries are constantly shifting. It is because gender touches on so many aspects of our lives, directly or by metaphorical extension, that it deserves detailed historical study. It is particularly important that historians of science and medicine take on the challenge of rethinking their fields in terms of gender.[6]

The reasons for this are the main concerns of *Sexual Visions*. First, what we recognize as gender stands as a putatively natural fact. It has been deemed a part of nature, and therefore as apt for scientific and medical scrutiny. We now perceive more readily that what appears natural is in fact a social-cum-cultural construct. Second, many different branches of the natural and medical sciences have focused their attention on the phenomenon of sex. It is therefore an area we must consider if we are to do full justice to the historical record. Furthermore, virtually all the sciences have employed ideas of sexual polarity; gender as a metaphor has had an exceptionally vigorous life in natural knowledge. Third, the very terms in which knowledge, nature and science are understood are suffused with gender, partly through the tendency, of ancient origin, to personify them, and partly because, as a result of personification, we think of the processes by which knowledge is acquired as deeply sexual.

It would be mistaken, however, to suppose that the goal is merely to add an additional consideration – gender – to the history of science and medicine. There are more general matters at stake. Over the last twenty years or so historians have become aware of the need to unpack the processes through which 'naturalization' takes place, whereby ideas, theories, experiences, languages, and so on, take on the quality of being 'natural', permitting the veiling of their customary, conventional and social characteristics. Understanding such naturalization is integral to the project of delineating and explaining the precise nature of scientific and medical power.[7] Of course, this power is of many different kinds, including economic, political and technological; it varies with time and place, but it very often involves presenting phenomena – racial difference, intelligence, gender, violence – as natural and hence as having a specific form of validity. Many domains possess and deploy such naturalizing capacities; yet, although not exclusive to the scientific enterprise, the special relationship long forged between science and nature gives its naturalizing potential special significance.

It follows from what has been said that the biomedical sciences deploy, and are themselves, systems of representation. If devices like personification and metaphor have been central to scientific thinking, then the notion of representation becomes a central analytical tool for historians. It can signal a number of important assumptions: that discourses are never simple descriptions or reflections of an actual state of affairs; that their rhetoric and their use of verbal and visual devices is constitutive of their character; and that no domain can be devoid of symbolic forms.[8] If all this is granted, then a number of consequences follow for the history of science and medicine. First, these disciplines have a deeper kinship with those in the humanities, like literary criticism, than is often recognized. Second, they must acknowledge the importance of textual analysis, because scientific and medical ideas cannot be separated from the language in which they are expressed. Third, these methods must be extended to images, for they too play a central part in scientific thinking, as the medium of theories, as heuristic devices, as speculative forms, as hypotheses and as sources of pleasure. The aesthetic dimensions of science and medicine are beginning to be paid the serious attention they deserve, not to display them as cultural ornaments but to demonstrate that aesthetics is constitutive of knowledge. We can see, for example, that 'realism', used as an aesthetic rather than a philosophical term, has been important within science and medicine in defining modes of illustration, and also, conversely, that scientific and medical ideas were central to realist artistic and literary practices, especially in the nineteenth century.[9]

The working assumptions outlined above are linked with the sources used and the way they have been treated. Readers will note a certain eclecticism with respect to primary materials, which include poetry, novels, magazines, advertisements, popular didactic works, film, book illustrations, prints, drawings and paintings as well scientific and medical writings. Whereas local studies, biographies or institutionally based research all have concrete foci of one sort or another, cultural studies generally enjoy no such advantage, because they have no natural boundaries; it is impossible to confine oneself to particular materials because they are inherently central to gender since almost anything is potentially central to such a theme. Gender, being a concept and also an individual, class, and even a national experience, is integral to many different concerns. Indeed, that is its interest. Thus I have no finite, self-defining body of materials to study. And, diverse primary materials are important if we are to convey the cultural presence of science and medicine.

Historians often imagine that it is possible, by using so-called representative sources, to avoid certain interpretative difficulties. This is an illusion. How can we treat a novelist like George Eliot, an historian like Jules Michelet or an artist like Thomas Eakins as 'representative'? Their work is important precisely because it is exceptional – a point too obvious to require mention among historians of literature, art and ideas, yet most historians resist its implications. Historians can find the exceptional valuable too, so long as they do not treat it, as is so often done, as a simple reflection of the historical setting that produced it.[10] It is more productive to see such exceptional cultural products as working in specific ways with themes of general historical importance. For this reason I have endeavoured to pay careful attention to the texts themselves, while drawing out of them larger themes.

Close reading of words and images is essential if we are to understand the ways in which mediations work, since language, in its most extended sense, is their medium. In employing such a method, it is important to be clear about the kinds of claims we can reasonably make. Since the meanings of texts always go beyond the explicit intentions of authors, it can be helpful to state the extent to which conscious designs are being discussed, if these are known. However, I have generally been less concerned to attribute motives or psychological characteristics to particular authors, than to draw out the implications of their works, whether intended or not, in so far as I can see them. To an extent, therefore, my reading is knowingly present-centred. At the same time, I have tried to avoid glaring anachronisms, partly by comparing a variety of texts with one another.

The multiple ways in which languages function are also at issue here. Writers and artists use devices, both consciously and unconsciously, which already carry complex historical and philosophical baggage. They respond to changes in ideas and language and also initiate such changes. A relatively small number of 'keywords' have been central to both the linguistic richness and conceptual complexity of scientific and medical discourses. Accordingly, there are a limited number of concepts to which I shall repeatedly return in what follows. These are of three main kinds. First, there are single terms of such outstanding significance, and with such a wide range of application, like 'nature', 'knowledge' and the vocabulary associated with sight, looking, vision and light, that they demand extensive analysis. Second, there are the binary oppositions; male/female, public/private, nature/culture, and so on, that have exercised great sway over the structures of Western thought. Paired terms work in special ways, a matter I have tried to explore. Here I want to emphasize, however, that we should be fully critical of dichotomous styles of thinking, not least in order to appreciate why they hold sway over us, and to discover the nature of their dominance. To discuss the ways in which they functioned in the past is emphatically not to endorse their general validity. The third category consists of current terms that are useful in historical analysis, such as gender, otherness, role, body image and realism.

I referred above to the existence of different levels in past societies that demand appropriate distinct analytical modes. The abstract nature of some of the following arguments can partly be explained in terms of these levels. The vast majority of the sources I have used deliberately pitched their arguments or images at an abstract level, and it is therefore necessary for the historian to respond by taking this seriously. The work of the French historian Jules Michelet, discussed in Chapter 4, is an excellent example of this. He revelled in terms like 'Woman', that global, universalizing idea of which nineteenth-century commentators were particularly fond. It is necessary to treat such abstractions seriously. They cannot be resolved into more limited components; indeed, they firmly resisted such resolution. The notion of 'Woman', although often used in ways that presupposed a specific class, conveyed the idea that all women, irrespective of class, race, creed or age, did indeed share certain essential characteristics. Of course, historians should not take such claims at face value, and should lay bare the assumptions such terms conceal. None the less, their generality is an important feature of the way they functioned and hence requires its own kind of historical account.

There are two further reasons why attending to an abstract level is important. First, it is a cardinal tenet of natural philosophical, scientific and medical thinking that it searches for a high degree of generality. The vast majority of writings on sex differences and sexuality were rooted in the search for lawlike statements which displayed male and female as natural facts. Second, the differences between men and women have long been thought about in our culture in terms of myth. 'Myth', by definition, and like 'science', enjoys general, abstract status. It lies beyond the here and now, having a special permit to tell specific stories that have general application. Christian, Greek,

Roman, and Pagan myths are central to the dominant ideas of gender in the history of Western European society. They are ever-present exemplifications of beliefs so deeply entrenched that enquiring about their origins seems fruitless. Although myths can be vehicles of ideologies, they are far more than this, in that, as stories about human doings, they are overtly powerful and emotionally dense. In this respect they differ from ideologies.[11]

Myths are always changing and new ones are constantly being added to our repertoire. Hence, to speak in terms of myth need not imply an ahistoricity of any kind, because myths are perpetually put to work in different, historically shifting ways. There is considerable suspicion among English-speaking historians of anything that is not firmly rooted in particular circumstances. Currently, the search for certain kinds of historical specificity, like that furnished by local studies, is so great that it seems necessary to show that abstract and general analyses can still be thoroughly historical. Of course, it is true that a number of recent trends in the humanities, and particularly in literary criticism, have proved in practice to be ahistorical, even anti-historical. Much of value can none the less be learnt from them that can be put to work in the service of a richer historiography. The rise to prominence of social history over the last two decades has encouraged the drive towards what I would call misplaced concreteness. This has involved a hostility towards theory, a naïve use of sources as directly descriptive documents, and the belief that particularity is somehow inherently superior to and more certain than generality. Although these trends are now less marked than they once were, the larger problem remains of historians' hostility to those traditions which take the analysis of ideas seriously. At the same time, the British intellectual scene, in marked contrast to North America, has never had much time either for intellectual history or the history of ideas. Much that goes under that name is now in any case more philosophical than historical and impinges little on run-of-the-mill history.[12] Generalizations and a degree of speculation are inevitable in historical writings about ideas and culture, and statistical underpinnings or direct archival support for such work may not be available.

Some of the topics touched on in the pages that follow have been much written about in recent years. The pre-eminent example of this is sexuality, around which there has been an astonishing deluge of literature.[13] *Sexual Visions* is not a work about 'sexuality', although it inevitably touches upon it. The recent secondary literature on sexuality has a number of important characteristics not shared by this book. Numerous recent publications have been heavily influenced by Foucault, many chart the development of attitudes towards what has been deemed 'deviant' sexuality, while others start from an elaborate theoretical position about sexuality, often influenced by Lacanian psychoanalysis. Sadly, academic voyeurism also plays its part in this literature – a fact that is much to be regretted. One only has to think of the historical work of Edward Shorter, which explicitly invites readers to imagine past sexual practices and female pathological conditions, to demonstrate the point.[14]

Sometimes, however, the voyeuristic position strikes rather close to home. Consider, for example, Paula Weideger's recent book *History's Mistress*. It is a selection of extracts from a well-known book on women, first published in 1885 by a German gynaecologist, Ploss, and finally made available in English in 1935 as *Woman: An Historical Gynaecological and Anthropological Compendium*. Weideger has chosen extracts from this work, provided an introduction and included a number of illustrations. Initially we note the suggestive title – chosen, according to the editor 'to keep reminding the reader . . . that this text is . . . one in which will be found only that part of woman's history that was attractive to the men who sought it out'. She calls the men who compiled the book over successive editions 'scholar-hunters who tracked down and recorded many wonderful and curious facts'. They hunted down the 'woman' of the title, and were 'terribly attracted' to her.[15] In the introduction Weideger imagines the original authors waxing lyrical about their work during after-dinner conversations about breasts. Her *fictional* scenario is supposedly to make the point that the thirty-two photographs of breasts in the 1935 English edition are included for prurient reasons. Yet the way she makes the point, her chosen title and the whole presentation of the book, serve to heighten any sense of titillation in readers and buyers.

History's Mistress is an affirmation rather than a critique of the very position Weideger purports to challenge. Alternative strategies were available and they include a careful study of the nature of the book and its circumstances of production in order to understand the project it represented. In particular, the mixture of natural history, medicine and anthropology, by no means unusual in the second half of the nineteenth century, demands detailed examination. Weideger assumes that the subject-matter of the book is self-explanatory, and that the motives behind its inception are equally clear. As historians we need to know why gynaecologists in particular, turned to anthropology, and what systems of meaning they used to frame their principles of collection and interpret their main findings.[16] Since Weideger wants to claim these as data for present-day women's history, she has no interest in asking questions about the construction of gender at a particular time and place. *Woman* is never located historically, a point which applies equally to the pictures. Ploss's book touches on numerous themes that are central to *Sexual Visions*, and Weideger's treatment of it can be used to point up some general historiographical issues.

All the editions of *Woman* are complex texts, composed of distinct kinds of discourse. To make sense, these have to be read against a historical context. This can only be done if we eschew facile assumptions about the motivations of the authors, especially with respect to their prurience. This is not to deny that they may have been so motivated, only that this needs to be established and then put to work as a significant feature of the text. Equally, to treat such a work as a source book for the late twentieth century seems naïve to say the least. We should come away from a study of Ploss's enterprise with a sense of what medical practitioners were doing in this period in relation to the construction of gender and the role that newly emerging domains like anthropology were playing in medical thinking. This could form the basis of a cultural history of the intersections between gender and medicine at that time. While we must recognize that a historically satisfying account of these matters cannot be given at the present time, when research into these areas is in its early stages, it is none the less important to cultivate a sense of what a new historiography might look like. This vision is essential if the shortcomings of much recent work on sexuality and gender are to be overcome.

Numerous reasons lie behind the recent explosion of scholarly interest in sexuality. Prominent among them is a preoccupation

with authenticity, which has been of particular importance within
the gay liberation movements. The concern has broad implications
since it is linked with a general trend towards thinking of sexuality
as central to human identity. Once this is assumed, the history
of how the identities of individuals and groups are formed takes
on new significance, especially if these have at some point in time
been defined as 'deviant'. There are two radically different styles
of historical scholarship in this area. The first seeks ways of
reconstructing historically what people actually did using civil
and church court records, private papers, data on illegitimacy,
and so on. In this way, it is thought, the 'real' experiences of
people in the past can be captured, and the past is often recovered
to form legitimating antecedents to the present.[17] The second
style, indebted to Foucault, studies discourses rather than
behaviour, on the grounds that the important issues in the history
of sexuality consist not of who did what but of who said what,
of the power relations embodied in discourses.[18] Both approaches
have their limitations. The former entertains an illusion about the
possibility of knowing about sexuality in past societies. Since all
records are accounts of something historians cannot know directly,
they must be treated accordingly and cannot be used as direct
records or reflections of earlier societies; there is no such privileged
path to the past. The latter approach avoids this problem by
focusing on discourses, but it tends to hover in an overly abstract
vacuum above specific historical circumstances, and fails to give
its favourite concept, 'power', a sufficiently vivid, graspable
presence. Although it is sometimes claimed that 'power' is
concretely embodied in and through historical circumstances, in
practice many analyses inspired by Foucault concentrate on
'power' in the abstract and hence lose sight of its complex material
manifestations. Such a split is unfortunate.

The theme of the search for authentic sexual identity is an
important, if not a new one. Montesquieu had a eunuch declare
in the *Persian Letters* (1721), that castration meant 'to be separated
from myself forever'.[19] This idea, that the core of a person's
identity is sexual, has been widely held at least since the eighteenth
century and has informed many scholarly accounts, especially
those of the history of male homosexuality. It is not necessary
to espouse such a position for the history of sexuality to be an
important field. I make no deliberate assumptions on this issue

beyond that already noted, namely that gender is fundamental to individual development, to human cultures and to social formations. Of course, such a formulation leaves open the relationship between gender and sexuality.

Gender is the more inclusive category since it includes areas of life where the difference between masculine and feminine is important yet not directly linked to sexual expression and experience. Whereas 'sexuality' implies the experience of sexual feelings, 'gender' can be applied to anything. Furthermore, if 'authenticity' is a guiding term, there is always a danger of Whiggishness, of searching the past for the appropriate precursors of contemporary modes of identity. Whilst clearly we cannot escape from our own context, there are ways of working which make unhelpful present-centredness more likely, and the preoccupation with authenticity is one of them. This is partly because it has a covert moral dimension: to attribute authenticity to a person or an object is to endow them with superior status.

More recently, the interest in sexuality has given rise to a fascination with 'the body'. To some extent such a shift was inevitable as many practices related to the control of sexuality functioned through attempts to regulate physiological processes. Foucault and many others have shown how the biomedical sciences played a special role in this respect – a role which included dealing with such matters as masturbation, birth control, abortion, sex-specific diseases, childbirth and so on.[20] Of necessity, human bodies were the medium through which sexual matters were represented and explored, and hence all the domains in which the body played a role have been central to the history of sexuality. Furthermore, some Western European traditions have indeed treated the body as a general category. Fine art practices are a good example, since it is clearly possible to speak of the norms applied to the representation of 'the female body' and 'the male body' at a given time and place, and to trace the theoretical debates artists engaged in about the essential characteristics of such bodies.[21] It does not, however, follow from this that we are entitled to use 'the body' as an unqualified abstraction. The phrase, 'the making of the modern body', to take the title of a recent book, and the claim that 'the human body itself has a history', from the same book, make little sense unless elaborately glossed.[22] I presume the title was modelled on that of Edward

Shorter's controversial book *The Making of the Modern Family*, where 'the family' can be justified by referring to the ubiquity of the phrase in modern parlance. Here is an abstraction of a quite different kind, since we deploy it constantly, knowingly and in a variety of ways.[23] This cannot be said of 'the body', which does not carry a similar ideological load and always demands further specification.

There is a notable asymmetry at work in terms like 'gender' and 'the body' as a result of which we as scholars, like the writers and artists we study, focus more on women than on men. It is not just, as Joan Scott observes, that historians of women talk about gender because it sounds more respectable, less 'biased', but that the very idea of gender leads more directly to women than to men.[24] The reasons for this are formidably complex. By a variety of means we have come to see women as the problematic sex, indeed as *the* sex. They are, as many feminists have noted, seen as relative to men who become the central term, the norm, against which women, as the deviations or variations, must be assessed. Strange as it may sound, we focus on notions like gender both in order to show how male and female are mutually defined and to pay particular attention to the feminine side of the dichotomy as that which has generally been construed as the more problematic.[25]

It is because of this asymmetry that the idea of otherness has seemed especially apt in relation to women. Woman is other to man, as Simone de Beauvoir argued; yet to unpack fully what such a statement implies is difficult. Although the idea now has general currency, it is best established in the fields of philosophy and anthropology.[26] The term helps us to think about the ways in which groups and individuals distance themselves from each other, often by unconscious means. Such separating devices are only needed, however, when the two parties involved are also deeply bound together, implicated in each other's characteristics. Otherness, then, conveys the kinship, the fascination and the repulsion between distinct yet related categories of persons. In the history of European culture, relations between the social realm and that of nature, however the latter is construed, are a paradigmatic example of this theme. Nature has been presented as other to culture, as different, as threatening or powerful, and by these very tokens, as an object of intense curiosity. The idea of conquering or mastering nature is a case in point, where the sense of otherness implied by the idea is also generally understood in terms of gender, with nature commonly, but by no means universally, being identified with woman.

There is an interpretative difficulty, however. In the search for a feminist identity during the late 1960s and 1970s, this identification with nature was often remarked upon. It seemed to have functioned historically as a way of dismissing women as primitive, babyish or in need of control. One response to this was to seek other values in nature with which women could more aptly be associated, such as nurturance or healing powers.[27] The woman–nature association was left intact and unchallenged; only the values assigned to both terms were altered. This is unfortunate, because it pre-empts a thorough-going analysis of the history of 'nature'. Such an analysis requires that we divest ourselves, in so far as this is possible, of our special commitments. Retaining a belief in the validity of linking women and nature makes it excessively hard to be sufficiently critical in the process of unravelling its history.

There are additional ways in which feminist scholarship has reinforced assumptions about womanhood of which it should be critical. The early work on women and medicine, for example, focused on pregnancy, childbirth, contraception, menstruation and gynaecological complaints – events and processes taken to be definitive of women's lives.[28] It is easy enough to see why this should have been the case. Medical theories and practices themselves privileged such subjects because they seemed central to 'Woman', while the equivalent masculine functions were hardly taken as central to men's lives. Furthermore, many (female) scholars were motivated to study these subjects because of their own experiences as patients. These pioneering researches have been of immense value, but taken collectively, they appear to reinforce that sense of female pathology about which eighteenth- and nineteenth-century medical practitioners wrote so eloquently. There may indeed be no easy way to escape this, just as the voyeurism we noted earlier may be all but unavoidable; none the less it is helpful to bring them up to consciousness if only to examine more closely the continued legacy of long-established modes of thought in our own times.

Early feminist scholarship on the life sciences and medicine possessed another striking feature. It generally employed the so-called use/abuse model, in that it was frequently assumed that when claims were made, for example, about the inferior mental capacities of women or blacks, an *abuse* of science had taken place.[29] This implied that scientific ideas were first formed and then, as a separate operation, applied in and to particular social situations. The further implication was that scientific theories were themselves value-neutral, only acquiring moral or ethical qualities in the process of deployment. This enabled people to criticize certain aspects of science and medicine, while leaving others, including their central core, intact. Such views have come under sustained, and to my mind successful, attack.[30] I mention the issue here to make it clear that this book does not employ the use/abuse model, a model which is incompatible with fully historical approaches to science and medicine, because these reveal that there are no firm boundaries between theory formation and use. Indeed, as more is known about the social and cultural history of the biomedical sciences, the less feasible it becomes to draw fixed boundaries of any kind around 'science'.

At this point it must be noted that the words 'science' and 'medicine' require careful handling. These are general terms which include diverse activities, institutions, social groupings, codes of behaviour and theoretical systems. Is it possible to justify their continued use given the range of phenomena subsumed under them? There are naturally occasions when such blanket terms would not be appropriate. For example, if in a specific social setting one wanted to distinguish science as it was practised in an elite institution from the ideas more widely disseminated, or to draw attention to the differences in organization, behaviour or value systems between scientific disciplines or from one country/community to another, then 'science' would be too coarse a concept. In other circumstances, however, these general terms can usefully signal the properties that all aspects of the scientific or the medical enterprise share. The common ground exists most powerfully at the level of ideas, not just in the sense of shared theoretical commitments, which is sometimes but not always the case, but rather as a distinctive orientation to the world, pre-eminently to 'nature', to the generation of coherent systematic understanding of the physical universe. This could and did take many forms at any one time. None the less, the existence of a shared belief in the value of producing general propositions about nature, the physical 'out there', that can be tested empirically where appropriate, and that are rational in character, is of sufficient importance to warrant using the term 'science' to draw attention to this core.

It is clearly not possible to treat medicine as simply a branch of science. Where I use the phrase 'science and medicine' no such implication is intended. Medicine has a history that differs from that of science in that the social diversity of medical practitioners has always been striking. Healing, a central aspect of medicine, has been part of the fabric of daily life for all social classes since written records began.[31] Medicine is primarily a practice, since interactions between people have always been fundamental to it. Practitioners deal with patients, and theories of diagnosis, prognosis and therapeutics arise out of, affect and are modified by medical encounters. The small number of practitioners who reflected at all systematically on their practice generally had well-developed scientific interests. In the eighteenth century this often took the form of a deep involvement with natural history, but an interest in experimental science was by no means unusual. Furthermore, since for many people a medical education was the most easily accessible, many 'scientists' were trained in this way even if they subsequently practised medicine little or not at all. There was therefore considerable overlap between science and medicine, which can be precisely described for a given social context. Many medical practitioners in fact shared the general orientation to nature described above, which entailed in their case the systematic unravelling of pathological phenomena. I argue, therefore, that there are related central cores of both science and medicine and that these must be understood at the level of ideas. However, this does not constitute a claim about the nature of the boundaries around those fields.

It is vital to recognize the fluidity of 'science' in particular. One reason for this is that it is a term of value – to call something scientific is to give it a specific kind of epistemological status – and attributions of value are always surrounded by conflict. Individuals, groups, disciplines and institutions fight over these matters, and hence 'science' cannot have a stable meaning. An analogous situation prevails in medicine whenever a group of practitioners seeks to restrict entry or control conditions of work, since conflict will ensue. Hence the meaning of 'medicine' cannot be fixed either.[32] The existence of contests around the legitimate meanings of science and medicine explains why the boundaries of these fields cannot be deemed constant. Furthermore, no domain is hermetically sealed off, politically, economically, ideologically or socially. Rather, there are continua between medicine and a whole range of other fields. Do discussions of medical theories, illnesses and operations in fiction cease to be 'medical' because they are also 'literary'? Clearly they cannot, unless we can construct clear-cut definitions which set literature on one side and medicine on the other. Since I do not believe it is possible to construct such definitions that are also consistent with historical evidence, the fluidity of science and medicine must be accepted, even embraced. It is then possible to develop approaches to them which take account of this feature – their constant interactions with the full range of social and cultural processes and their consequent occupation of the imaginative realm. I am thus committed in *Sexual Visions* to a form of interdisciplinary history.[33]

Two main features of interdisciplinary history are relevant here. First, it is characterized by a willingness to use theories, techniques, terms and ideas from other disciplines. Accordingly, there is no single methodology that defines such history. Second, it entails using a wide range of materials; indeed, no category of primary sources can be excluded a priori. Beyond this it is not helpful to attempt further abstract definitions of what interdisciplinary history involves, since *Sexual Visions* is an attempt to put it into practice.

2

Natural Facts: An Historical Perspective on Science and Sexuality

The distinction between women as natural and men as cultural appeals to a set of ideas – with a long history – about the biological foundations of womanhood. To understand the historical dimensions of these interrelated pairs of dichotomies, it is necessary to consider the close relationships between natural knowledge and notions of sexuality. Although I shall focus here on the biomedical sciences in eighteenth- and nineteenth-century France and Britain, the links between nature/culture, woman/man, are both ancient and widespread; they may be found in numerous other domains besides science and medicine. However, sex roles have long been discussed in terms of what is deemed natural and authoritatively uncovered by systematic, that is scientific study. Equally, the natural sciences have found sexuality appealing not just as a subject for intensive investigation but as a source of images, metaphors and symbols. The distinction between nature and culture, like that between women and men, is one of value. However, the term that is given greater value can shift dramatically in both cases, hence it is not surprising to find that the two dichotomies have been combined in different ways and given a variety of meanings. In what follows I explore the association between women and nature because it has been one of the most pervasive historically, not because there are essential connections between them.

Perhaps we should dispel a common misapprehension right at the beginning. Associations made in the past between women and nature did not arise out of attempts to capture social life in abstract terms. The associations have always existed as representations not as descriptions. There is no longer any doubt about the diversity of female social and economic roles in the past, a diversity that co-existed with inflexible contemporary ideas about those roles.[1] It is now frequently suggested that during the eighteenth century a process of hardening began whereby gender polarities were understood as firmer, less flexible than they had been previously. This stiffening inspired numerous attempts to bring social life into line. Such a dramatic and persistent lack of fit between ideas and experience clearly points to the ideological function of the nature/culture dichotomy as applied to gender.[2] It was in the domain of medicine above all that these ideological matters were canvassed in eighteenth- and nineteenth-century Europe.

As there seems to be no easy way to reconcile material conditions with ideas about sex roles, we are left with a problem as to how the identifications between women and nature, men and culture, are best understood. It may appear tempting to solve the problem by adding a far less ambiguous dichotomy to the existing ones:

nature	culture
woman	man
oppressed	oppressor
(i.e. powerless)	(powerful)

A model of oppression, assuming clear-cut power relations, takes a social relationship – in this case between men and women – and finds a basis for it in the distinction between nature and culture. But in doing so, a single aspect of the dichotomy has been abstracted out, reducing it to a one-dimensional construct directed solely at oppressing women. Accordingly, discrepancies between women's lives and ideas are, like the prevalence of the nature versus culture idea itself, explained in terms of the ineffectiveness of, or resistance to, an ideology that sought to control the female lot. Unfortunately, historical evidence does not support such an interpretation.

The notion that women are closer to nature than men contained numerous elements, including the claims that women are more emotional, credulous, superstitious and less analytical than men. It could equally effectively express the idea that they were the carriers of a new morality through which the artificiality of civilization could be transcended. Similarly, taking men as cultural could imply either the progressive light of masculine reason or the corruption and exploitation of civil society. Next to what is presented as the desirable domination of superstition by reason, and women by men, in Mozart's opera, *The Magic Flute* (1791), one must place repugnance for the exploitation, suffering and inequality generated by masculine domination expressed in the eighteenth-century French novel *Paul et Virginie* (1788). It will therefore be important to chart the diversity of the woman/nature and men/culture associations. What is already apparent, however, is that radically different meanings can co-exist in the thought of a single individual even, as we shall discover in the popular writings on women by the mid-nineteenth-century French historian Jules Michelet (1798–1874).[3]

In our attempts to understand the deployment of symbols and metaphors, we must recognize the fact that one of their most powerful forms in our culture has been the dichotomy, where two opposed terms mutually define each other. It is not just male/female and nature/culture but also town/country, matter/ spirit, mind/body, public/private, capitalist/worker and so on. Our entire philosophical set presents natural and social phenomena in terms of oppositional characteristics.[4] Each polarity has its own history, at the same time as it develops related meanings to other pairs. For instance, church and state, town and country, also contain allusions to gender and to nature and culture. Transformations between sets of dichotomies are performed all the time. Thus man/woman is only one couple in a complex matrix; it cannot be understood in isolation.

The power of dichotomies such as man/woman, nature/culture, city/country, does not just consist in the apparent clarity of definition by contrast. There can also be a dialectical relationship between the members of each pair. The fact that there are a number of related pairs, connected in complex ways, demonstrates the point that we are not speaking of simple linear hierarchies. Especially since varied values could be assigned to individual terms, to pairs and whole clusters of dichotomies, a single, continuous scale was never at issue. Frequently, it was precisely the degree of fuzziness between the two sides that was most attended to. For example, debates about sex and sex roles, especially during the nineteenth century, hinged on the ways in which sexual boundaries had become blurred. It was as if the maintenance of the social order depended on clarifying certain key distinctions whose symbolic meanings spread far beyond their explicit context. At certain times, perhaps those of perceived rapid change, medical practitioners were at the forefront of serious concerns about the feminization of men, for which homosexuality could be adduced as evidence and the masculinization of women, which was believed to result from excessive physical and mental work.

Raymond Williams has suggested that oppositional pairs provided a way of exploring the parameters of change without directly challenging the social order. He takes a specific case – analogous and closely related to the nature/culture distinction – the long-established Western dichotomy between the city and the country:

> On the country has gathered the idea of a natural way of life: of peace, innocence, and simple virtue. On the city has gathered the idea of an achieved centre: of learning, communication, light. Powerful hostile associations have also developed: on the city as a place of noise, worldliness and ambition; on the country as a place of backwardness, ignorance, limitation.[5]

Williams indicates something of the complexity that can be held within dichotomies. We can also see from his comment how the city/country opposition could have a sexual dimension. The innocence and simple virtues of country people were typically expressed through the simple, unaffected sentiment of women. The negative image of the country, pervasive in Enlightenment writings, portrayed the superstitious and credulous behaviour of peasant women. The 'light' and civilization of city culture were symbols of the male capacity for abstract thought and intellectual genius. The negative side of urban life was often expressed in terms of exploitative domination and economic competition – metaphors of masculinity.

Despite the superficial clarity of the country/city polarity, Williams stresses that the relationship between these two terms has been ambiguous and problematic. Cities arise out of the countryside, urban and rural life are inescapably linked, while between cities and the country lie a whole host of intermediate forms of human settlements: villages, towns, suburbs, garden cities. The sharp dichotomy seems to deny historical reality, suggesting that there must be powerful imperatives behind the persistence of these archetypes. Possibly the way the polarity can provide coherence in the face of threatened social disorganization, has been, as Williams suggests, the key to its enduring vitality. Indeed, the same may well be true of the nature/culture and woman/man polarities.

The oppositions between women as nature and men as culture were also expressed concretely through common distinctions, for example, between men's work and women's work. These did not describe occupational structures but served to prescribe appropriate behaviour through metaphorical associations between the type of work and gender. The ideological dimension to these oppositions is discernible in contrasts promulgated by medical opinion, such as that between male strength (especially muscular) and female vulnerability (especially nervous).[6] But the dichotomies we are exploring in this chapter did not manifest themselves in a neat, consistent manner. This is partly because social and conceptual changes take place slowly, erratically and in piecemeal and fragmented ways. It is also because the polarities themselves were riddled with tensions, contradictions and paradoxes.

There are strong reasons for beginning a consideration of nature, culture and gender with the Enlightenment. Shifts in the meaning and usage of words such as 'culture', 'civil', 'civilize', 'nature' and 'life' indicate far-reaching changes in the way human society and its relations with the natural world were conceived. 'The Enlightenment' is, of course, no easier to define than notions of nature and culture are.[7] In the very term we see an appeal to light as a symbol of a certain form of knowledge, which had the potential for improving human existence, and which was based on first-hand observation whenever possible. Rational knowledge rooted in empirical information derived from the senses was accordingly deemed the best foundation for secure knowledge. Starting with a sensualist epistemology and a number of assumptions about the potential social application of an understanding of natural laws, many Enlightenment writers critically examined forms of social organization. They employed a language rich in sexual metaphors and systematically examined the natural facts of sexuality as integral parts of their programme.[8]

Science and medicine were fundamental to Enlightenment investigations of sexuality in three different ways. First, natural philosophers and medical writers addressed themselves to phenomena in the natural world such as reproduction, sexual behaviour and sex-related diseases. Second, science and medicine held a privileged epistemological position because their methods appeared to be the only ones which would lead away from dogma and superstition towards a secular empirically-based knowledge of the natural and social worlds. Third, as activities, science and medicine were understood through sexual metaphors, for example by designating nature as a woman to be unveiled, unclothed and penetrated by masculine science. The relationships between women and nature, and between men and culture, can therefore be examined productively through the mediations of science and medicine.

In the self-conscious scientism of the Enlightenment, the capacity of the human mind to delve into the secrets of nature was celebrated. Scientific prowess could be conceptualized as a male gift, and nature could be, among other things, the fertile woman or the archetypal mother. People had explored their capacity to master and manipulate nature for many centuries, but the powerful analytical tools of the natural sciences and techniques of engineering and technology enhanced their confidence that human power over the environment was boundless. The desire for dominance over nature was above all fuelled by an imaginative fervour. Francis Bacon (1561–1626) is often taken as one of the most influential and enthusiastic exponents of human ascendancy. As he expressed it in the early seventeenth century, 'My only earthly wish is . . . to stretch the deplorably narrow limits of man's domination over the universe to their promised bounds'. And the process by which Bacon thought this would be achieved was a casting off of 'the darkness of antiquity' in favour of the detailed study of nature: 'I am come in very truth leading to you Nature with all her children to bind her to your service and make her your slave'.[9] Bacon is considered important not just because he couched his arguments in gendered terms but also because he was taken by future generations as the validating figure of natural philosophical enquiry, especially of its observational commitment. He was not, however, unique in this respect, since we find the same sexually tinged language about mastery in, for example, the writings of René Descartes (1596–1650), another central figure in the 'scientific revolution'.[10] Although it is usual to contrast Baconian empiricism with Cartesian rationalism, the shared ground in relation to images of knowledge and its acquisition is striking.

In discussions of human domination over nature, the concept of environment comes to hold an important and complex place from the late eighteenth century onwards. The environment was construed as that cluster of variables that acted upon organisms and determined many of their characteristics. Human sickness and health could be understood in terms of powerful environmental factors such as climate, diet, housing, work, family and geography.[11] This notion of environment had two aspects. First, there were variables such as custom and government – human products amenable to direct manipulation. Second, there were parameters, such as climate and geography, in the province of immutable natural laws, and these were infinitely more challenging to human power. In the first case environment denoted culture, in the second, nature. Unpacking this concept of environment enables us to recognize two important points. First, it demonstrates that a single term or cluster of ideas can hold within it both sides of a polarity. Second, at a more specific level, it reveals one of the main conceptual tools for thinking about gender, which was understood in environmental terms during this period.

It had become clear by the end of the eighteenth century that living things and their environment were continually interacting and changing each other in the process. This was true of sexuality, for, although sex roles were seen as being in some sense 'in nature', because of their relationship to physical characteristics, they were also seen as mutable, just as physiology and anatomy in general were taken to be. The customs and habits of day-to-day life such as diet, exercise and occupation, as well as more general social forces such as mode of government, were taken to have profound effects on all aspects of peoples' lives; their sexuality was no exception. The foundation for this was a naturalistic conceptual framework for understanding the physiological, mental and social aspects of human beings in a co-ordinated way. This framework underlay the relationships between nature, culture and gender in the period.[12]

In the biomedical sciences of the late eighteenth and early nineteenth centuries, mind and body were not generally seen as incommensurable, absolutely distinct categories. Mental events such as anger, fear or grief were known to have bodily effects, while illnesses such as fever produced emotional and intellectual changes. A model of health and illness was dominant in the eighteenth century according to which life-style and social roles were closely related to health.[13] The model was applied to both men and women, but with different implications. A tight linkage was presumed between tasks performed in the social arena and health and disease. For women these jobs included the production, suckling and care of children and the creation of a natural morality through family life. They thereby became a distinct class of persons, not by virtue of their reproductive organs but through their behaviour. This implied both that female physiology was to be understood as a totality and that health and pathology could be defined in terms of life-style and social roles.

The model applied to both sexes. For example, people who lived in certain settings, such as those who worked in mines or at sedentary occupations, were known to be susceptible to particular diseases. Practitioners therefore advocated health precautions; the appropriate diet, exercise, housing, clothing, behaviour, regimen. The same argument applied to women. Each way of life held its own particular health dangers, which could be held at bay by preventive measures. In the case of women, permissible occupation was tightly defined according to putatively natural criteria. There was thus a close relationship between habit and life-style. Through habit and custom, physiological changes took place which had been socially induced, with the result that each human body was a tangled composite of nature and culture.[14]

The radical boundary drawn between the sexes through life-style and occupation was based on a physiology that was sensitive to the interweaving of physical and moral, mind and body.

The language of this physiology brought together biological, psychological and social considerations largely through the use of bridging concepts such as 'temperament', 'habit', 'constitution' and 'sensibility', which were technical medical terms. This framework offered a naturalistic account of gender, race and class differences, which captured the complexity of individual lives while also offering avenues for detailed medical investigations.[15]

The logic of this approach allowed both individuals and groups with shared characteristics to be understood from a biomedical perspective. Although it acknowledged the plasticity of human beings, there were considered to be limits on the extent to which people could be changed. For example, variation among women from different climates and occupations was often noted. Nevertheless, all women had certain physiological features in common, but not as a *direct* result of their reproductive organs. It was a basic premise of many late eighteenth-century medical commentators that women were distinct from men by virtue of their total anatomy and physiology. As the medical philosopher Cabanis (1757–1808) put it at the end of the eighteenth century, 'Nature has not simply distinguished the sexes by a single set of organs, the direct instruments of reproduction: between men and women there exist other differences of structure which relate more to the role which has been assigned to them'.[16]

The teleological argument was made even more explicit by his contemporary, Pierre Roussel (1742–1802): 'The soft parts which are part of the female constitution . . . also manifest differences which enable one to catch a glimpse of the functions to which woman is called, and of the passive state to which nature has destined her'.[17] It is significant that both men were deeply indebted to Rousseau (1712–78), whose vision of woman was so powerful and enduring and whose strongly dualistic style of thinking had placed gender alongside other dichotomies in a political context.[18]

We can see some of the ways in which the nature/culture and female/male pairs worked together in medicine by taking a specific example – the concept of sensibility.[19] This was a physiological property which, although present in all parts of the body, was most clearly expressed through the state of the nervous system. For many the nervous system indicated most precisely the total state of an individual, especially with respect to the impact of social changes. Thus it was said that increases in female hysterical illnesses (understood as nervous phenomena) during the eighteenth century, were evidence of the growing use of luxuries such as tea and coffee.[20] By virtue of their sex, women had a distinct sensibility that could be further modified during their lifetimes. They were taken to be highly *'sensible'* (i.e. sensitive or even sensitized) like children, and more passionate than men. This is because of 'the great mobility of their fibres, especially those in the uterus; hence their irritability and suffering from vapours.'[21] The distinctive sensibility of women could also be used to explain their greater life expectancy by associating life-style with the physical consistency of the constituent fibres of their bodies. As Barthez (1734–1806), a prominent French physician explained:

> Probably women enjoy this increase in their average age because of the softness and flexibility of their fibres, and particularly because of their periodic evacuations which rejuvenate them, so to speak, each month, renew their blood, and re-establish their usual freshness. . . . Another important cause of women living longer than men is that they are usually more accustomed to suffering infirmities, or to experiencing miseries in life. This habit gives their vital sensibility more moderation, and can only render them less susceptible to illness.[22]

However, he went on to say that because of their 'delicate and feeble constitution', women feel things more deeply than men. Again we meet the ambivalence already noted in the woman/ nature association. Women are tougher and softer, more vulnerable and more tenacious of life than men.

The idea of the softness of women took a particularly strong imaginative hold upon people. The metaphor was extended by Cabanis to construct an elaborate image of the dependent nature of woman:

> This muscular feebleness inspires in women an instinctive disgust of strenuous exercise; it draws them towards amusements and sedentary occupations. One could add that the separation of their hips makes walking more painful for women. . . . This habitual feeling of weakness inspires less confidence . . . and as a woman finds herself less able to exist on her own, the more she needs to attract the attention of others, to strengthen herself using those around her whom she judges most capable of protecting her.[23]

Although the logic of these arguments was the same for men

and for women, there was an important asymmetry in their application, since women's occupations were taken to be rooted in and a necessary consequence of their reproductive functions, teleologically understood in terms of roles rather than organs. Men's jobs were unrestricted. Women's capacity to bear and suckle children was taken to define their physical, psychological and social lives. Men were potential members of the broadest social and cultural groups, while women's sphere of action was the private arena of home and family. As wives and mothers, women's role in the family – the natural basis of social life – was central and its importance was registered in extensive contemporary debates on the subject.

These debates provide the immediate context for the emphasis on the breast – the epitome of feminine softness – in much medical literature. It is a misconception to imagine that medical practitioners were exclusively preoccupied with the uterus or ovaries. The breast was of particular interest to eighteenth-century practitioners concerned with moral philosophy and ethics. It symbolized women's role in the family through its association with the suckling of babies; it defined the occupational status of females within the privacy of the family, as opposed to public life. It was the visible sign of femininity that men recognized:

> Nature destined this organ to nourish the new-born human being; she gave to the breast a seductive charm by virtue of its form and bloom which powerfully attract men; this is why jealous husbands and discreet wives, do not permit its charms to be paraded.[24]

It could thus be said to be a social law that sexual attraction was founded on the breast, and a natural law that women should breastfeed their own children. If this natural law was thwarted, the child suffered and the mother endured punishment, including the miscarriage of subsequent children: 'It is thus that one exposes oneself to cries of pain for having been unfeeling about those of nature'.[25] Breasts not only symbolized the most fundamental social bond – that between mother and child – they were also the means by which families were made, since their beauty elicited the desires of the male for the female. Such claims, which brought together social, medical and aesthetic arguments, took place in a historical setting where closely related issues, such as the use of wet-nurses, were immensely controversial. These debates negotiated definitions of the natural in relation to class as well as to gender, since the wet-nurses were frequently of lower social status than their employers, those women who did not suckle their own children. Although the refusal to breastfeed was stereotypically associated with self-indulgent aristocratic women, in fact women of diverse social and occupational status employed wet-nurses.[26]

In general there was a strong aesthetic component in medical writings on women in this period. Discussing the beauty of the breast in the same breath as its vital nutritive function indicates how tightly linked and highly charged medical and social values were. The breast was good, morally and biologically, hence its attractiveness and the resultant sociability between the sexes. The social and natural domains were brought together here; furthermore, medical thinking depended on a rich set of images and metaphors that appealed not only to the imagination but specifically to visual pleasure.

The question of visual pleasure should alert us to the ways in which the woman/nature and man/culture associations functioned at different levels, from the aesthetic to the social, embracing literary and artistic as well as medical and philosophical discourses. But more than discourses were at issue. Taken as oppositions, women versus men, and nature versus culture, became key terms in medical conflicts of the period. They were especially prominent in the heated debates, rivalries and struggles around child care and midwifery, which hinged on the ideological tensions between superstition and tradition on the one hand and enlightenment and progress on the other.[27]

The theme of the irrationality and irresponsibility of women's ways with small children was articulated in Britain by William Cadogan (1711–97) in a pamphlet *An Essay upon Nursing and the Management of Children*, first published in 1748. He argued that 'the Preservation of Children [should become] the Care of Men of Sense' because 'this Business has been too long fatally left to the Management of Women, who cannot be supposed to have proper Knowledge to fit them for such a task'. And by proper knowledge he clearly means science: 'What I mean is a Philosophic Knowledge of Nature, to be acquired only by learned Observation and Experience, and which therefore the Unlearned must be incapable of'. This is contrasted to the 'superstitious

Practices and Ceremonies', inherited by women from 'their Great Grandmothers'. He recommended a transfer from female to male authority regarding infant care. He was not simply co-opting a new field for medical practitioners, since he wished fathers to take on a more active role: 'I would earnestly recommend it to every father to have his Child nursed under his own Eye, to make use of his own Reason and Sense in superintending and directing the Management of it'.[28] Paternal authority, then, takes the form of active management, for which the sense of sight is the key metaphor. This echoes not only Cadogan's own insistence on observation but also a widespread association between looking and the knowledge that leads to power and control.

Cadogan thought that women perpetuated ancient practices, such as swaddling, which should be abolished, in favour of the forms of care advised by physicians. He never suggested that men should take over the daily care of children, only that mothers should perform their allotted tasks under the advice of men, husbands and medical practitioners. So, it was not that female functions had been abolished and co-opted, but that a hierarchy had been established where women acted under the supervision of men. It was a changed division of power not of labour that he was after. Cadogan mobilized contemporary ideas and metaphors of medical antagonisms between men and women in an effective manner. His argument could be summarized as follows:

women	men
superstition and custom	Philosophic Knowledge
learning from kin	learning by observation and experience
unlearned	scientific
daily care	direction, superintendence, and management

For the most part these dichotomies are of a particular kind, where the two sides are antithetical to each other. The last pair, uniquely, is composed of complementary terms and it expresses the ideal form of childcare where women and men work together.

Despite the apparent neatness of Cadogan's position, there are two revealing fissures in it. He does not in fact treat all women

as if they were the same. Artificial, aristocratic women are singled
out for special denunciation, the poor (and natural!) for special
praise, while neither of these groups fits the stereotype of women
elaborated elsewhere in the pamphlet.[29] Although by and large
women are presented negatively, Cadogan personifies nature as
a woman, in positive terms.[30] Thus, although he maintains a
dualistic position throughout, the terms are not given stable
values. Such reversals are, of course, common.

The same theme of female irresponsibility was prominent in
attitudes towards midwives. The relationships between midwives
and other categories of medical practitioners were complex. There
was an element of competition for patients and for fees.
Eighteenth-century writings by male practitioners commonly
implied that midwives were dangerous and ignorant by comparison
with surgeons and physicians. The claim was made by potentially
rival practitioners in the context of widespread concern about
the control of medical practice. Midwives appeared especially
suspicious to enlightened savants because their territory was the
intimate and tightly knit circle of women, at least in the
imagination of their detractors. Midwives, being generally women
with children themselves, and being associated with birth, were
at the centre of feminine stereotypes. In fact, numerous attempts
were made, especially in France, to regulate midwives in a manner
that suggests they were feared as morally and sexually polluting.[31]

One of the principal themes in the polemical literature on the
subject was 'decency'. On the one hand, it was claimed that it
was indecent for men to deliver women, and on the other that
midwives were of doubtful decency themselves. The delivery of
babies was in fact performed by both men and women, so that
here we have a situation where the actual occupational divisions
between the sexes were blurred. In addition to midwifery, women
from all social strata practised a wide range of medical techniques.
We can detect enormous unease about the demarcation between
male and female medical practitioners that was as much about
sexuality, sex roles, science and nature as it was about professional-
ism. The result was recurrent attempts – in words and pictures
as well as in practice – to control and clarify the gender boundaries.

The midwifery debates clearly depended on a set of tacit
assumptions about sexuality and medicine and, perhaps more
important, on an accepted vocabulary through which discussions

could be conducted. The currency and content of such a language can be neatly confirmed by an examination of an early nineteenth-century poem by the medical practitioner turned parson and poet, George Crabbe (1754–1832). He was perfectly explicit about the conflict between midwives and male practitioners and about the language through which it was expressed. In *The Parish Register* of 1807 he narrates the battle between an established village midwife and the new Doctor Glibb. Crabbe subtly deploys the contrasts between male and female, science and nature, urban and rural, upwardly mobile and socially unpretentious. Of particular relevance here is Glibb's speech in which he denounces the midwife in the name of science and progress by associating her with Nature:

> And what is Nature? One who acts in aid
> Of gossips half asleep and half afraid;
> With such allies I scorn my fame to blend,
> Skill is my luck and courage is my friend:
> No slave to Nature, 'tis my chief delight
> To win my way and act in her despite:
> Trust then my art, that, in itself complete,
> Needs no assistance and fears no defeat.[32]

Crabbe locates the conflict not just between two individuals, classes or professions, but between modernity and tradition and between their related stances towards nature, the one either aggressive or modernizing, depending on your perspective, the other either respectful or retrogressive, according to the speaker's vantage point. The vocabulary the doctor used to press his case was full of implied, sexually tinged aggression.

The fraught position of the midwife illustrates one of the ways in which beliefs in women as bearers of tradition and men as bearers of modernity worked. The fact that forceps were used by men may have further reinforced their image as the possessors of new, progressive power by linking them with innovative techniques. The professional struggle hinged on who should have charge of birth, an event which occupied the centre stage of many women's lives and of the symbolic structures associated with them. Indeed, the issue of midwifery touched masculinity and femininity so deeply that the man-midwife could be portrayed at the end of the eighteenth century as a bizarre monster. The

frontispiece to a diatribe of 1793, entitled *Man-Midwifery
Dissected* shows a figure half man, half woman. Whereas the
female side includes in the background only a few simple
accoutrements, the male side includes fearsome instruments and
drugs. According to the caption the print depicts 'a newly
discovered animal, not known in Buffon's time'; 'this Monster['s]
. . . Propensities to crudity and indecency' are detailed in the
text. There can hardly be a more dramatic illustration of the way
in which changing midwifery practices threatened conceptions of
gender. Each individual had to possess a unified, coherent gender
identity, the print implies, since the splitting it portrayed was
monstrous.[33]

Linking women and nature could lead to passivity being stressed
as a significant common feature. However, in other formulations
a more active image was presented. When the capacity of women
to give and cherish life was emphasized, they could be understood
as active, especially with respect to morals. We can see this clearly
in the work of a prominent disciple of Rousseau, the naturalist
and writer Bernardin de Saint-Pierre (1737–1814).[34] As he said to
the female sex in 1806, 'You are the flowers of life . . . You
civilize the human race . . . You are the Queens of our beliefs
and of our moral order'. He explained:

> Women lay down the first foundations of natural laws. The first
> founder of a human society was a mother of a family. They are
> scattered among men to remind them above all that they are men,
> and to uphold, despite political laws, the fundamental laws of
> nature. . . . Not only do women bind men together by the bonds
> of nature, but also by those of society.[35]

These words were written for a new edition of his best-known
work, *Paul et Virginie*, first published in 1788, which explored
in fictional form the relationships between sexuality, sex roles,
nature and culture. Woman can not only be nature and culture,
but can also link these two areas, performing the role of a moral
suture.

Paul et Virginie was a moral fable, one which the 1806
introduction suggests was consciously built on the capacity of
women to redeem the ailing civilization of the *ancien régime* and
the chaos of revolution. Yet Bernardin offers no political solution
to the social decay of Europe. Despite his celebration of women

quoted above, with its monarchic image, he idealized women as mothers above all, the core of a 'natural' society. To find out how the women/nature and the men/culture pairs were given political inflection, we shall move away from science and medicine for a moment.

The Magic Flute by Mozart (1756–91) presented female/nature and male/culture as locked in a struggle for political dominance.[36] Just as *Paul et Virginie* presented clusters of images about women and nature, so did *The Magic Flute*, but the moral judgement went in quite the opposite direction. In the opera there was a struggle between a patriarchal lineage (Sarastro and Tamino) and a matriarchal one (the Queen of the Night, and, initially, Pamina). It is well known that the opera contains many allusions to freemasonry, a considerable radical force in late eighteenth-century Vienna.[37] The opposition between the enlightenment of freemasonry, from which women were generally excluded, and the darkness of evil was expressed in sexual terms.

The Queen of the Night was the wife of the Priest of the Sun. She was part of a matrilineal succession but, before his death her husband had handed to Sarastro, the ruler of the temple of wisdom, an emblem of sovereignty to be kept for his male successor. Sarastro kidnapped Pamina, daughter of the Queen, to marry her to the new king. One surmises that such a marriage would legitimate the substitution of a patriarchy for a matriarchy. Throughout the opera the native ignorance of women is shown as needing to be tempered by male reason and wisdom. The three ladies of the Queen of the Night represent the state of unenlightenment of the Catholic Church. They describe to Tamino, the chosen male prince, how 'a powerful, evil demon' has taken Pamina and the suffering this has caused the 'loving maternal heart' of the Queen. In alluding to the pain caused to the Queen by Sarastro, a brief attempt is made to exploit the nature/culture metaphor to win sympathy for feminine vulnerability, but the opera as a whole firmly places right on the side of male reason. This moral superiority is reinforced by scenes in the temple of wisdom, nature and reason where 'prudence, work and art dwell'. Women are constantly and denigratingly informed of their inferior position: 'women do little but chatter much'. Sarastro chides Pamina, 'a man must guide your heart, for without one every woman seeks to exceed her rightful place' and describes her mother as 'a woman who vaunts herself and hopes to delude the people by trickery and superstition'.[38]

However, the symbolism is by no means unequivocally demeaning to women, and the treachery in the opera is perpetrated by the Moor, Monostatos, who wants Pamina for himself. One commentator has claimed that the marriage of Pamina and Tamino at the end of the opera mitigates the generally violent anti-feminist tone by 'a proclamation of the redemption of Woman and her rise to equality with Man in the Mystery of the Couple'.[39] But in fact the nature of the ultimate victory is unambiguous; light triumphs over darkness, men over women, patrilineal over matrilineal succession. Another reading, therefore, is that 'The entire opera legitimizes the principle of patriarchy through its assignment to men of the realm of reason, to women the realm of emotionality; its assignment to men, but not to women, of the realm of power and the right to pass it on, including the right to give the daughter away'.[40]

The richly inventive imagery in *The Magic Flute* provides some useful clues as to how the sexes were conceptualized at the end of the eighteenth century. Its late eighteenth-century audience would have certainly found the political message about the bankruptcy of absolute monarchy and the need for a new secular order, quite obvious. Presumably they also took the point that this could be seen as a battle between women and men, femininity and masculinity, and their associated symbols. In other words, the ability to move between social, cultural, political and symbolic registers in relation to sexuality and sex roles was taken for granted in late eighteenth-century Europe. Furthermore, the range of writings, artefacts and so on in which we can find these assumptions suggests that the associations, made for example by Mozart, between women and darkness were not merely arcane but part of a widespread cultural repertoire.

The ideology of progress, which was so deeply entrenched in Enlightenment thought, meant that the growth of a humane, rational and civilized society could be seen as a struggle between the sexes, with men imposing their value systems on women to facilitate social progress – a theme which remained influential during the nineteenth century. The nature/culture dichotomy thus had an historical dynamic. We often think of oppositional pairs in terms of static types; I suggest that during the eighteenth and nineteenth century these dichotomies were endowed with a temporal dimension. Human history, the growth of culture through the domination of nature, was represented as the increasing assertion of masculine ways over irrational, backward-looking women. The very concept of progress was freighted with gender.[41]

A brief examination of 'culture' may throw light on this point. There was a transition in the meaning of 'culture' during the eighteenth century from a noun of process, denoting the tending of something, such as plants and animals, to a more abstract usage, often associated with the state of development of human society. Not only did this concept of culture incorporate a historical dimension, it also allowed the possibility that each nation, each people and its constituent groups had its own distinctive culture – an idea sustained by the environmentalism discussed earlier. In tying culture specifically to the state of civilization, it was logical for writers to stress those features of civilized life they considered paradigmatic of their own society's achievements.[42] Starting in the eighteenth century, and becoming more marked in the nineteenth, was the trend towards identifying these with science and technology, with the capacity for abstract thought. The relative strength of nations was not just a matter of military or economic prowess, but of the extent to which science was cultivated and rewarded. This is the background to the 'decline of science' debates of the mid nineteenth century, when considerable fears were expressed in Britain about the ascendancy of French and German science.[43] National competition expressed through science was a recurrent theme during the nineteenth century articulated by French, German and American as well as British commentators. This notion of progress was one in which men played the dominant role; women were deemed incapable of contributing because of their lack of analytical modes of thought. Other models of progress also embodied gender assumptions. Yet this is not to say that women were thought incapable of contributing to *any* sort of progress. On the contrary, there were many proponents of the idea that woman was a powerful civilizing influence, but generally the feminine form of the civilizing process stressed emotional and moral rather than scientific, economic, technological or political progress.

I have suggested that a particular scientific style of studying

human beings sustained the relationships between nature, culture
and gender. It was characterized by an interest in people as
integrated units, drawing on the combined resources of what we
would now call physiology, anatomy, psychology, sociology and
anthropology. In relation to the medical domain in particular, it
was evident that moral and aesthetic considerations were insepar-
able from other elements. It is therefore inappropriate to treat
any of these ideas as if they directly reflected material conditions.
They stand to them as representational systems do to that which
inspires and occasions them. They mediated social relations in
that they constantly addressed social relations indirectly, offering
ways to reassess, manage and diffuse conflict – a conflict that is
readily discernible in the conception of nature and culture as two
opposing forces.

This struggle was also given a psychological cast. In the
eighteenth century a struggle was imagined inside each individual;
between those elements designated masculine – reason and
intelligence – and those deemed feminine, that is the passions and
the emotions. Stereotypically, men were portrayed as serious and
thoughtful, women as frivolous and emotional. There was not a
total division of mental properties by sex, but a continuum,
registering the degree to which reason dominated, that was fully
consistent with the physiology based on life-style. Two points
stand out. First, there was battle envisaged between the two
aspects of an individual's psychology, just as there was between
masculine and feminine elements in society as a whole. For many
commentators, reason should prevail over the passions, while for
others the latter were paramount.[44] Second, this sense of
psychological division between the sexes became rigidified during
the nineteenth century. The historian Jules Michelet, for example,
questioned whether women were responsible from a legal point
of view in the sense that men were. The German physiologist
Lotze (1817–81) claimed in 1852 that 'analytical reflection is so
little natural to women that it may be asserted without risk of
being far wrong that words like to the right, to the left, across
. . . do not signify any mathematical relationships in women's
speech but a certain peculiar feeling which one has in following
these instructions while working'.[45]

Some decades later Durkheim (1858–1917) expressed similar
views in *Suicide*, first published in 1897. He asserted the greater

devotion of women to religious practices and summarized the differences between the sexes thus: 'Woman's sexual needs have less of a mental character because, generally speaking, her mental life is less developed. These needs are more closely related to the needs of the organism, following rather than leading them. Being a more instinctive creature than man, woman has only to follow her instincts to find calmness and peace'.[46] The precondition for Durkheim's statements was a well-developed biological and medical science which gave meaning to such terms as 'organism' and 'instinct' – terms already bearing implicit sexual meanings. By using these same terms in a sociological context, Durkheim was able to conjure up a set of biological assumptions which gave extra dimensions to the woman = nature stereotype, and embodied a far more deterministic social understanding of women than of men. We can, of course, locate Durkheim's approach in a well-established biomedical tradition going back to the mid eighteenth century which offered a naturalistic perspective on all aspects of femininity.

Two interrelated features of Durkheim's ideas that depart somewhat from tradition should be noted. He was interested in the notion of the 'organic', in the way in which societies could be seen as made up of functionally interdependent parts. Such a concept was hardly new, but in the late nineteenth and early twentieth centuries it achieved a novel prominence and fresh inspiration from the biomedical sciences. In a later chapter we shall examine an example of how the organic analogy itself is gendered.[47] The sense of hierarchy in Durkheim's ideas is also quite marked. Invoking organisms, needs and instincts in connection with women led the reader to suppose a more material, demanding and delimited existence for them in marked contrast to that of men. Once again, the sense of hierarchy did not originate with Durkheim or the late nineteenth-century social sciences; it had been forcefully affirmed in the wake of anti-Enlightenment feeling earlier in the century.[48]

We can understand that the nature, culture and gender associations, historically varied as they are, were ideological constructs, systems of representation and that they contained normative, reformist programmes. We are therefore entitled to analyse them in terms of the interests they served and the cultural patterns they contained. In this chapter, as I shall do in others,

I have focused on the latter. It may therefore be appropriate to comment briefly on the issue of 'interests' here. The literature I have been discussing was certainly generated by a small group, despite being directed at a wider audience. The members of this group were not, on the whole, aristocrats or politicians, that is people wielding traditional or official forms of power. Rather, they were intellectuals, professionals or creative artists who came mostly from the middle social strata, who gained their positions and influence precisely by virtue of their ideas, talents and knowledge, not inherited wealth or rank. Their concern was to establish the validity of their vision of the world, and above all their right to intervene in social debate. Many shared a view of science and medicine as the motors of social advance, and hence as the harbingers of a rational future to be managed by people like themselves. Women occupied a peculiar position in the march of progress. On the one hand, what was conceived of as their traditionalism had to be fought to the death, while on the other they were assigned the role of putting the family on a secure moral footing – a necessary step for the improvement of social and cultural life.

It is particularly helpful to understand the dichotomies explored in this chapter in terms of myth. In *The Second Sex* (1949) Simone de Beauvoir (1908–86) rightly emphasized the importance of myths in the ways women are seen.[49] She appeared to take for granted, however, that polarities are basic to the way the human mind works. Thus, for her, it is inevitable that woman has been taken as 'other' by man, and so seen only in relation to him. In her state of otherness, woman is the repository of the myths and stereotypes that de Beauvoir analysed. Unfortunately, she omitted from her analysis the historical importance of science, medicine and technology in the promulgation of myths of femininity. Precisely through the study of nature as it was conducted after the 'scientific revolution' of the seventeenth century did the stereotypes of the sexes become reified and hardened – stereotypes that drew on and themselves had the quality of myths. These notions of sexuality and sex roles were far from consistent, but riddled with tensions. It was in elaborating paradoxical yet compelling images of women and men that the myths became powerful. These different elements sometimes clouded and veiled each other, partly perhaps to disguise deep antagonisms between the sexes, and partly because a simple debasement of women by men would not have commanded assent, or spoken to the complexities of social relations between the sexes.

In her emphasis on myths of otherness, de Beauvoir eschews an evolutionary perspective on the different social positions of women and men. Other approaches, including some anthropological ones, presuppose clear ranking systems within societies. Even if we separate issues of value (bad/good) from those of control (sub/superordinate), there are no simple scales on which men and woman can be ranged. Women, for example, are deemed both good and bad, and both evaluations may be represented as stemming from their naturalness. Similarly, they may be subordinate in some areas of life, such as legal rights, and superordinate in others, such as control of the household, and again, *both* of those could be based on their putatively natural qualities. Simple hierarchies, a hangover from the impact of evolutionary ideas on the nineteenth-century social sciences, simply fail to do justice to historical materials.

As we well know, nature was endowed with a remarkable range of meanings during the period of the Enlightenment.[50] However, one common theme stands out. Nature was taken to be that realm upon which mankind acts, not just to intervene in or manipulate directly, but also to understand and render intelligible, where 'nature' includes people and the societies they construct. Such an interpretation of nature led to two distinct positions: nature could be taken to be that part of the world which human beings have understood, mastered and made their own. Through the unravelling of laws of motion, for example, the inner recesses of nature were revealed to the human mind. Nature was also that which had not yet been penetrated (either literally or metaphorically): the wilderness and deserts, unmediated and dangerous nature.

To these two positions correspond two radically different senses in which women are identified with nature. According to the first, they stand as repositories of natural laws to be revealed and understood. This was the point Michelet made when he denied that women were unpredictable but fully subject to nature's rhythms and laws – as the menstrual cycle, which enabled their states of mind and body to be read off, amply demonstrated. According to the second, women's emotions and uncontrolled passions, including those of a sexual kind, gave them special qualities. Women, being endowed with less reason than men, even with less need for reason, since their social lives required of them more feeling than thought, were more easily dominated by their sentiments. It was then quite easy to conceptualize women as wild and dangerous because less amenable to the guiding light of reason.[51] According to this second perspective, moves to contain women's disruptive potential were required; scientific scrutiny – a prelude to control – was but one route by which the wild was rendered tame. Women's potential for disorder could be minimized by drawing and maintaining strong boundaries around them, using the full range of social, cultural, political and economic practices. Such a situation, far from giving the male/ female dichotomy a fixed quality, made it constantly in flux. Furthermore, these two positions gave rise to a variety of moral evaluations of womanhood.

The nature, culture and gender matrix in the history of our own society has served to express the desire for clarity in profoundly unstable and inherently problematic areas. The historical interrelatedness of these ideas shows how apparently distinct domains are linked through sets of symbols and metaphors, which at some times persist for generations and at others shift over shorter periods. Although the terms 'man' and 'woman', 'masculine/feminine', 'sexuality' and 'sex roles' pertain to phenomena of different kinds and of different degrees of abstraction, they are none the less linked through imagery. Science and medicine have acted as major mediators of ideas of nature, culture and gender, with verbal and visual images as the tools of that mediation. One of the most powerful aspects of scientific and medical constructions of sexuality is the way in which apparently universal categories were set up. These implied that there were profound similarities among all women; to a much lesser extent among men. The precise characteristics thereby attributed to the two sexes – the constituent elements of gender imagery – were thus composed both of those given currency in the immediate historical setting and of those more abstract ones of mythic proportions.

3

Body Image and Sex Roles

'Body image' is a term from psychology, used to express an individual's subjective picture of his or her own body. When employed psychoanalytically, it suggests the centrality of the body in child development and hence also its centrality in any psychic disturbance.[1] The notion of body image evokes both a dynamic internal life and a visual aspect of identity formation. The historian can add further dimensions to the term. The internal, picture-making life of people is part of social and cultural life, so that the experiences, models and resources present at a given place and time are integral to the formation of body images. To the internal life of body images, we can add their external existence in which they are the very medium of social interaction. Individuals form images of themselves and each other, which come to shape their reaction to and feelings about their fellows. These images carry within them prevailing values and preferences, which surface and take on what appears to be 'a life of their own' in a range of cultural forms. Here we shall be concerned with the ways in which images of male and female bodies carry assumptions about sex roles.

Some traditions and institutions explicitly focus on picturing the body. To an extent, all human endeavours bear on this question – art, literature, politics, economics, myth and so on, but some do so with a special intensity and authority. One such case is medicine in the eighteenth and nineteenth centuries, and it is a leading theme of this book to explore how the medical sciences in this period were bound up with a particular aspect of body image, namely the differences between men and women. The use of 'body image' and 'sex roles' in relation to this larger theme is intended to show that we must bring together the imaginative realm, especially the visual language of the body, naturalistic accounts of anatomical, physiological and pathological characteristics. and beliefs about how men and women inhabit a

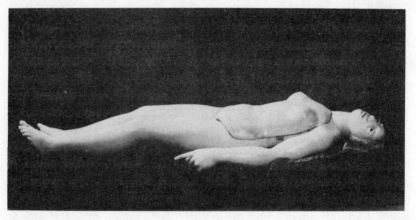

Plate 1 Wax model with removable torso.

world deeply marked by gender.

In this chapter we shall look at wax anatomical models, particularly of female bodies, as a jumping-off point from which to explore the relationships between body image and sex roles, and to examine more closely the assumptions about gender and its representation that the models express. Many of these waxes were made in northern Italy towards the end of the eighteenth century and dispersed all over Europe. These 'Venuses' as they were significantly called, lie on silk or velvet cushions, in passive, yet sexually inviting poses. Not all wax models were of female bodies. Some show only a small body part, illustrating specific diseases or pathological conditions. Others represent men, either the whole body or sizeable parts of it. Yet, I know of no male models which show the complete body either covered with flesh or recumbent. Instead there are either upright muscle men, with no flesh at all, or severely truncated male torsos. The differences between the male and female models go further than this. Many of the female ones are adorned with flowing hair, pearl necklaces, removable parts and small foetuses.[2] It is therefore apparent that many distinct visual signs of gender are present in the waxes, and that the process of looking into the female ones by removing successive layers of organs may be understood in terms of the sexual resonances attached to the coupling of seeing and knowing – a theme discussed elsewhere in the book. It is equally important, however, to examine the representational logic of these models.

Visually speaking, they possess three notable features. First, the use of wax to imitate flesh produces texture, and colour, which eerily resemble 'the real thing'. A first glance at the models produces a sense of verisimilitude, mixed with an equally vivid sense of the uncanny. Second, the naturalistic colouring of all the anatomical parts together with the meticulous details such as eyelashes and eyebrows further reinforce a simultaneous admiration of and unease about the likeness. Third, many, although by no means all of the models repeat positions and gestures from well-known works of art. The faces of some recumbent women recall Bernini's Saint Theresa with its ambiguous mixture of sexual and religious ecstasy, while there are male figures based on the Sistine Chapel ceiling and the Pietà.[3] All these features facilitate associations between anatomical models and the representation of the human figure in a range of non-medical settings. At the same time, they also trade on a form of 'realism'. Slippery though this term is, it is exceptionally apposite for an understanding not just of wax models but of a wide range of medical images in the eighteenth and nineteenth centuries.

In general usage, 'realism' refers to two distinct areas; philosophy and the creative arts. According to the *Oxford English Dictionary*, all the main uses of the term date from the nineteenth century. Here I shall be particularly concerned with the way realism has been used to understand art, but 'the view that the physical world has independent reality' was clearly of the utmost importance for scientific and medical traditions, not least in validating the palpability and material intricacy of the physical world, features which underwrote an insistence on exploring and representing human anatomy and physiology.[4] None the less, if we wish to

comprehend visual artefacts, it is to the question of likeness that
we must turn. For those writing about medical imagery in
particular, 'realism' implies a progressive move towards accuracy,
which takes as a paradigm the supposedly unmediated eye of the
camera. This is built on the assumption that the camera, like the
eye, sees what is really there and that the goal of representation
is the recreation of an original perceptual act. Representation
accordingly consists of recording or transcribing an objective,
natural world. This approach is as seductive as it is fallacious. It
is possible to challenge every one of the foregoing assumptions;
that the eye simply records the real world, that the camera does
the same, that unmediated perception of any kind is possible,
that historically we move ever closer to clear vision and hence to
accurate representation and so on. Particularly telling is the
critique of such unthinking uses of realism by Michael Fried in
relation to a controversial nineteenth-century painting of a surgical
operation by the American artist Thomas Eakins (1844–1916). It
has been argued, Fried claims, that because:

> The Gross Clinic is a work of undeniable and . . . uncompromising
> realism, it therefore represents with something approaching total
> fidelity the painter's perception of an original, actual situation,
> from which the further conclusion is drawn that any features of
> the painting that are at all unusual have their rationale in the
> specifics of that situation . . . this explanation is unsatisfactory,
> first, because it confuses effect with cause . . . and second, because
> . . . it implies a prejudicial conception of the realist project as
> merely photographic.[5]

In effect, those who offer representations are always selecting and
choosing, both consciously and unconsciously, rather than merely
reflecting a pre-given world. The job of historians is unravelling
such processes. The fact remains, however, that realism was an
important goal towards which writers, artists and medical
practitioners among others deliberately worked in the past. We
need to understand what realism meant to them and to beware
of using it uncritically now.

Yet this proposal is far from unproblematic for a historian. It
is not merely pedantic to point out that before the second half
of the nineteenth century, and possibly not even then, 'realism'
did not carry the sense in which use the concept now. This
throws the burden back on us to find ways of using the idea that

are in harmony with historical materials, even if realism is defined in terms of twentieth-century criticism. For my purposes I take realism to be an impulse towards forms of representation which insist that the viewer be convinced that they have a referent beyond themselves, in a supposedly objective world, and that they closely resemble that referent. It is important to note that this can be achieved in a number of different ways, all of which are based upon convention. For example, Norman Bryson has suggested that the inclusion of detail extrinsic to the central purpose of the work concerned, be it visual or literary, constitutes the core of realism. He argues that it is precisely by filling cultural productions with unnecessary objects and information that we create a sense of reality.[6] Wax anatomical models, with their meticulous hair and facial details exemplify the point. Eyebrows, lashes, head and pubic hair were added painstakingly and serve no other function than to make the body as lifelike as possible. They add nothing to the anatomical detail of the model; they even form a bizarre and striking contrast to the exposed internal organs and muscles that look like chunks of meat. Here we have more than realism; a verisimilitude so relentless that it becomes hyper-realism.[7]

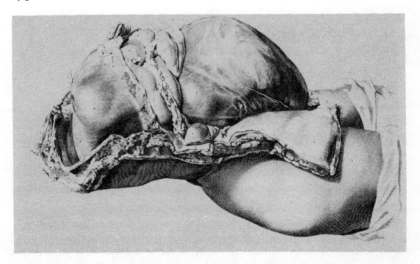

Plate 2 According to William Hunter, this plate was 'made from the dissection of a woman, who died suddenly in the end of her ninth month of pregnancy, in the year 1750'. It showed 'the whole mass of the abdominal visera . . . in its natural situation'.

But this is only one form of realism, a form where the term seems appropriate once the object is examined in detail. We can contrast the waxes with the illustrations to William Hunter's obstetric atlas (1774), which can be described as realistic in a quite specific but different sense, not to be accounted for by the generic differences between modelling and engraving. Drawn from actual dissections, they take a form of literalism as their starting-point and are drawn in such a way that the three-dimensional quality of maternal and foetal tissue is foregrounded. This is a result not only of printing and drawing techniques and conventions but also of Hunter's sense of himself (and by extension of the artists he employed) as topographers, recording details of the organic terrain as faithfully as possible.[8] In this sense his atlas – to extend the geographical metaphor – is an example of 'realism' in that he opposed idealization and generalization, being dedicated instead to capturing particularities accurately. A satisfactory definition of realism must be able to embrace divergent visual practices; not all realist representations look alike. Obvious as this may sound, it is an important corollary to the claim that photography/unmediated perception cannot be treated as a universal paradigm, since such a claim implies that there is only one proper kind of realism and that this is, by implication, scientifically validated.

Art historians commonly employ realism in a range of senses we have not yet mentioned, arising out of what is perceived as a specific historical movement in the nineteenth century.[9] In this connection science and medicine have an explicit and central place in historical scholarship, as indeed does gender:

> In reference to art and literature, [realism is] sometimes used as a term of commendation, when precision and vividness of detail are regarded as a merit, and sometimes unfavourably contrasted with idealized description or representation, in recent use it has often been used with implication [sic] that the details are of an unpleasant or sordid character.[10]

So, realism is ambivalently associated with value, and in both cases science is implicated. In the first, where realism is precision, it is understood as betokening a concern with objectivity modelled on scientific lines. In the second, where realism is baseness, as in the subcategory of naturalism, it is linked with pathology, either literally as in an interest in disease and death, the monstrous and the morbid, or metaphorically, as in the fascination with low life, the dangerous, even contagious classes. And, in each case, a preoccupation with gender animates the realist project.[11]

The discussion of realism indicates that such representations must be understood in a number of mutually reinforcing ways. They speak at once to social, sexual, epistemological and pictorial preoccupations. Bearing this in mind, let us reconsider the wax models, although these points could equally well be applied to other medical artefacts. If we want to recover their social significance, studying the uses to which they were put is one possibility. We can find references to them in medical teaching, in art academies, in public exhibitions of various kinds, and in private collections. The important point is that they were not restricted to a narrowly medical context but enjoyed wide circulation.[12] We still know very little about exactly how medical practitioners employed them, and their functions need to be uncovered rather than assumed. It seems reasonable to conclude, however, that they appealed to a variety of audiences who used them for quite different purposes. It is also possible to see them as cultural products, and compare them with other, similar artefacts, like contemporary or pre-existing art works. Such an approach has already been hinted at when the waxes were shown to closely resemble a Bernini sculpture and a Michelangelo painting. The waxes could also be compared with two-dimensional representations, especially prints. Of course, one of their most important if unusual features was naturalistic colour, a respect in which closely related works are hard to find. Useful as such studies are, they are also limited because they do not address directly two issues which must be considered if we are to do justice to anatomical models and other medical representations: their meaning and their emotional power. This is to enter dangerous territory because speculation is necessarily involved. That such objects now elicit powerful reactions in no way tells us that they did so in the past, still less that those reactions were similar to our own. Yet without direct evidence, which will almost necessarily be absent, such reactions have a heuristic value. Indeed, it could be argued that illustrations and models are designed in such a way as to make certain reactions very likely.

Examining the wax models with such considerations in mind leads us to focus on the questions of sexuality and of reproduction.

These matters are closely related not because the link between them is intrinsic, but because it has been forcefully made at certain times and places, for example those which idealize, romanticize or mystify a closeness between mother and child and lend it at the same time an erotic quality. This blending of sexuality and reproduction is evident in much eighteenth- and nineteenth-century painting, from Greuze's openly erotic *Much Loved Mother*, from the salon of 1765, and the sensuous woman breastfeeding her child in a wood (salons of 1810 and 1814), by either Constance Mayer or P.-P. Prud'hon, to Maurice Denis' *Maternity* (c. 1896) and Eugène Carrière's mystical treatments of mothers and children.[13] The wax models of recumbent women are highly sexualized by virtue of their conspicuously feminine features: long hair, smooth skin, passive pose and so on. Equally, they indicate female reproductive capacities through the presence of the foetus. In theory, not even this would be needed, since breasts can perfectly well act as signs of gender, although it is noteworthy that the breasts of the recumbent figures are only visible when the outer flap, the 'skin', is in place. It is, I think, undeniable, that the wax 'sleeping beauty' figures are knowingly erotic. At the same time they invite us to peer into bodily recesses and to find there evidence of reproductive capacities. Three distinct issues can be discerned here: the evocation of an abstract femininity, the route to knowledge as a form of looking deep into the body, and the material reproductive processes associated with women. Not only were these three aspects bound together, as an ensemble, but they were also political in a quite direct way.

Two senses of the term 'political' are involved here. The gendered nature of body images, and the ways in which the signs of these work, express relations of power and authority. In addition to this general meaning of 'political', body images have a direct and specific connection with political theories through the persistent use of analogies between parts of society or the state and the human frame – a subject to which we shall return later in connection with organicism in the early twentieth century. In order to show exactly how it was that medical representations were political, it is necessary to remember the central features of medical theories underpinning ideas of femininity. In the second half of the eighteenth century especially, life-style and social roles were deemed integral to health. Naturalistic ways of thinking about gender did not locate sex differences in organs but in the interaction between a way of life and an organism considered as a totality. This approach persisted into the nineteenth century, despite the prevalent interest in, for example wombs, ovaries and breasts as emblems of femininity, because how women lived as women never ceased to be a matter of concern.

We can recast the emphasis on occupation, life-style, environ-ment and custom in such a way as to reveal its political aspects. Women and men, it suggested, are formed through experience. Their physiological completeness demands the appropriate behav-iour, although to different degrees – it was certainly deemed a far more urgent problem for women than for men, as the extensive literature on female education reveals.[14] Certain body images represented degrees of conformity to a variety of ideals, which were social, political and mythic in nature. Here was a medical framework that focused on and explained the origins of social difference; it was political at its very core. In later chapters we shall return to the key mythical structures that have served to link gender and sexuality with natural knowledge. For the moment I want to note that assumptions about how the sexes were to inhabit the world, what I am here calling sex-roles, were built into representations of the human body, and that this was so in a historical setting where links between behaviour and the body were commonplace, as the examples of masturbation and diseases specific to particular social strata indicate. These were common eighteenth-century preoccupations, among the mainstays of the deluge of advice books.[15]

During the eighteenth and nineteenth centuries it was taken for granted that the human body was legible, even if there was no consensus on exactly how it could and should be 'read'. Without minimizing the undeniably major shifts that took place over this period in bodily decoding practices, such as the rise and fall of phrenology and the transformation of physiognomy, the general adherence to the principle of legibility should none the less be stressed for two reasons. The existence of ancient traditions that systematized body signs had rendered such interpretative acts commonplace and familiarized people with the idea of the body as a bundle of signs – an idea formalized in medical theory and practice. The principle of legibility was also important because it sanctioned a particular form of inferential thinking, that moved

from visible indicators on a surface (either the body itself or
clothes) to invisible traits inside the body.[16] A common currency,
a shared language and a resource pool therefore existed which
produced and sustained the linkage between gendered body images
and sex roles.

The easy movements I have assumed took place between the
biomedical sciences, social and cultural processes and representational practices could only exist under certain conditions, the
most important of which is the presence of mediating terms. By
this I mean verbal and visual languages which were sufficiently
rich in their application and meaning both to appeal to different
constituencies and to convey complex ideas. An excellent example
of this is 'public', 'private' and their cognates. Since the distinction
between public and private spheres is deeply entrenched in
Western culture, it can be applied to an infinitely wide range of
phenomena. It is a profoundly gendered dichotomy.[17] However,
we must be clear about the status of these concepts. They function
not as descriptions but as types or ideals. They serve to organize
ideas, reactions, prescriptions. And, perhaps most important,
they can be invested with fresh significance by different groups,
in various periods. I shall argue in a later chapter that medicine
bears an especially ambivalent relationship to the public/private
dichotomy, in being rooted in the latter yet making claims in the
former, a situation that explains the predisposition in medical
writings and representations to the breaching of taboos.

The public/private pair is central to relationships between body
image and sex roles in the eighteenth and nineteenth centuries,
because it provided one of the principal vehicles for thinking
about social roles, and thus for the naturalization of these in
images. This explains why we find Rousseau, for example,
bringing together the political, medical, social and psychological
aspects of femininity in *Emile* (1762). Like many other writers
he was anxious about such matters as the education of girls,
breastfeeding, virginity, the quality of mothering, and marital
fidelity. While his originality in these matters is frequently
exaggerated, his writings can be used effectively to demonstrate
the existence and principal characteristics of powerful images of
womanhood, both positive and negative. His starting-point was
the assumption that men and women play quite different roles
within the family and in society as a whole, and that these are

sanctioned by nature. From here Rousseau proceeds in two directions. First he vividly evokes feminine and masculine attributes – 'girls are from their earliest infancy fond of dress' – in order to set in place a vocabulary with which gender difference, as natural difference, can be discussed. Second, he presents male and female roles as deriving from a proper education, an education that initially addresses the bodily signs of gender: 'as the body is born, in a manner before the soul, our first concern should be to cultivate the former'.[18] Rousseau thus effects a naturalization of both body image and sex roles which are compatible with his vision of society as divided into distinct, complementary spheres. It is not just that he was an 'influential' writer, although this can scarcely be doubted, but that the language he used was exceptionally effective in conveying dominant ideas about the proper role of women, and especially their sexual and maternal duties – ideas to be understood in the context of an increasingly elaborate sense of the private.

We can recover a sense of Rousseau's ideological legacy in these matters from the vehement repudiation of it by Mary Wollstonecraft in her *Vindication of the Rights of Woman* (1792). It is surely significant that not only does she take particular care to undermine the whole tradition of advice books for women – a central location of gendered body images presented as 'natural' – but also that medical examples are prominent among the works she criticizes. In addition, Wollstonecraft's book illustrates a further reason for Rousseau's importance – his centrality as a political theorist – because she shows how his ideas on the nature and health of women had political bite. For her, he was a prime example of 'writers who have rendered women objects of pity, bordering on contempt' because, by educating women as different, and above all as creatures of feeling, he made them incapable of being citizens, that is, of entering the public realm.[19] For him adultery and illegitimacy undermined social stability, which was predicated on a secure and moral domestic (i.e. private) life for all citizens. The adultery of women, and their capacity to bring the children of another man into the family were to be feared precisely because husbands relied on their wives to maintain a literal and symbolic sanctuary in the home. Rousseau clearly thought in terms of there being two gendered realms, the public and the private, whereas, for Wollstonecraft, it was women's maternal duties, as makers of future citizens, that drew them into, and gave them rights in, political life.

Although not novel, Rousseau's arguments about nature, health, sex roles and child care demonstrate the manner in which female 'nature' was invested with social and political significance through the images of femininity it contained. Of course, despite her disagreements with him, Wollstonecraft makes the same assumptions. However, she extends her arguments to the mind, which must, like the bodies of both men and women, be formed in accordance with her own political goals. These images of femininity were weapons in conflicting conceptualizations of gender. It is worth remarking that all the topics Rousseau and Wollstonecraft dealt with were common subjects in prints and engravings, as they were also in contemporary fiction. In other words, there was a close relationship between literary and visual culture and natural knowledge in connection with sex roles and the family.[20] No matter how deep the differences between contemporary commentators, they shared significant common ground in that they took body image and sex roles to be inextricably linked; they stressed education as the means by which these were constructed, and their touchstone was 'nature'.

The debates in which those like Rousseau and later Wollstone-craft were engaged constitute the setting for the wax models and for other depictions of women in a medical context. These debates were hardly confined to 'major' figures but were enjoined by literally hundreds of medical writers, ideologues of all persuasions and middle-class reformers. To describe these debates as 'context' is, however, unsatisfactory because the term betrays a dualism between artefacts on the one hand and their setting on the other, with the implicit assumption that the latter influences the former. I do not wish to imply such a separation. Indeed, the discussion of the public/private dichotomy above is intended to suggest that themes, ideas, preoccupations and images could move effortlessly from one domain to another, and that, by acting as mediators between them, representations of the body created a cultural matrix scarcely captured by the language of influence. The late eighteenth-century wax models occupy the same space as political theory, advice books, medical theory and practice, art and literature, and accordingly, we can see this space as having political, social, cultural, ideological and aesthetic dimensions.

This is not to suggest that such spaces are occupied by seamless, consistent discourses; quite the contrary is the case. It is rather to indicate the centrality of medicine and science in the culture of the period.

Let us return to the waxes. The way in which the recumbent women are presented as objects rather than as subjects, as in the throes of experience rather than as active, as both pregnant and erotic, has to be understood in general historical terms. Of course, these were not the only ways in which women's bodies and gender differences were portrayed, but such polarities have occupied a dominant place in European culture over long periods of time. In the final chapter I shall suggest some of the forms in which they persist.

It is possible to use the wax models to examine another theme equally central to my purpose here. We have concluded that the viewer was intended to respond to the model as to a female body that delighted the sight and invited sexual thoughts. One form such thoughts can take is of mentally unclothing a woman. Of course, these models were already naked, but they gave an added, anatomical dimension to the erotic charge of unclothing by containing removable layers that permit ever deeper looking into the chest and abdomen. It is certainly possible to speak of shared metaphors at work here, such as penetration and unveiling, which are equally apt in a sexual and in an intellectual context. These will be discussed in Chapter 5; for the moment, however, I want to go in a slightly different although related direction. A leading image is that of depth, an idea inevitably evoked to some extent by dissection, by the successive removal of layers, but not brought into prominence before the eighteenth century.

The new preoccupation with depth took on a number of forms in the life sciences. It is hard to do more than tentatively suggest the reasons behind the related shifts towards a hierarchical approach to living phenomena. This involved studying organ systems, finding lesions and generally investigating in the insides of organisms, none of which had been as prominent in the earlier, more mechanical approach to the body, with its commonplace terminology of pipes and pulleys. Such a manner of imaging body parts had excited curiosity of a mechanical kind and a search for how the bits worked together. An explicitly anti-mechanistic, organic physiology, by contrast, generated a distinctive curiosity about the intricate, often invisible, but always dynamic processes that made up living things.[21] It is exceptionally clear in the natural philosophy and medicine of the late eighteenth and early nineteenth centuries. Five related factors seem to have been involved.

First, during the eighteenth century a serious search was conducted for a human centre, as it were – for example, in the study of the sensorium commune, which took the form of elaborate experiments on the brain and nervous system. The idea of working through layers to get to a central core was implicit in this search.[22] Second, the study of physiological systems produced a strong sense of a hierarchy among those systems, even if the exact order was disputed. This is beautifully exemplified in the *Recherches physiologiques sur la vie et la mort* (1799/1800) by Xavier Bichat (1771–1802), in which having divided 'life' into two kinds – of different degrees of complexity, organic and animal; the former common to all living things, the second peculiar to animals – he worked through the main organs (heart, lungs and brain) in order to show the effect of the death of each upon the others and upon the body as a whole. Such an analytical technique presupposed an elaborate formulation of the interaction between organs and organ systems and a concern for the different degrees to which they are fundamental to the two kinds of life. Bichat's approach, like that of many other anatomists and physiologists, was based on assumptions about bodily depth – literally, through dissection, and conceptually through the method known as 'analysis'. For natural philosophers and medical practitioners of the second half of the eighteenth century, it was the philosopher Condillac (1715–80) who was deemed the major progenitor of the analytical approach, decomposing phenomena into their elements.[23] This need have no direct implications of bodily depth, although it does presuppose distinguishable degrees of incremental complexity. Those who used it in the biomedical sciences were indeed employing it to capture different levels of vitality.[24]

Third, during the eighteenth century techniques of dissection became increasingly refined, and greater emphasis was given to first-hand anatomical study in medical education. William Hunter exemplifies this trend, with his private anatomy classes and his own publications which portray, in the *Gravid Uterus*, for example, a careful peeling off of layer after layer of organic tissue to reach the foetus itself.[25] Fourth, there was a growing interest in the nature of tissues and membranes in this period, which nurtured the idea that organic layering was an important phenomenon. This interest culminated in Bichat's work on both tissues in general and membranes in particular, issuing from his passionate engagement with dissection.[26]

Finally, in a somewhat different key, layering in both the organic and physical worlds became a prominent issue once a historical approach to nature came to the fore. Geologists and paleontologists saw sedimentation processes and the distinctiveness of strata with new eyes once the detailed examination of the history of the earth became the dominant approach in the eighteenth century. The exact study of each layer, conceptualized as having a unique place within a time sequence, involved going deeper and deeper into the earth.[27] Time as a real factor in nature gave impetus to a study of sequences of all kinds, through which notions of organic depth in particular developed. We can see this in the natural philosophy of Lamarck (1744–1829), for whom the increasing complexity of organic life, over time, allowed him to designate some forms as simpler than others because historically prior. His method could be applied to biological systems as well as to whole organisms. The highly developed human nervous system displayed many stages of the history of life, in its levels of anatomical and functional complexity. For example, in human beings the front of the brain was the most historically recent innovation in living creatures, while the core of the nervous system had been in existence longer. The base of the brain, present in the most primitive vertebrates, was a sign of a prior organic state: going deep into the body meant going deep into time. In effect, then, penetrating inside organisms was a way of approaching the origins of life. Lamarck is a particularly interesting example, because he himself had no special interest in dissection, did not use a microscope and therefore his commitment to the idea of a historical, organic hierarchy, and to understanding levels of differing complexity was independent of many of the factors already outlined.[28]

By the end of the eighteenth century, then, there were a number of ways in which the idea of organic depth manifested itself, through changing practices, ideas and metaphors. This interest in depth was especially significant for the construction of femininity in two distinct although related ways. The first was by promoting the actual unveiling of women's bodies to render visible the emblematic core of their sex in the organs of generation. The second was by giving expression to a model of knowledge, based on looking deeply into and thereby intellectually mastering nature – a model infused with assumptions about gender.

It is fairly easy to see that parts of the body like the breast, uterus, ovaries and so on can provide vehicles through which sex differences of all kinds from the anatomical to the social can be rehearsed. However, organs common to both sexes also carry deeply gendered metaphorical loads. One example of this is the feminization of the nervous system and the masculinization of the musculature in the eighteenth century. Such associations, however, are never historically stable, and their viability particularly depends upon the social and cultural apparatus of class and racial divisions. For example, there are very few female wax anatomical models that are erect. Most of the erect models are male, displaying muscles contracting and relaxing in athletic poses. A rare upright female model displays the nervous system and includes prominent genitals and pubic hair.[29] The idea of the nervous temperament of women and their heightened sensibility was a commonplace in medical writings, which associated hysteria with the nervous system in the eighteenth century.[30] Similarly, such writings abound with assertions of the muscular weakness of women. There is a special kind of 'classism' built into such assertions, which embody a distinctively middle-class notion of femininity as sedentary, domestic and emotional, yet a much more populist image of masculinity as physically active.

To note this is not to imply that associations of the form female and nerve, or male and muscle should directly reflect social conditions, for this would be naïve. Ideas or ideology, and material conditions simply do not relate together in any one to one manner. None the less quite tangible consequences can flow from, for example, treating woman or man as universal categories, as scientific and medical discourses tend to do. Such consequences, while often not consciously intended, were nevertheless far from inadvertent; they were part of systematic sets of associations that gather around our ideas of each sex. We can see this quite clearly from the metaphorical extensions the gendering of body parts gave rise to, such as the denunciation of effeteness or effeminacy in men with what was deemed an overdeveloped sensibility, which was appropriate only in very specific social settings. For example, melancholia was acceptable in men of a certain kind, usually those who were in some occupation linked with learning or the fine arts, but for other occupations or social strata it stood for a feminized identity and was presented as socially undermining.[31] Disequilibrated social relations have frequently been signalled by a language of gendered anatomy and pathology.

There are, of course, powerful polarities at work here (and in all the examples used in this chapter), the mark of centuries of dichotomous thought:

active	passive
muscles	nerves
action	experience
male	female
public	private/domestic
subject	object
self	other
seeing	seen
reason	passion/desire

Taking the list as a whole it is immediately apparent that the pairs are not consistently or logically related to one another. For example, there is no clear reason why men should be seen as both more muscular *and* better fitted to be subjects than women, when subjectivity might be more plausibly seen as issuing from a highly developed nervous system. A similar point might be made about reason and muscularity, although the related linkage between women and the passions seems perfectly clear. These tensions if they are indeed tensions do not, however, undermine the historical force of such associations. They can be explained by showing that the various dichotomies perform different social functions and insert themselves at different places, and by reminding ourselves that the meanings we give to all these terms are profoundly labile. None of this lessens the importance of the gendered associations of body parts and their metaphorical extensions; rather, it underlines once again that body images and sex roles are necessarily intertwined.

The lectures on design given by James Barry (1741–1806) at

the Royal Academy offer a perfect example of this point. Indeed, that these matters should have been discussed in detail at an art academy points to their importance for representational practices:

> The whole and every part of the male form, generally taken, indicates an aptness and propensity to action, vigorous exertion, and power. In the female form the appearance is very different; it gives the idea of something rather passive than active, and seems created not so much for the purposes of laborious utility, as for the exercise of all the softer, milder qualities. How admirably does this gentleness of frame correspond with the mild and tender pursuits for which female nature was intended. . . . Hence it appears that this superior tenderness and soft affecting sensibility . . . are only the legible, agreeable exteriors of necessary utility.[32]

Here Barry has been able to combine an evocative word-picture of femininity and masculinity with assertions about female roles, about the visual pleasure women afford men, about the nature of the sexes, and about the legibility of the body with respect to gender.

The multiple intertwinings between body image and sex roles thus gave rise to a range of cultural phenomena going far beyond the domain of the natural sciences and medicine in their significance, finding expression in art, literature and political theory. The special kind of eroticism at issue here had a further aspect not so far discussed: violence. Let us consider for a moment the kinds of violence sometimes present in medical representations of women and in the use of gender imagery in natural philosophy and medicine. We will want to distinguish here between three sorts of violence: epistemological, actual and representational. In the first case it is of a metaphorical character, easily explained through the example of Bacon speaking about wresting knowledge from (female) nature, enslaving her and so on.[33] Here it is the very manner in which knowledge of nature is acquired that constitutes a form of violence because it involves struggle, conquest and force.

In the second case the violence is quite literal – the actual dissection of female corpses or the performance of experiments or surgery upon women. We know, for example, that William Hunter performed many dissections on women who had died during pregnancy. In the popular imagination the dissection of any body was perceived as a massive violation.[34] Although we may wish to explore the ways in which medical practice singled women out for 'dubious' procedures, this second kind of violence is best explained in terms of the other two. Of exceptional importance is the third kind, namely representational violence. I include here any literary or artistic device, or indeed any idea, which invites readers and viewers to collude with sexually aggressive fantasies and practices. I stress this form, not to minimize the suffering of women as patients but because representational violence acts to permit, legitimate and even encourage actual abuse, a phenomenon with which we are only too familiar from, for example, long-standing and deeply entrenched arguments about pain thresholds varying with the sex, class and race of the subject. This form of violence has all the tools of representation at its disposition.

Historically, there have been many different places where these kinds of violence surfaced, often through concrete struggles like those that took place in the nineteenth century over the speculum, which split the medical profession itself.[35] There can be no doubt that violence has been focused particularly on women's genitals. In performing dissections to reveal the gravid uterus, for instance, William Hunter also sectioned the clitoris, although this was not the object of his enquiry.[36] Medical texts of the eighteenth century contain increasingly explicit illustrations of female genitals, which in earlier periods had mostly been discreetly covered. Of course, there had been illustrations of the reproductive organs, but these were presented as disembodied parts and hardly represented in directly erotic terms. The more 'accurate' representations of the Enlightenment are not indicative of a matter-of-fact acceptance of 'private' parts, but of increasing scrutiny and voyeurism. Such phenomena can hardly be unproblematic. A revealing example is to be found in the anatomical plates of the *Encyclopédie* (1751–77) which show, for instance, the genitals of hermaphrodites in a naturalistic manner. Complete figures are shown in a variety of realistic poses, including the subjects looking at their own sex organs.[37] These images are not themselves violent, although they do indicate that most insistent curiosity about sexuality in nature which was so prominent a feature of the period and which I am using the term 'voyeurism' to evoke. Other anatomical illustrations directly embody violence. The example of William Hunter has already been mentioned. I have argued elsewhere that in relation

to the *Gravid Uterus* plates, the position of the viewer relative
to the corpse, which has the effect of drawing the eye into the
vagina, the cut-off thighs, the sectioned clitoris may all be seen
as implicitly violent.[38] The anatomical atlas of 1754 by William
Smellie (1697–1763) might be cited as another example. There he
had the genital area depicted from below during the crowning of
a baby's head. The unfamiliar angle and the powerful image of
taut skin join together to produce a shocking and violent effect.
Smellie's book also contained a plate showing forceps being
applied to the head during birth. Set in the context of the heated
controversy about man-midwifery and the use of forceps, such
an illustration contained its own form of implicit violence.[39]

Violence towards the female body surfaces most plainly in
pornography, and medical practices can provide a suitable occasion
for (gratuitous) bodily violence. Yet it would be wrong to
conclude from this that medicine is an area that more or less
directly sanctions men's sadism towards women. In fact, an
idealization of women is as prominent a theme as violence –
possibly these constitute two sides of the same coin. The same

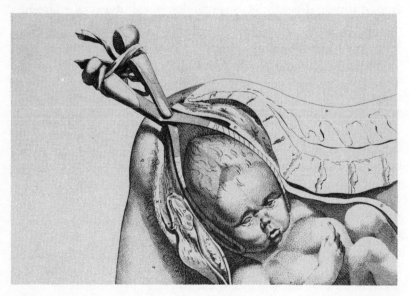

Plate 3 Smellie included this plate to 'shew in what Manner the Head
of the *Foetus* is helped along with the Forceps as artificial Hands, when
it is necessary to assist with the same for the safety of either Mother or
Child'.

body, the reproductive capacities of which performed venerable, even sacred functions, was also to be profaned. We can see this double female body image with exceptional clarity in late eighteenth-century France when medical writers frequently invoked Rousseau while discussing women in lyrical terms. At the very same time, de Sade (1740–1814) directly attacked the idea that women had special qualities and privileges because they bore children. This was integral to his social critique. Although not confined to women, the acts of sexual violence portrayed in his writings encompass an astonishing range of bodily violation. It is as if he represented an inversion of the celebratory mode, so that his work constitutes a perpetual reaction against it, even as it is bound to it. In both the idealizing and the violating modes, body image and sex roles remain welded together.[40]

It may appear unreasonable to set so-called 'pornography' next to medical texts, since the former intentionally sets out to shock, provoke, titillate and excite while, at a conscious level at least, the latter set out to edify. There are, indeed, major generic differences here, but they do not invalidate comparisons. All texts work at many different levels, and beyond the expressed intentions of their creators. We are as entitled to find a form of violent eroticism in medicine as we are to note the philosophical dimensions of 'pornography'; neither case need involve the attribution of conscious motives to authors. This does not mean, however, that the expressed intentions of cultural products are uninteresting.

The role of intention can best be indicated by a specific example. The fact that the famous wax modeller Zummo (or Zumbo as he is sometimes called) intended his scenes commemorating the Naples plague that ended in 1656 to function as *memento mori*, is of the utmost importance. Warnings about death are ubiquitous in anatomical depictions of the early modern period and also in medical writings of the eighteenth century, although the languages in which these warnings were expressed varied.[41] In addition to the insights the ghastly scenes of destruction, decay, pain and suffering can offer us about attitudes towards death, they also reveal something important about the nature of representation. Zummo's scenes of rats, corpses and general devastation contain the same relentless, literalistic naturalism mentioned earlier, and it was clearly integral to his moral purpose. There is a bond here

Plate 4 This wax *memento mori*, *The Triumph of Time*, contains many of the objects commonly associated with death

between verisimilitude (i.e. 'realism') and morality, a bond which endures to this day in the waxworks of Madame Tussaud's. These were initially designed to bring the lessons of the French Revolution to the British populace. An ardent Royalist, Madame Tussaud (1761–1850) believed that seeing exact likenesses of the major revolutionary protagonists would have a beneficial moral effect on her audiences.[42]

Although we could see modern waxworks as providing simple, mass entertainment, the fact that social extremes are represented, the rich, the royal and the famous on the one hand, iniquitous criminals on the other, suggests that moral purposes lie just below the surface. If so, the link between body image and social roles remains unbroken. It is important, therefore, never to leave technical virtuosity unexamined, but to try to tease apart what lies behind a search for extreme versimilitude. What lies behind it, of course, depends on the time and the place, and encompasses a variety of goals, some stated quite openly, others unacknowledged or even suppressed. In the case of the latter, historical discussions necessarily entail a degree of speculation. It is not speculative, however, to note that medical and scientific images of the body were gendered in rather complex ways, that they served to differentiate masculine and feminine, not because putatively natural differences and sex roles were stable but because they were not. Furthermore, such representations acted as naturalized bases to which other attributes of masculinity and femininity could be added, by tradition, by metaphorical extension, by contingent demands.

4

Gender as a Cosmic Metaphor

Both the persistence and complexity of dichotomous styles of thinking have been discussed in earlier chapters. Gender itself constitutes a paradigmatic example of this in that masculine and feminine can hold an impressive variety of contrasting meanings and be applied to an extremely wide range of instances. It is vital, however, to keep reminding ourselves that gender is not intrinsically dichotomous, that we can derive no sanctions from nature (with its impressive plurality of reproductive styles) for our insistence on duality. As a result, we have to comprehend how polarities are made and given credibility. In order to grasp more fully the implications of these points for the nineteenth century, we will trace them in the ideas of a single person – the French historian Jules Michelet. Michelet's diverse writings can be used to illuminate a specific set of cultural themes, since his work brought together a remarkable number of the major issues of the day.[1] To appreciate these we need to consider the whole spectrum of his activities from the history books to the natural history publications and including works on women and the family. In all of these gender plays a central role; furthermore, it is a concept that he understood in large measure through medicine and natural history.

Michelet's whole stance towards the areas he studied is indicative of his thought patterns. His method involved an intense and intimate identification with his subject-matter rather than a distancing from it. His prose style follows logically from this; devoid of cool objectivity, it is full of naked emotions and is florid, even euphoric. For these reasons modern commentators often treat him with disdain, with the result that he is now discussed largely by literary critics who are attracted above all by the qualities of his writing.[2] The interest of his non-historical, popular books is now being recognized, again largely for stylistic reasons. Indeed, these are also documents of unusual value for historians concerned with the relationships between science and gender.

Michelet's emotional attachment to the people, things and processes he studied constitutes an important link between his history writing on the one hand and his books on natural history and women on the other. When Michelet studied the world of nature, for example, he did so in a thoroughly anthropomorphic way. This is perhaps too bland a formulation, since in imposing the human viewpoint upon the living world, Michelet projected his whole personality onto organic processes, and this personality was, to be truthful, obsessed with sexual difference. Accordingly, the nature books are permeated by a language which refers to his own life and preoccupations, conveniently acted out before his eyes in the theatre of nature. Similarly, his enthusiasm for medical knowledge and for doctors derives from a belief in medicine as a humanizing field, which enables him to comprehend the life experience of women more fully. The post-mortems so vividly evoked in *La Femme* (1859), for example, serve to convince him of the inherent vulnerability of women. Science and medicine thus serve as convenient instruments for heightening Michelet's capacity to understand, through identifying with, natural processes in general and the female sex in particular.

Michelet took woman and nature as two intimately related terms. He also possessed a profound sense of the 'otherness' of woman. This is because gender as a metaphor underlay all his work, allowing him to stress the deep gulf between the masculine and the feminine, which are distinct modes of being. He argued, however, that the gulf must be bridged and the sexes brought together. Behind so much of what he wrote lay a vision of the ideal relations between the sexes, which, if realized, would revolutionize, or rather cleanse, French society. Nature and gender thus also constitute major forces in the history of France. We can understand them both as systems of representation; they constitute flexible patterns of images, generally applicable to other phenomena. Michelet's highly symbolic and metaphorical view of the world is worked out by means of complex analogies that permeate his works. Before exploring these in more depth, I shall say something about Michelet's education and origins, since it is instructive to see how these, together with the historical circumstances in which France found herself during his lifetime, shaped his views of gender and nature.

Jules Michelet was born in 1798, the son of a Paris printer who found himself in financially precarious circumstances but who, at some cost to himself, encouraged his son to acquire a good education. Michelet considered himself a man of the people – a concept of particular importance in his social theorizing and historical work. He prided himself on coming from peasant stock, on his early years of hardship and on his political inheritance as a member of the Parisian populace with revolutionary sympathies. Until 1848 he enjoyed a prestigious career with posts at the Archives Nationales, the Collège de France and the Sorbonne, a career that finally disintegrated following his refusal to take the oath of allegiance to Napoleon III in 1852. He died in 1874, dispirited by France's defeat by the Germans.[3]

Michelet was a prolific man who produced books on a number of themes: the multi-volume histories of France and the Revolution, the short popular work Le Peuple (1846); the natural histories L'Oiseau (1856), L'Insecte (1858), La Mer (1861) and La Montagne (1868); works on women – L'Amour (1858) and its sequel La Femme (1859); and several other volumes on religion, history and autobiography. It was the popular books with a strong moral element that found particular favour with the public. Michelet claimed that when it first appeared in 1846, Le Peuple sold a thousand copies on a single day in Paris alone. L'Amour, first published in 1858, sold 5,700 copies in the first year and was in its fifth edition by 1861. Its sequel, La Femme, sold 13,000 copies in its first year and was in its fifth edition by 1861. By contrast, Volume 1 of his History of the French Revolution, 1847, sold only 2,500 copies in six years.[4] The evidence suggests that

Michelet's views on women and the family in particular were widely known and responded to in contemporary periodicals. His preoccupation with these topics was far from unusual, and many other authors were producing similar works at the same time.[5]

In terms of politics, the most accurate label we can apply to Michelet is 'populist' in that he consistently argued for the nobility and rights of the common people, but this does not make him a socialist, just as his writings on women do not make him a feminist.[6] Although not directly politically active himself, Michelet was passionately interested in contemporary affairs, and was deeply saddened by the events of both 1848 and 1870–1. His views took the form of social critique rather than political analysis. The overall tone of his writings was cosmic; invoking the destiny of France, universal forces, and feeling on a grand scale.

A specific target for attack was the Catholic Church. He had been baptized a Catholic at the age of 18 (1816), but by the early 1840s began to feel distinctly critical of the Church in general and of Jesuits in particular. Michelet's anti-clericalism was closely linked with his concern for family life and for women, since he saw the priest as the evil interloper between husbands and wives. His *Du Prêtre, de la Femme, de la Famille* was published in 1845, and enjoyed considerable success. It was in its third edition by the following year, with, according to its translator, 50,000 copies sold and an English edition.[7] Over half the book is devoted to an analysis of seventeenth-century religious thought and the behaviour he considered it to have sanctioned. In the book Michelet argued against what he called *'direction'*, that is the spiritual guidance of women by priests, which created a schism between husband and wife. His violent attacks on Roman Catholicism are also closely linked with his commitment to France as a nation. The nation was the supreme, the sacrosanct unit, not to be interfered with by outside interests.[8] Yet Michelet was also a deeply spiritual man, who believed in ethical systems so long as they were rooted in nature and a love of humanity – features he found in non-Christian religions such as Hinduism. It was the institution of the Catholic Church and its celibate clergy that he found offensive and threatening to the health of French society.

It is not hard to see how Michelet's ideology was moulded by his intellectual concerns, his political opinions and his religious views. Those who have written about Michelet have usually attributed particular significance to his private life as the source of his ideas. He was married twice, first in 1824 to a woman with whom he had been living for six years, by whom he had two children. His first wife died in 1839, and some years later he married a woman considerably younger than himself. She shared his intellectual interests and took some credit as the inspirer of his nature books. His intimate record of their conjugal life was an important source and expression of ideas on the nature of woman.[9] His writings are, naturally enough, profoundly marked by his personality and he was more than usually willing to commit details of his private life to paper. But there is no reason to suppose that his ideas are best understood principally in terms of his biography, or that they were peculiar to him. In order to lay out some of Michelet's key concepts, I want first to examine a work about neither medicine nor natural history, yet which offers an exceptionally clear illustration of his ideas, because his historical writings were equally rich in ideas about gender and nature.

I therefore propose to examine Michelet's approach to history and to women by discussing briefly one of his best-known works, *Joan of Arc*, considered by many to be his masterpiece. It was first published in 1841 as part of Volume 5 of his *History of France*, then reissued as a separate work in 1853. Michelet was writing at a time when interest in Joan was dramatically accelerating in a 'climate of romantic patriotism'.[10] The central themes of her biography had long been established: her donning of male clothing, her virginity, her amenorrhoea, her childlike qualities. Thus we can immediately appreciate how gender is pivotal to the retelling of her story.

Joan of Arc is a chronological account of her life, from childhood to death, written from an openly partisan perspective. As one critic has put it, 'Michelet and Joan of Arc are one'.[11] Certain themes, concerning the special qualities Michelet discerned in the Maid, dominate the work. First, he drew the reader's attention to the many manifestations of her vitality: the vividness of her religious convictions, the poetry of war, her leadership of the ordinary people, her intellectual acuteness and her ability to make mind triumph over body. All these traits convey a sense of her peculiar personal power and vital strength. At the same time, however, Michelet stressed a second set of characteristics pertaining to her innocence; her virginity (literal and metaphorical), her modesty, which led her to wear men's clothing to help her avoid any sexual contact, her childlike qualities, an affinity for animals, the fact that she never menstruated, and her capacity to ward off an attempted rape. Both sets of qualities indicate that although Joan possessed a certain kind of potency, affirmed by her role in the history of France as a nation, her power had no *sexual* dimensions to it -- to the extent that Joan never attained full womanhood. Rather, she had a 'vital force' that was 'pure'.[12]

Michelet's intensely personal account of Joan of Arc offers us some interesting insights into his notions of gender; it indicates one way in which metaphorical and symbolic elements are woven into his history, and it reveals how he raised certain historical actors to the status of mythical heroes. Yet Michelet was totally committed to offering a naturalistic explanation of Joan's actions. No miracles explain her initial success. Hence, the cult of spirituality surrounding her was not presented as magical but as rooted in her human capacity for transcendence, which derives from her simplicity, her closeness to nature. She was astute, full of native wit – 'Joan's eminent originality was her common sense'.[13] Above all, she had a vision of France that her religious convictions helped her to make real. Her beliefs were thus a vehicle for political goals, for seeking the geographical and spiritual integrity of France as a nation. Michelet had considerable emotional investment in the supremacy of France, and at one historical juncture, Joan of Arc stood for this dream. Hence, Michelet's method involved both an intense identification with his subject-matter, and the use of figures and images to represent, with considerable imaginative power, his principal historical and social tenets.

Joan's relationship to the lot of women in general was complex in that Michelet found her feminine in some respects but not in others. Joan was doubly distanced from the women he saw around him in being first a national hero and second a figure from the distant past. She resembled them, however, in that she was childlike, natural, creative. What is elided here is class. At one level, Michelet spoke of woman as a universal category, but at another he was, as we shall see, addressing the problems of

working women and seeking to promote a petit bourgeois life-
style for them.

At this point we should note two terms from religious discourse
which crop up all the time in relation to Michelet's approach:
resurrection and redemption.[14] Resurrection refers to his goal of
making the past come alive again; redemption, to his idea that
there were crucial historical moments at which the French national
destiny was saved through suffering. Joan of Arc was one such
saviour. For Christians, redemption contains just these elements
of identification and representation that have already been noted
as characteristic of Michelet's thought. The Christian feels, as it
were, Christ's pain and identifies with His bodily suffering. He,
through His death and salvation, represents the entire human
condition in the same way as Joan represented France when she
was burnt as a witch but lived on through her contribution to
the nationhood of her country. Similarly, by bringing the past
to life, Michelet's method of resurrection was designed to make
people feel part of it, to fuse their identities with the great
waves of history. Accordingly, personification is a general
characteristic of Michelet's thought, a device which serves to
encourage the reader to feel rather than to analyse and so
yields a particular form of understanding through empathetic
identification. It enables Michelet to present historical movements
in human terms and so achieve a more vivid representation of
past processes.

On the basis of these remarks about *Joan of Arc*, it is now
possible to be clear about why Michelet's approach has proved
so disturbing to later commentators. First, it is unashamedly
partisan, and second, it displays a vigorous commitment to a
nationalist ideology (pro-French, anti-English). Michelet brought
together features in history writing which we have become
accustomed to keep distinct. This point is exemplified by Stanley
Mellon's undisguised distaste for Michelet by comparison with
François Guizot (1787–1874) the historian and statesman. For
him, Guizot's liberal commitment to historical objectivity is vastly
to be preferred to Michelet's partisan, nationalist style, which he
characterizes as '*Einseitigkeit*' – the fault of only seeing one side
of things. He is particularly critical of Michelet's resurrection
technique, which involved searching for that which embodies an
epoch, or for the forces representing the true France.[15] The danger

of Mellon's approach is that since it takes modern historiographical values for granted, it leads us to miss important features of Michelet's world-view – features which are central to the ways in which he conceptualized gender and the natural world.

It is precisely because Michelet blended together description and fantasy, politics, ethics and history, that scholars have preferred to seek out specific facets of his work and concentrate on those. It is, I think, more productive to emphasize the unifying features of his work without presenting these as purely psychological traits. I have suggested two themes which run through his writings and which link his historical works with those on nature, women and the family: first, his method of identifying with his subject-matter, and second, his search for meaning which led him to use gender as a cosmic metaphor. I mean by this that Michelet displayed a cosmological drive to assign meaning to everything; accordingly, anything can be seen as gendered, and since gender is part of a larger system of signification, to speak of something as male or female implies sets of other, related characteristics. Gender functions in this way because it is seen to be part of the natural world, the source of all morality and ethics, and animated by the same forces as the human world. Nature and society mutually illuminate each other, each can be used to represent the other. The nature books and the works on women exemplify these points. I stress the interrelatedness of Michelet's thought because it is the source of the power of his ideas – his writings speak to the imagination in a particularly vivid way, they engage our attention, hence the potency of their constituent scientific and medical ideas.

It has often been suggested that Michelet should be seen as a Romantic writer.[16] Thinking critically about the term 'Romantic' is important if we want to understand Michelet's concern with science and medicine in the context of his work as a whole. Three general senses in which the term has been used are particularly apposite. First, there is the emphasis on feeling as distinct from reason, an interest in subjective experience and a celebration of the imaginative faculties often presented as a reaction against classicism and the Enlightenment.[17] Second, there is the stress on the authenticity of the individual personality and on the capacity of individuals for liberation. Third, there is the fascination with the erotic, the funereal and the demonic described by Mario Praz as an interest in 'everything that exists only in aspiration and in remembrance, everything which is remote, dead, unknown'. He added, 'the essence of Romantic . . . comes to consist in that which cannot be described'.[18]

Let us examine what implications these senses of Romanticism have for the natural sciences and medicine as they enter Michelet's work. The polarization between subjectivity and objectivity implied by the first sense would suggest that 'Romantic science' is a contradiction in terms, and hence Michelet's concern with science, natural history and medicine becomes a 'problem', an anomaly, in that he is assumed to be bringing together two irreconcilable elements. In fact, this is a false dichotomy. Michelet's writings show very clearly the marriage of 'scientific' and imaginative elements; for him each reinforced the other, as when he saw the cold facts of the dissecting room as heightening our appreciation of human suffering, or when he examined anatomical plates of the female reproductive system in order to understand the mysteries of femininity.[19]

For Michelet, knowledge of nature was an important source of individual liberation since it enabled people to attain a cosmic perspective. Assuming an opposition between feeling and reason seems historically unhelpful when it applies to a period in which such crude polarities were not universally assented to. Furthermore, Michelet was particularly indebted to the science of the late Enlightenment and early nineteenth century, as is clear from his admiration of Lamarck and Geoffroy Saint-Hilaire. He dubbed this period 'the French Revolution in the natural sciences'.[20] Thus we could say that Michelet is indeed an exponent of a Romantic science, not in the sense of celebrating feeling at the expense of reason, but in the sense of encouraging a sympathetic relationship with nature that enables people to combine knowledge of the natural world with an enhanced awareness of the human condition. In fact, this approach informed his entire mental framework: his history as well as his scientific and medical ideas.

The second definition of 'Romantic' pertained to the role of the individual and the cultivation of fresh, authentic feelings. Mid-nineteenth-century science and medicine assiduously cultivated the idea of the single creative scientific mind, of the doctor or scientist as hero. We can illustrate this theme by referring to Michelet's contemporary, the experimental physiologist Claude Bernard (1813–78). In his widely read *Introduction to the Study of Experimental Medicine* (1865), Bernard set out the philosophy underpinning his scientific practices. The experimenter is presented there in truly heroic terms; he is 'at once theorist and practitioner', with an active, controlling stance towards nature: 'the experimenter doubtless forces nature to unveil herself by attacking her with all manner of questions . . . he must submit his idea to nature'. According to Bernard the experimenter 'must note her [i.e. nature's] answer, hear her out and in every case accept her decision'. This privileged role in relation to nature encouraged scientists to present themselves and each other as heroes. As Bernard said of himself, 'my whole scientific life is devoted to contributing my share to the immense work which modern science will have the glory of having understood'.[21] One of his pupils described him as a 'great and noble character', a 'true genius' with 'a sureness of vision, an astounding penetration', 'one whose gaze is undismayed by the unknown'.[22] Although he enjoyed unique prestige in nineteenth-century France, the instance of Bernard is of general interest and of particular relevance to Michelet, who was prone to idealize practitioners of science and medicine. The grandness, the global significance attributed to the encounter between a human consciousness and nature is clearly a common theme. More telling, however, is the fact that for both men the momentous meeting between a masculine heroic mind and feminine nature is an imaginative engagement, in which the sense of sight plays a central part. I am not suggesting that Bernard be understood as 'a Romantic', only that he vividly exemplifies the point that there was no incompatibility between playing a scientific or medical role and celebrating human creativity on a heroic scale.

Turning now to the final sense of Romanticism, we can see immediately that Michelet's preoccupation with death, sickness, and the 'otherness' of women fits comfortably into this category.[23] Indeed, the very elusiveness of these phenomena led him to seek scientific and medical knowledge of them. The notion of a Romantic science/medicine seems to be particularly useful because it can help us to understand strong traditions, especially prominent in France, that combined literature, science and medicine to express a restless fascination with the dead and the morbid.

Michelet found women to be inherently morbid, hence pathology
was also an especially appropriate tool for the study of gender.
The success of writers in these traditions, many of whom presented
themselves as disciples of Rousseau, depended on the existence
of a language, both visual and verbal, of social pathology – that
is on established ways of discussing, in agreed-upon terms, the
relationships between social positions and roles, and bodily states.
It further depended on the reading public accepting that the
vocabulary of health and disease could legitimately be applied to
the social body.[24]

It would, of course, be possible to offer a far more sophisticated
and sustained analysis of Romanticism in relation to science and
medicine than the brief one offered here. My concern has been
simply to show that no wedge should be unthinkingly driven
between the world of the imagination and that of science. Since
Michelet is often presented as a 'Romantic' writer, partly in order
to make sense of his prose style, investigating the extent to which
this is a useful label and its implications for our understanding
of his vision of nature is important. However difficult the term
is to use in practice, it helps us to think about Michelet's
fascination with nature and with death, morbidity and the erotic
in a broad historical context.

We have already discussed the way in which Michelet used
Joan of Arc to epitomize a stage in the national development of
France, with an historical actor representing a historical period.
Michelet also used diseases in this way. In *L'Amour* (1858), he
argued that each century is characterized by a great illness: leprosy
– thirteenth century; black death – fourteenth century; syphilis
– sixteenth century; and in the nineteenth century it was the
ulcerated womb of women and the paralysed brain of men that
summed up the epoch.[25] Michelet evoked the state of French
society in his own time by making the illness or death of
individuals stand for the condition of entire groups. By presenting
information about an individual life, in recounting a life history,
Michelet invites the reader to emotionally identify with their
plight, to feel the depth of the social crisis as if it were the
suffering of a dear friend.

In the lengthy introduction to *La Femme* (1859), Michelet
wished to establish that 'Woman does not live without man'. He
meant this quite literally: just as children left in foundling hospitals

expire because they have been robbed of their mothers, women die from illness or suicide if they do not enjoy the protection of a husband. In order to establish his point, Michelet turned to the dissecting room. First, he related how he was invited to participate in the autopsies of a number of children, waxing lyrical about the moral value of anatomy: 'It is death above all that teaches us to respect life, to take care of and not to overtax the human race'.[26] It therefore followed quite naturally for Michelet that great doctors are also the best, the most humane people.

Michelet had some specific anatomical interests. It was the brain in particular that fascinated him. He noted a close relationship between the brain and the face. More specifically, he claimed that the lower edge of the brain reveals the person even better than does the face itself. Studying the brain of an individual permits the anatomist to reconstruct their life, and examining the outside of a human body allows the viewer to infer the state of the brain. In women, the uterus can be used in a similar way.[27] Having established that a person's life is engraved in their organs, Michelet recounted a specific life history. He began by describing the corpse of a young woman in some detail, allowing his imagination full play before telling her, presumably fictional, story. In essence the account is very simple, and totally familiar in its stereotyped elements. An unmarried mother from the provinces, in poor health, comes to Paris in search of work. The only job she can find, doing ironing, causes her health to deteriorate. Michelet drew here on an occupation commonly associated in his society with difficult working conditions for women, and with somewhat loose sexual conduct.[28] Spending the nights in the room where she worked, she grew worse and finally died alone in hospital. Since no one claimed her body, it was sent to Michelet's anatomist friend for dissection. To his satisfaction, Michelet has established through this tale that, 'Woman dies if she has neither home nor protection'.[29]

This interest in illness found its most elaborate expression in Michelet's work on women, because the female sex was, for him, inherently morbid. It is vital to stress, however, that he meant this in a rather particular way. He did not, for example, believe that women's brains are inferior to men's or that women are essentially more animal-like than men. It is rather that women's vulnerable physiology is perfectly complemented by men's more

robust one, from which it follows that health, both individual
and social, lies in the union of male and female elements.
Addressing men, he claimed, 'you are her health, and she is your
illness. A cure for her involves coming back into harmony with
you'. Michelet's definitions of health and illness were closely
bound up with his notions of gender, of sexuality and of the
couple: 'illness is discord; health, unity'.[30]

We can now see how, by metaphorical extension, he could use
health and illness as structuring concepts in his historical as in
his moralizing writings. To an extent, Michelet is merely one
example of a very old tradition, which explored analogies between
the human body and the body politic or social, and which laid
particular stress on maintaining the integrity and stability of those
bodies. Like so many of his contemporaries, Michelet drew on
organicist ideas, but his use of pathology was especially far-
reaching in that it was a central component of his social theories.
Pathology was an imaginative trigger that generated metaphors
of social relations of all kinds, including gender. In other words,
Michelet used pathology as part of a representational system,
while he simultaneously naturalized social phenomena by means
of it. Furthermore, since diagnosis and therapy are closely linked,
Michelet prescribed certain cures based on his analysis of the
sickness in nineteenth-century French society. These included
lessening the power of the priest, encouraging marriage and
improving the lot of women.

In *L'Amour* (1858), Michelet stated that men and women have
different characteristic illnesses. Among men's diseases those of
the digestive organs were prominent, women's ills included those
of the womb: 'she is ill from love, the man from digestion'.[31]
Michelet's diagnosis was that men's ills derive from eating and
drinking too much, activities he deemed characteristic of the life
of the working man in mid-nineteenth-century France. As in his
story of the unmarried mother, Michelet was invoking a familiar
social type. The quintessence of working-class manhood is
reluctant to marry, spends his earnings self-indulgently in the
cabaret rather than using them to provide a home for the woman,
who works in worse conditions than he does and for such low
wages that she can barely afford to eat. The characteristic diseases
of men and women thereby encapsulate the entire condition of

'the people'. From this the appropriate social therapy becomes self-evident; men must be urged to marry, women not to work but to remain in the home, as civilizing agents and as the architects of a bourgeois or petit bourgeois life-style. Money previously spent on pleasure, should go on the accoutrements of domesticity.[32]

Other social changes were also implied by Michelet's analysis of the condition of women in French society: women should marry men older than themselves, they should use doctors rather than priests as confessors, they should not work during pregnancy and may on no account receive the death penalty. It was the fact of menstruation that convinced Michelet of women's need for special protection.[33] He saw this process not as repellent but as a glorious natural rhythm which harmonized women with the great patterns of the universe – tides, phases of the moon. Furthermore, he claimed that chemical evidence showed that menstrual blood was just like other blood and hence not impure. Religious orthodoxy that women were defiled by their periods was therefore to be forcefully condemned. In Michelet's hands, menstruation was no longer an unpleasant subject about which silence should be maintained, but an exciting one, linked with the mysteries of femininity, about which he incessantly felt the need to speak and write.

Despite his celebration of it, menstruation must none the less be understood as a wound: 'It is the healing of an internal wound which, in the last analysis generates this whole drama. It follows that in fact for 15 or 20 days out of 28 (one could say almost perpetually) woman is not only ill but wounded.'[34] Medicine provided Michelet with a language of nature through which to express his reactions to his own society and its history. Organs could be symbols of the state of specific social groups, diseases could stand for centuries, physiological systems could stand for the sexes, and conversely, to speak of either sex evokes their distinctive physiological and pathological profiles. Michelet elevated the anatomist to the position of moral arbiter, the doctor to that of priest and confessor.[35] But above all, medicine moved him, it nourished his imagination and enabled him to conceptualize the complex blending of nature and society in gender differences.

Given Michelet's concern with the material conditions in which 'the people' lived, it is not surprising to find that he made use of a number of the medical surveys conducted in France at this time. For instance, he warmly praises the work of Louis-René Villermé (1782–1863), well known for his studies of prison conditions and of textile workers, and one of the most prominent hygienists in France during the first half of the nineteenth century. The work of Villermé and others has been seen as a significant step in the development of statistical methods in medicine, as the product of liberal political economy, whose appalling findings challenged *laissez-faire* orthodoxy, and as the result of sincere commitment to reform.[36] In *Work and Revolution in France*, Sewell presented Villermé in a somewhat different light, one which makes Michelet's indebtedness to him all the more interesting. The particular attention Villermé paid to the poorest workers indicated to Sewell that he was using them to epitomize a larger labour problem.[37] His horrified fascination with their degraded state, which allowed him to jump effortlessly from poverty to incest, closely resembled Michelet's extrapolations from the weakened bodies of women workers to their overall debasement. In both cases the sight of misery and suffering acted as an imaginative trigger that enabled Villermé and Michelet to leap from knowledge of material deprivation to the assumption of sexually related degradation.

Furthermore, Villermé exploited the metaphorical associations of darkened damp and dirty cellars in which the poorest workers lived, especially in Lille, to dramatize the abject decay of the poor. As Sewell has said, attics have less rhetorical potential than cellars. We might add that the attic was an appropriate image for the plight of some social groups, such as artists and students, but less so for the 'dangerous classes'.[38] Villermé's perspective was fundamentally a moral one, within which vice like disease was contagious and the proper relations between the sexes stood for a well-regulated society. Thus the language of social pathology, with its sexual allusions, which was well-established within the medical literature and statistical surveys, employed the same methods of inviting the reader's emotional response. As in Michelet's writings, it represented social conditions through naturalistic and medical metaphors.

It was Michelet's deep commitment to the study of nature that made gender and sexuality of such overwhelming importance in his work. Yet his writings contain no overt traces of an aggressive attitude towards women, or of unbridled male desire. Indeed, those were aspects of male sexuality that Michelet explicitly condemned, as we might expect given his conviction that women were masculinized by sexual intercourse.[39] It was rather gender and sexuality as metaphors that concerned him. This is evident in his descriptions of the reproduction of insects, the song of birds and the character of the sea, which symbolized femininity. He saw the whole world in sexualized terms, so that by characterizing male and female as distinct, although complementary and interdependent, everything could be represented as either one or the other. This included inanimate objects like Mother Earth or the Sea as vagina, as well as abstractions like disciplines and religions. Thus history was masculine, while natural history, like Christianity, was feminine.[40]

Corresponding to the two sexes of the universe were two ways of understanding it: 'the two sexes of the mind'. There were male and female mental powers, each of which was sensitive to a different aspect of the world and fulfilled a different function. The female principle is characterized by emotion, spontaneity and religion, it attains *certum*, the truth of collective feeling. By contrast, the male principle is characterized by reason, reflection and philosophy. To the female *certum* corresponds the male *verum*, intellectual truth. Man, therefore, 'perceives', having 'reflection of the wise', while woman 'feels' with the 'instinct of the simple'.[41]

Michelet was giving voice to ideas about the nature/culture distinction which had long been familiar in Western thought since classical political theory, and now generally discussed through the terms made familiar by anthropology. Equally in keeping with ancient ideas was Michelet's conviction that the fusion of two distinct elements was necessary if creative and truly moral consequences were to result – hence, he argued that it will only be when history and natural history come together that truth can be found. Furthermore, Michelet denied any simple or rigid hierarchy between the sexes; in fact, each is dominant at certain times in the life cycle. However, his stress on the complementarity of the sexes was perfectly compatible with an influential nineteenth-century view of women which linked them with domesticity through a dense cluster of closely related images of the feminine. Michelet loved to fantasize about the details of domestic life – sheets, linen, flowers and so on – to which it was woman's

Plate 5 Michelet's ambivalence towards women was shared by many of his contemporaries, for whom it was often focused, as it is here, on their sexual attraction and their danger.

destiny to attend. When Michelet extolled women's home-making activities in the following terms, 'The woman represents economy, order, and providence in these households. Every increase in her influence is progress in morality', he was drawing out the effect of cheap cotton goods on the poor through the 'advance in cleanliness' they allowed. Thanks to textiles, women could stabilize the family.[42]

In assigning to women the realm of nature, Michelet was not giving a single value to femininity, which for him contained contradictory characteristics – a Marie-Antoinette as well as a Joan of Arc. Good women could save and civilize a nation as well as their own families; bad women could be correspondingly destructive, especially when under the thumb of the priest. But whatever the circumstances, women were first and foremost members of their sex, being unable in the ordinary course of events to transcend their femininity. This idea was already commonplace in Enlightenment writing and had been particularly vividly expressed by Rousseau. For Michelet, this perspective does not reduce womanhood to a biological condition, rather it finds in biology a spiritual dimension. So, in saying that women are more 'natural' than men, he was certainly not attributing crudity to them, in fact quite the reverse. Women of the working class, he claimed, are more refined than their menfolk: 'the women of the people . . . are by no means coarse like the men, and [they] feel the need of delicacy and distinction'.[43] Michelet was quite explicit about the dual nature of womanhood: 'Higher and lower than the man, humiliated by nature whose heavy hand she feels, but at the same time lifted up to dreams, premonitions and higher intuitions that man will never have, woman has fascinated him, innocently enchanted him for ever.'[44] And, the key to this special, 'natural' status of woman is menstruation. Despite the euphoric, even mystical language he uses on the subject, Michelet presented the regular, predictable menstrual cycle as an example of the complete transparency of natural events.

Michelet's attitudes towards nature, whether in relation to women, to animals or to the environment, had two elements. First, he wished to understand its physical aspects, principally by detailed observation. Second, he sought to record the spiritual potential of nature. The very idea of nature being base was contradictory for Michelet; nature was on the contrary full of non-material powers. The evolutionary process showed the progressive liberation of spirit from matter. His model of development was a non-materialistic one, as we might expect from his adulation of Lamarck and Geoffroy Saint-Hilaire, both of whom were claimed by later nineteenth-century thinkers for the cause of transcendent transformism and a 'vitalistic' approach to biology. Michelet's kinship for these naturalists is not without its irony since they were also seen by some as materialists and claimed accordingly by subsequent generations.[45] Michelet's 'vitalist' sympathies are also evident in his enthusiasm for the work of Felix-Archimède Pouchet (1800–72), biologist of the mammalian reproductive system and staunch defender of the reality of spontaneous generation. He was the author of an important work published in 1847 on mammalian and human ovulation, but is best known for his defence of spontaneous generation against Pasteur's attack. Michelet's admiration for him is especially interesting in the light of Pouchet's activities as a popularizer of science – his successful *L'Univers* first appeared in 1865.[46]

The capabilities of life forms was one of the major themes of Michelet's nature books (1856–68), which are parables of human life as well as lyrical accounts of the complexities of the animal world.[47] Michelet used individual animal species to represent human qualities, urging readers to identify with them and to find meanings in nature from studying them. We may want to see this as employing a similar strategy to his deciphering of the meanings of women's lives by examining parts of their bodies. In both cases, items in nature stand for larger human concerns, and in both the anthropomorphic form of the arguments suggests a kinship with physiognomy with its sense that human and animal faces mutually illuminate and represent each other and that visual inspection permits the inference of invisible moral qualities.[40]

Michelet's works sought to establish a particular relationship between the author, the reader, and the subject-matter, which in the natural history books and those on women, is nature itself. As their author, he was the agent of a particular relationship between the knower and that which is known; he encouraged the reader to identify with the cosmic processes of nature, as he did himself. To this end he used specific cases – the bird, the spider, the unmarried mother, and so on. It is not those beings in themselves that are important, but the meanings their lives generate, the qualities of which they are emblems and the relationships between Michelet's readers and 'nature' that they facilitate. We find in Michelet, then, a matching between particular ways of knowing, specific parts of nature and the social urgency of the issues he focused on. And, all of these are gendered.

Michelet's own way of knowing was based on a fusion between subject and object – striving for fusion is a general characteristic of his thought, and it is, as many commentators have noted, erotically charged. It is summed up in the importance of the idea of the couple. This shows why his belief in two sorts of knowledge is important – both kinds are needed, *certum* and *verum*, just as Michelet wished to unite men and women, history and natural history. Thus the couple is a basic structure, composed of complementary elements. For Michelet, the fundamental natural, universal paradigm of the couple is gender. Paired terms embody old themes in Western thought and express ideas specific to Michelet's time. He therefore has to be understood both in terms of his lively sense of immediate social problems and of the mythic dimensions of his ideas, which are not directly tied to immediate historical circumstances.

An understanding of Michelet encourages us to appreciate more fully the conceptual and imaginative richness of science and medicine. It would be misleading to describe him as someone who took 'facts' of nature and dressed them up in a fancy language to appeal to ordinary folk. The ideas he used were already dense with associations. We now recognize the value of treating scientific and medical writings as literature – a point which has particular relevance to Michelet since he responded to the imaginative dimensions of the biomedical sciences and was also the author of popular works that epitomize the union of science and literature.[49] Furthermore, this union was thoroughly political in every sense.

It is the political significance of Michelet's treatment of nature and gender that is of special importance. His work in general, of course, reworked political myths according to the circumstances in which he found himself. His monumental history of the Revolution and his careful attention to the conditions of 'the people' exemplify this. Successive generations of historians have shrouded Michelet with their own myths, myths that have to be carefully peeled away for a more realistic assessment to take place. The fairly widespread but profoundly misleading conviction that Michelet was a pioneering feminist is an excellent example of such a myth. He held complex views on women which are not adequately summed up in the term 'feminist', but which did engage in complicated negotiations about power relations between the sexes. Analysing the construction of myths, in the past generally and by historians in particular, is an important task. It is exceptionally important that we develop a critical understanding of the processes of myth-making in relation to nature and gender, because without such a perspective the cultural power of figures like Michelet will never be comprehensible. This form of historical understanding will then in turn bring with it greater appreciation of the relationships between science, medicine and gender.

5

Nature Unveiling Before Science

I take the title of this chapter from the inscription on a late nineteenth-century statue in the Paris medical faculty. An almost identical, though polychrome one was on display at the exhibition of French nineteenth-century sculpture held in Paris in 1985. It was by Louis Ernest Barrias (1841–1905), and made in 1899 for the Conservatoire National des Arts et Métiers.[1] The figure of the young woman is covered except for her breasts, and she raises both her hands to the veil on her head in order to remove it. Once seen, the statue appears almost banal, with its personification of nature as a beautiful woman, only her breasts showing, and its choice of the very moment of unveiling as its subject-matter. It implies that science is a masculine viewer, who is anticipating full knowledge of nature, which is represented as the naked female body. This statue is easy to understand despite the fact that it brings together a number of distinct, abstract ideas – presumably because such ideas have acquired a degree of familiarity. It mobilizes, in fact, a number of devices commonly used over many centuries: personification, veiling, the use of breasts to denote femininity, the gendering of both science and nature. We will want to examine the ramifications of these representational

Plate 6 Nature Unveiling Herself Before Science.

practices to see what they reveal about the relationships between
gender and scientific knowledge.

   Although the statue itself is legible, the concepts it deploys are
not easily teased apart. If we look, for instance, at veiling
and gender, the issues become altogether more complex. This
complexity stems on the one hand from the deep ambivalence
already encountered in earlier chapters in the relationship between
gender and knowledge, and on the other from the multiple uses
and meanings assigned to veils. In the case of the statue, there is
an implication that unveiling nature is of positive value, yet it is
essential to note that it is only the head and upper part of the
body that are to be revealed, not the lower part, the unveiling
of which can be deemed profoundly threatening.[2] Thus, even in

this case the veil is doing two different jobs, in that its removal will give rise to knowledge at the same time as its presence is preserving decency. There is a powerful moral ambivalence at work here, stemming from the absence of any stable value attached to the female body and hence to its visibility or concealment.

This chapter focuses on the veiling/unveiling of women's bodies as vehicles for thinking about knowledge, especially of a scientific or medical kind. We can readily agree that veiling is an idea peculiarly associated with women and with female sexuality. In the case of brides and nuns, veils seem to be linked to female chastity and modesty on the one hand and to their submission to authority on the other. Women also veil themselves during mourning. In all these cases, the head and particularly the face – the part of the body most expressive of individual identity – is the crucial area. As such, the face is the locus of shame and guilt, to be covered in gestures or by material in public, acts of social acknowledgement of moral transgression. In this case, men as well as women may be involved in literal or symbolic veiling, as Nathaniel Hawthorne's story *The Minister's Black Veil* (1836) shows. None the less, there are special senses in which femininity and shame are linked.

Veils have also been associated with the explicitly sexual modesty of women, as in the wispy little bits of material strategically placed in much Renaissance painting. As Leo Steinberg has put it, 'these veils charming a woman's flanks were meant to delight'.[3] The whole question of appropriate female dress raises intricate issues of sexual modesty, since women were not to flaunt their charms, yet these should be decorously hinted at in their clothing. Of course, the exact costume requirements vary with period and class, but it is none the less striking how many instances there are during the eighteenth and nineteenth centuries of attempts to conceptualize what the basic requirements of women's clothing were and to police female sartorial behaviour.[4]

Unveiling also has specifically female connotations, not just because of the eroticism of the female body, but because of the female personification of both Nature and Truth. Here a positive value is given to nakedness. Both painting and sculpture abound with examples, as Marina Warner has shown, where the general beauty and specific admirable features given to the female figure of Truth or Nature serve as indicators of the esteem in which they are held.[5]

We have already noted that what is unveiled can, in other contexts, have a more ambiguous status. Of course, there are many places where the different associations of women and veiling are mixed together, a fact which makes the complex nexus of femininity and veils especially interesting. We can usefully examine this complexity through the meaning of the term 'veil'. Veils offer a rich metaphorical field. Some uses are openly pejorative – in the words of the *Oxford English Dictionary*, 'to draw a veil over' means to hide or conceal, to refrain from discussing or dealing with, to hush up or keep from public knowledge. While other meanings simply stress physical concealment, the verb to veil also denotes 'to conceal (some immaterial thing . . .) from apprehension, knowledge, or perception; to deal with . . . so as to hide or obscure; to hide the real nature or meaning (of something)'. We gain two insights from this: first, veiling has to do with knowledge and truth, and second, quite obviously, it implies a link between such knowledge and the capacity for unimpeded vision.[6]

One significant feature of veils is that unlike most other types of material or clothing they reveal and conceal at the same time. The whole point about veils is that they are sufficiently translucent to hint at what lies beneath them and hence they invite the viewer to fantasize about 'the real thing' in anticipation of seeing it. This combination of hiding and revealing accounts for the erotic dynamic of veils. It also implies a form of truth beneath a layer which only certain people (generally men) may reveal.[7]

We find these points neatly exemplified in visual form in a painting by the American artist Charles Wilson Peale (1741–1827), entitled *The Artist in His Museum* (1822). Here Peale is holding aside a heavy curtain so that his museum containing both an orderly arrangement of natural objects and pictures of exemplary persons painted by himself is unveiled to the viewer. He saw the portraits as 'represent[ing] man as "the head of the Linnean order" of nature'. His subjects were those who had distinguished themselves during the American Revolution. Just as interesting is the way in which his museum project changed his artistic practices: 'To preserve his human specimens in portraits, Peale felt he had to achieve as close a likeness as possible. Therefore, he began to render even the smallest details of his sitter's features with great fidelity. He also devised a special format for the museum portraits, which set off the likeness and minimized distracting details.' In a number of distinct, although overlapping senses, Peale unveiled nature and human nature to allow the spectator's unimpeded vision of them and presented himself, since the picture is also a self-portrait, as the principal agent of these multiple revelations. Another painting by Peale makes the point even more forcibly. He was one of the originators of a *trompe-l'œil* tradition in America. Among the best-known examples of his work in this genre is a picture of his two sons ascending a staircase, painted to be visually continuous with an actual wooden step. One of the boys is holding an artist's palette. Peale's preoccupation with clarity of vision is dramatically portrayed here, and it is associated with art, in the staircase picture, and with science, in the museum painting.[8]

There are three aspects to the question of veiling/unveiling. First, we can attend to the veil itself, to its qualities, metaphorical associations, its contrasting uses and meanings. Second, we can focus on what it either conceals or reveals – woman/nature/truth – that is, on what lies behind the veil. Third, we are drawn to consider the very act of looking itself, an act that lies at the heart of our epistemology. All three bear on the relationships between science and gender. The metaphorical associations of (un)veiling are rich and diverse, going far beyond their direct connections with scientific knowledge, encompassing religion (nuns, ideas of revelation, the cover of a chalice), clothing, crime, mystery, horror and deceit of all kinds.[9]

The process of looking is central to the acquisition of valid knowledge of nature. From classical times, science and medicine have been explicitly concerned with the correct interpretation of visual signs, and skill in those fields was pre-eminently seen as a form of visual acuteness. Of course, other skills were also highly prized, such as computational abilities, but even in fields where mathematical methods were central, like astronomy, some form of observation or visual discrimination was nevertheless involved. Western scientific traditions have customarily placed 'looking' at centre stage, although, to be sure, they have done so in historically specific ways. But this point alone would not establish the significance of *veiling* as a focal metaphor in scientific culture.

We also know, however, that the ancient Greeks and Romans were deeply interested in physiognomy, a subject which was based on the premise that what we want to know is not on the surface of objects but has to be elicited by decoding visual signs.[10] This gave rise to a scientific and medical tradition which presented itself as an agent of the unveiling of the true inner nature of things, and dominated thinking about the acquisition of natural knowledge for centuries.

The following statements are used in the *Oxford English Dictionary* to illustrate the use of the word 'veil', 'of material substances'; 'between us and the invisible world there is a gross cloud and vail of flesh which interposes', and 'I am sure, within this veil of flesh there dwells a soul'.[11] Clearly they principally reveal the significance of veiling for religious language, but they also indicate a general mentality, that I would call physiognomic, which encouraged people to think in terms of getting behind appearances, to some deeper level – by means of a process of unveiling. In physiognomic traditions, moving inferentially from visual signifiers to other, invisible, inner signifieds was the central operation. Perhaps physiognomy, as an exceptionally pervasive historical phenomenon, offers one clue as to why scientific knowledge was associated with vision, and why its success was linked with removing the impediments to vision.[12]

Why then, we must ask, is it the *female* in particular that is to be (un)veiled? Un/covering women's bodies has two implications that may be pertinent here. First, covering them implies shame and modesty, originally, presumably, that of Eve, but by the eighteenth century women's modesty carried less overt religious significance – it was seen rather as a guarantee that women will veil their voluptuousness in the service of social and possibly psychic stability. This point was made especially forcefully by Rousseau, and by his disciple Bernardin de Saint-Pierre, who both gave positive value to the veiling of women, precisely to preserve their femininity without it being disruptively flaunted. Modesty was a concept through which, especially in the eighteenth century, the contradictory effects of seeing women's bodies were negotiated.[13] Second, veiling implies secrecy. Women's bodies, and by extension feminine attributes, cannot be treated as fully public, something dangerous might happen, secrets be let out, if they were open to view. Yet, in presenting something as inaccessible and dangerous, an invitation to know and to possess is extended. The secrecy associated with female bodies is sexual and linked to the multiple associations between women and privacy.

In this connection we can compare the statue of *Nature Unveiling Herself Before Science* with a contemporary wooden statuette entitled simply *The Secret* of 1894. It depicts a naked woman incompletely covered by a long veil, holding to her chest a box. Her belly and one of her legs are bare, although her head and her mouth are covered. This piece, by Pierre-Felix Fix-Masseau (1869–1937), is medieval in style, and it effectively brings together woman, the veil and secrecy.[14] Here, as in the Pandora story, secrecy is reified as a box. Furthermore, it is tempting, if somewhat speculative, to think of the gift in this connection, with its associations with religion, inspiration, property and natural endowments.[15] Yet none of these constitute the essence of a gift, which, in its material form, is linked with unfolding the unexpected. In the specific sense of gift as an unsolicited present, surprise, pleasure and visual discovery go hand in hand. It is clear why the idea of unveiling secrets seems to lead inexorably to femininity, the visual manifestations of which generate both excitement and fear. We will return shortly to the gendered nature of secrecy.

It is striking that secrets, like women and knowledge in general, are thought of as things to be possessed, and they remain, for that very reason, elusive – in what sense can one own a fragment of knowledge, an idea or another person? This elusiveness is closely bound up with both desirability and danger, features associated particularly with magic and the occult. The drive to possess the secrets of the universe, the philosopher's stone and a whole range of magical powers was bound up both with material possession – the search for gold – and with the possession of women, as is made clear in the Faust story:

New roads lie open to me. I
shall pierce the veil that hides what we desire,
break through to realms of abstract energy.

Faust exclaimed as he strove to unlock 'Nature's secrets'.[16] Here it may be helpful to remember the impossibility of neatly separating science and magic historically until natural philosophers themselves began self-consciously to effect a schism, a process which really only gathered momentum in the eighteenth century. Before then much knowledge was essentially arcane, even dangerous, but certainly mysterious, reached through many different forms of revelation – a point to which Newton's life and ideas stand as eloquent testimony.[17] What we call the Enlightenment became a significant turning-point in this connection precisely because people strove to redefine proper knowledge as deriving from the open study of what could be viewed, hence valid knowledge came to lie exclusively in the public domain. In medicine, for instance, secret remedies inevitably suggested quackery and hence unprofessional behaviour.[18] This shift did not damage the basic conviction that visual signs in nature required interpretation, although it made the articulation of clear rules of inference for doing so far more important. However, it also inadvertently gave a new attraction to the idea of illegitimate knowledge, of forbidden insight, as the considerable literary attention given to this theme in the late eighteenth and nineteenth centuries suggests.

Science and medicine, since they claimed special truth status for themselves, were drawn both to personifications of nature as woman and to the image of unveiling in order to represent their privileged relationship to Truth and to Nature. They thereby become the domains strong enough, as a power nexus, to grapple with the complex forces that nakedness unleashed. Yet brute force was by no means the leading image here, because the metaphor of unveiling could be used with considerable rhetorical elegance. An illuminating example of this is to be found in the new edition of a medical treatise on woman prepared after the author's death in 1803. The book in question was Pierre Roussel's *Système Physique et Moral de la Femme*, which was an instant success when it first appeared in 1775 and became, as befitted the work of a disciple of Rousseau, a part of literary culture. Alibert, the editor, said, 'I would like to see the author [Roussel] . . . portrayed receiving . . . homage from the enchanting sex whose organism he has unveiled with so much delicacy and so much insight [pénétration]'. For Alibert, Roussel personified science and gallantry, women personified nature; she was a specific kind of organism and a special sort of mystery.[19]

But what is the mystery that lies behind the veil? In a poignant novella, written in 1859, George Eliot (1819–80) explored precisely this question. *The Lifted Veil* concerns a young man who knows what others are thinking, and has visions of the future. This 'superadded consciousness' is only a curse to him, bringing him infinite pain and almost total isolation. Although she did not link his 'unhappy gift of insight' directly with science, the general implications for ideas of unveiling, especially in relation to gender, are important. The story is written autobiographically by the man in question, and the plot is driven by his attraction towards a young woman into whose mind he cannot, initially, see. He reaches the depths of despair when this particular veil is finally lifted in a 'terrible moment of complete illumination . . . the darkness had hidden no landscape . . . only a blank prosaic wall'. What the narrator bemoans is exactly the loss of secrecy and mystery, which is generally indispensable for happiness, and which is particularly crucial for his relationship with the woman who became his wife. The gender implications are quite specific, since what animates the story is the loss of female mystery with the advent of a specific kind of vision, given here to a man. Eliot presented a black abyss beyond the veil that covers other human beings and the woman loved by the narrator.[20]

In the case of Oriental women who remain veiled in public, it is presumably their full femininity, their private personhood that lies behind the veil. In his 1820 article on 'physiognomonie' in the *Dictionnaire des sciences médicales*, Virey (1775–1847) explicitly presented his subject as one which 'unveiled the nature of individual character', before referring to the veiling of Eastern women, an example which he used to assert that unless people use their faces in speech (i.e. in public intercourse) they don't have a physiognomy to interpret![21] For Virey, therefore, nothing lies behind the veil of Eastern women, so that for a Western European man, they are blank. The veil far from concealing something enticing, has become a barrier to its development. Virey's argument, maverick though it may be, contains an interesting assumption, that layers of identity, truth or meaning form dynamically during a lifetime and are not pre-given, from which it follows that what is unveiled is not just static natural objects but the presence or absence of temporal processes.

More conventional in its meaning is the dance of the Seven Veils, where the mystery of feminine sexuality emerges gradually into view. In the personifications of woman as Naked Truth it is no less than reality itself which is finally exposed, so that the secrets of nature/the universe are identified with the secrets of women's bodies, at least at an abstract level. The linked myths of Prometheus and Pandora may be instructive here. Both the stories involve secrecy and deception, yet with a significant difference. Prometheus, in stealing fire from the Gods and giving it illicitly to people, deceives in the interests of the human race, and then suffers on their behalf. Pandora, by contrast, deceives in a way that acts against human interests, for she makes others suffer as a result of her insistence on opening the jar containing 'all the Spites that might plague mankind'. In this she is presented as a typical woman, who is only able to succeed in her deception because of her stunning beauty: she was 'as foolish, mischievous and idle as she was beautiful'.[22] These myths could be seen as showing that revealing secrets is a bad thing. But this depends on the point of view taken. In the case of Prometheus it was only bad from the divine viewpoint; he transgressed against the rules of the Gods in order to bring knowledge to human beings. When a man is in conflict with supernatural power, the issue hinges on secrecy and knowledge. When a woman transgresses, as it happens in this instance against the human race, the issues are secrecy, visual deception, and suffering. Hence, in these myths men and women have a different relation to secrecy and knowledge. Men desire to possess both women and knowledge, and they pay a cost for both. Women and their secrets have a profoundly ambiguous status, being both desired and feared. So far we have discovered that although (un)veiling has a wide range of associations, which are not necessarily gendered, there are a number of senses in which these ideas are intimately intertwined with conceptions of femininity.

By contrast, the idea of unveiling men is comic, implausible and unthreatening, presumably because their bodies are not the symbolic carriers in modern society either of creative or destructive forces. We can imagine women being 'unveiled' in a way men cannot be. Also suitable for unveiling are plaques, statues, indeed prized possessions or items of special public commemoration. Unveiling women is an idea that remains acceptable, since it fulfils masculine desire allied with fantasies of ownership and display. Unveiling women is not just a prelude to possession but an encounter with risk and danger and so also with excitement and pleasure.[23] In speaking of our own society some particular conditions obtain which make associations between women and the desire for possession of material objects perfectly explicit. They are actively encouraged through advertising, among other things, which repeatedly portrays sexual and material possession together.

I have digressed somewhat in speaking about the late twentieth century in order to make the point that we now have in a mass society a number of quite concrete ways of thinking about 'having' and a ready source of images, which, with varying degrees of sophistication, draw on our assumptions about femininity, knowledge and looking. When we turn to a historical setting, the repertoire of instances and the means by which these were generated are profoundly different.

In dealing with science and medicine in the eighteenth and nineteenth centuries, we have to come to terms with a greater degree of conceptual abstraction than is found in the mass media of the twentieth century, and with socio-cultural settings containing neither many material embodiments of these ideas nor the technology to reproduce them, especially in their visual form. Furthermore, the closely related languages of mastery, control and property, of material and personal possession are now so elaborate and widely disseminated, that it is hard for us to imaginatively enter a society where such associations were less ubiquitous. Equally important here is the fact that, in Britain at any rate, there was a paucity of bodies available for dissection until the mid-nineteenth century.[24] One result of this was that models and pictures of the human body had a value that they have long lost for us. There was also a lack of popular illustrations of the body beyond the very crude, as in chap books, until the late nineteenth century. Hence the links between gender, knowledge and unveiling were not proclaimed in common images, but were worked through in a number of ways, which ranged from the mythical and the literary to images that were relatively specific historically. We therefore have to search for cases where these themes were brought together. One example would be the frontispieces of scientific and medical treatises, which contained many examples of the personification of knowledge, or particular sciences, as women, as well as of the theme of unveiling knowledge.[25] Here, however, I shall be concerned with a rather different case where the themes of this chapter are brought together with particular force – representations of dissection, using the female corpse.

The representation of a woman's body in the process of being dissected appears to be a historically specific theme. It bears directly on the idea of unveiling, which has, at any one time, both a mythical dimension and a rooted socio-cultural one. In the case of dissection, an actual female body could be possessed, made to yield up secrets, generate knowledge. In early depictions of dissections, the corpse is generally either male or un-sexed, although there is evidence to suggest that female corpses were dissected and some illustrations depicting such events exist, including the frontispiece of Vesalius' masterpiece of 1543.[26] The obsession with the female corpse in particular, seems to be a late-eighteenth-century and a nineteenth-century phenomenon. In a sense this is not surprising, since the erotic was an integral part of the fascination with death characteristic of, for want of a better word, Romanticism. This mixture of morbid and erotic ideas has been brilliantly described by Philippe Ariès in *The Hour of Our Death*. In his chapter on 'The Age of the Beautiful Death', he uses writings from the mid nineteenth century by members of the La Ferronays family to illustrate a historically specific preoccupation with 'the death of the other', as opposed to the self. He associated 'the death of the other' with privacy, the nuclear family, and what he called 'absolute affectivity'. Most pertinent, however, is his comment that '[death] had become moving and beautiful like nature'.[27] Both death and nature were erotically charged. We have already encountered one version of this constellation in Michelet's enthusiasm for the dissecting room. The language of death as described by Ariès, although verbal, had clear visual correlates.

A particularly vivid example of this is the German painting and lithograph of a beautiful young woman, who had drowned herself, being dissected by an anatomist, Professor Lucae (1814–85), who was interested in the physical basis of female beauty. A group of men, comprising both artists and anatomists, stand around the table on which the corpse is lying.[28] She has long hair and well-defined breasts. One of the men has begun the dissection and is working on the belly and chest. He is holding up a sheet of skin,

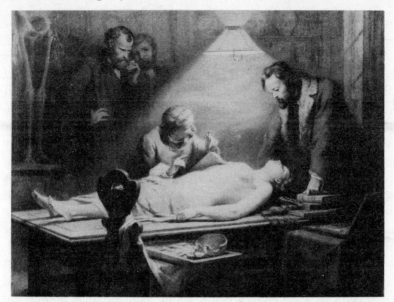

Plate 7 Lucae and his Assistants Dissecting a Female Cadaver.

close to her breast, as if it were a thin article of clothing so delicate and fine is its texture. The corpse is indeed being undressed scientifically; the constituent parts of the body are being displayed for scrutiny and analysis. The sense of enquiring into nature, for both aesthetic and scientific purposes, is conveyed by composition and lighting: a group of men peer at a female corpse, and, in the background are an array of skulls, a skeleton and glass jars. This sense is considerably heightened by the fact that the dissection is actually in progress, as we can see from the piece of lifted skin. The picture leads us to the idea that dissection is itself a process of unveiling, of removing layers of organic tissues.

The notion that dissection was a form of unveiling can be supported in a number of ways, some of which have been touched on in earlier chapters. Of particular interest is the common device, used on the title pages of several anatomy and surgery books, of the corpse being unveiled, sometimes by female personifications of medicine, surgery or learning. These images made perfectly explicit the assumption that anatomical and surgical knowledge unveils the human body. The corpses in these cases are in the process of being revealed by having their delicate covering tissue removed.[29]

The term 'tissue' is itself significant, as we noted in Chapter 3, since it was a key concept in the pathological anatomy of Bichat. Through the dominance of Paris hospital medicine, this field endowed the act of dissection with a special status in nineteenth-century medicine. Dissection became the symbolic core of scientific medicine – the place where signs of pathology were revealed to the medical gaze. Tissues are both thin layers, that is veils in general usage, and in anatomy, basic components of living matter. Indeed, the word 'veil' itself has a biological meaning – a membrane, membranous appendage or part, serving as a cover or screen; a velum. These usages began in 1760 for botany, 1829 for anatomy and 1810 for zoology.[30]

To return to the picture of Professor Lucae by Hasselhorst (1825–1904), it is significant in two respects. First, it gave visual expression to a general curiosity about women, their bodies and death that was especially widespread during the nineteenth and early twentieth centuries. This curiosity was present in Lucae himself, who sought to learn about feminine beauty through anatomy, as did his artist friends. They sought the origins of visual-cum-sexual pleasure in the construction of the physical world, that is in the body. Second, the picture initiated a visual tradition. We can illustrate the first point by returning once again to Jules Michelet, who exemplifies the particular kind of curiosity I just alluded to, with its twin emphases on nature and on woman. We have noted how in *La Femme* (1859), he described the post-mortems he attended, in order to demonstrate his thesis about the inherent vulnerability of working women. He recounted the story of a young woman, her sad life, her lonely death. In the dissecting room her body allowed a broader narrative to take shape, that of 'woman', her social and moral condition. It was by seeing her body being dissected and analysed that Michelet imaginatively constructed a general scenario. In his writings, a number of different elements worked together – woman, other, nature, death and pathology, feeling and identification – and these elements became manifest, visually, in the dissecting room. Michelet's fascination with these matters was far from unique.

We find the motifs of Hasselhorst's picture repeated in *The Anatomist* (1869) by Gabriel Max (1840–1915). A beautiful girl is once again lying on a slab under the male gaze. But where Lucae's team were under way with their dissection, Max's anatomist is lost in thought, his chin in his hand in a typical melancholic pose. The location, given the books, papers and skulls strewn on a desk in the background, would seem to be his study, and he is alone with the body. Max himself was both a painter and an amateur of science – anatomy, anthropology and astronomy – as well as being an anti-vivisectionist. His painting of 1883 in which a beautiful young woman personifying virtue admonishes an old man about to undertake a vivisectional experiment, played a part in the anti-vivisection campaigns. Photographs of it were sold, and it was a favourite of a prominent American activist. It has been claimed that the picture was even reproduced in the New Yorker in 1882 and that postcards of it were also available.[31] It therefore seems at least possible that the American artist and anatomist John Wilkes Brodnax (1864–1926) could have seen a reproduction of it.[32]

Brodnax is an example of someone who took up the themes of Hasselhorst's and Max's images, as was the Spanish painter Enrique Simonet (1864–1927), who produced a picture of a female corpse and male anatomist in 1890 while he was in Rome. This too was apparently available in cheap print and postcard form.[33] Brodnax undertook his first picture along these lines in 1897, although how consciously he was echoing earlier examples we do not know. In his first version he depicts himself sitting, scalpel in one hand, chin on the other, near a beautiful female corpse, naked to the waist. The thoughtfulness is reminiscent of Max, but Brodnax is not touching the veiling material as Max's anatomist was. And, in the later picture more of the body is visible. There is a light, similar to the one in Hasselhorst's picture, shining on the male figure and the female body from one side. Thus several elements from the earlier pictures recurred here, the recumbent woman, the signs of death, the male onlooker. Yet there are also significant differences. Hasselhorst depicted an anatomist and his colleagues dissecting a woman. Brodnax's paintings are primarily self-portraits; on one occasion he appears twice in the picture. He thereby made the theme of fantasy in relation to dissection in particular and to anatomy in general, quite explicit. There were, of course precedents for the self-portraiture – Peale's representation of his museum gave prominence to a self-portrait,

Plate 8 Only a Dream.

while Hasselhorst included himself in the background. Brodnax introduced novelty by giving prominence to his own inner life and, curiously, to humorous touches.

It was as an anatomist, an artist and a subject, that is as a multiple participant, that Brodnax created these images. He appears contemplative and almost melancholy. One is entitled *Only a Dream* (1922), yet it remains unclear what is dreamlike – the chance to dissect a beautiful woman? Or is it the chance to work with three famous anatomists – Cunningham, Gray and Morris – who are also shown in the picture.[34] In *Only a Dream* just the upper part of the body is revealed, somewhat like the Hasselhorst. Is this a classical allusion, in that it allows a certain amount of nakedness while avoiding charges of indecency and hence appears to evoke a timeless female image? In *The Anatomist* (1924) the body is completely covered with thin veiling, so that she is clothed but in a highly suggestive manner. As in the other two pictures, Brodnax is sitting thoughtfully in somewhat chaotic surroundings that include books, bones and skulls. Is Brodnax pondering on mortality – in which case the images are somewhat

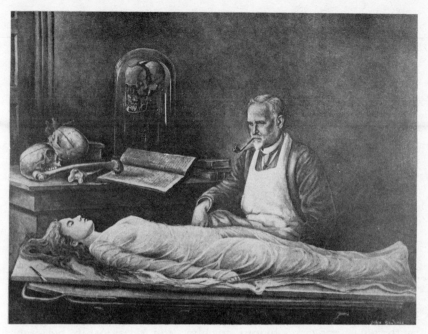

Plate 9 The Anatomist.

banal – or is he reflecting upon the nature of dissection and of medical knowledge? It is worth noting that the pictures are far from simple. We might see the knives and scalpels as obvious phallic symbols, indicating that Brodnax was commenting on male fantasies of dissection, but then a humorous note is introduced by the skull, a figure of death, with a pipe in its mouth (Brodnax was a pipe smoker), suggesting playfulness.

The historical interest of Brodnax lies in his unselfconscious use of an imagery that reveals the connections between medical knowledge and sexual fantasy. As a teacher of anatomy at the Medical College of Virginia and a coroner for the city of Richmond, he had to constantly manage his reactions to death and to the macabre business of preparing bodies for the use of medical students. His artistic activities are best understood in this context. In addition to the pictures discussed here, Brodnax prepared anatomical drawings for use in teaching and to illustrate his publications and worked as a sculptor. The artistic side of his life was well known and widely admired locally – he was written about in newspapers, gave lectures and had his prints sold on a commercial basis.[35]

It is evident from the college yearbook, *The X-Ray*, dedicated to him shortly before his death, that his students revered him. They stressed 'his high character and rectitude', his concern for 'the ethical criteria of the profession'. Included in the volumes are three poems, each to accompany one of Brodnax's pictures. The two he wrote himself concerned *Old Chris* and *The Anatomist*. It must be admitted that both his poems deal, predictably, with well-worn matters – mortality, dissection, and science – and as with the pictures, it is this very predictability that reveals received ideas about gender, science and medicine:

> This comely maiden, once buoyant in life,
> By the dread hand of disease expires,
> Is now subject to the dissector's knife,
> To carve and mutilate as he desires.[36]

I read Brodnax, not as revelling in or celebrating male medical power over the female corpse, but as attempting to come to terms with what appears obvious to him: the relationship between anatomist and anatomized is quintessentially gendered. It is remarkable that Brodnax was able to present these issues in a form that elicited admiration from his contemporaries, despite the fact that he touched on some very delicate matters.

It should be pointed out that when Brodnax painted such pictures he was treading a difficult path between a 'realism' that might be seen as offensive, since images of female corpses easily breach taboos, and a generalized depiction that would not offend because it dealt with long-established abstract themes such as mortality and *vanitas*. A particular kind of realism is at issue here. It was not the literalism of Brodnax that could cause offence, but the implications of a sexual dynamic embedded within the brutal facts of life. It seems he avoided the threat that was always latent in the subject because the women of his images are dead and generalized, and are presented as remote, almost classical entities, so that despite the specificity of the self-portraits, the corpses simply stand for 'beautiful, young dead woman'. The touches of humour, like Brodnax placing himself alongside the great anatomists, possibly also served to lighten the pictures' effect.

That opinion was roused in cases where the individuality of the woman was at issue is clear from the controversy surrounding the picture *William Rush Carving the Schuylkill River*, painted by Thomas Eakins in 1876–7. The controversy concerned the naturalistic treatment of individual nudity. Eakins's painting, showing Rush carving from life, used a named model who was a local teacher for wayward girls. To defend himself against criticism, Eakins claimed that Rush had also used as his model a named person – the daughter of a colleague and friend. Eakins made explicit an association between the personified river and real women. By forcing such a connection on the viewer's attention, by using a style not in the tradition of idealized nudes, and by insisting on drawing from life using totally nude models in mixed classes, Eakins scandalized his contemporaries, resigning from his position at the Philadelphia Academy for Fine Arts in 1886.[37]

Significantly, Eakins also painted a number of medical subjects; his controversial pictures of surgical operations are relevant here. Their literal rendering of a medical event, and their gory details, invited viewers into scenes that had not been traditional subjects in high art. In his concern for exactitude, Eakins also used photography, for example of himself and his friends naked, to help him paint. Furthermore, he was a highly skilled anatomist, who was totally familiar with the operating and dissecting rooms. Eakins breached conventions relating to the body; even where the body was male, as in *The Gross Clinic* (1875), the picture caused offence. Of course, in this case, as in his later canvas *The Agnew Clinic* (1904), the bodies were alive, and a documented event is depicted. It is never easy to explain why some images elicit a violent response, while others fail to do so. Much was at stake in the furore surrounding *The Gross Clinic*, since the nature of the fine art establishment was involved, and the immediate historical situation, the centenary celebrations of the American Revolution, was one likely to heighten sensitivity about whether images for public display were fitting or not. Artists could easily use such scenes to introduce female nudity as Henri Gervaux did in *Before the Operation; Dr. Péan Explaining the Use of Hemostatic Clamps*, exhibited at the salon of 1887. The patient's breasts are exposed, with her long hair falling over the sheet on which she lies, while the male doctors, with a couple of nurses in the background, crowd around her. One doctor is holding her wrist, his hand just beneath a breast. Eakins's own *Agnew Clinic* contains a female patient undergoing an operation on one breast, while the other is plainly visible. In this case, however, since the operation is in progress and her hair – a potential sexual signifier – is barely visible, the overall effect is one of engagement in a task, not of contemplation or display of a body, as it is in most of the pictures so far discussed.[38]

Representations of medical events, be they operations, dissections or the anatomist contemplating a corpse, raise issues of unveiling in three ways. First, the body itself can be unveiled by the removal of its enveloping tissues. Second, a particular person, procedure or piece of information can be revealed in the process – an identity made manifest. Third, at an abstract level, nature can be unveiled by science. These elements may be present simultaneously, although they need not be, but in all three the dimension of gender intensifies the relationships involved, thereby bringing them to a point of danger. The representations I have discussed hover around this point; some have caused offence, others not, while it is perfectly possible for an image to transgress only at some times or in the eyes of particular groups.

Although we have already mentioned unveiling of a number of different kinds, one more remains to be added. In order to examine this we can use the memorial pamphlet published by the Medical College of Virginia shortly after Brodnax's death. It contained a short appreciation of his artistic work by F. William Sievers (1872–1966), sculptor. This offered guarded praise for Brodnax's work, while placing him firmly as an amateur (he had attended the Art Students League in New York before studying medicine). Sievers mentioned briefly the *Only a Dream* picture to criticize the use of the double self-portrait. However, he reserved special praise for a picture Brodnax produced of a helper at the Medical School

> I will make special mention of his wash drawing entitled 'Peyton'. It represents a seated, full length figure of the colored janitor at the Medical College of Virginia. There he sits, comfortable and unmindful of what to some might seem ghastly surroundings, scraping the boiled flesh from human bones. . . . One wonders

Plate 10 Peyton.

whether the several cats feed on the cooked human flesh. . . . The mood and lack of emotion in the darky are perfect . . . The spirit [of the model] is correctly portrayed . . . the darky is alive.[39]

One picture of Peyton shows him sitting down wearing an apron, and scraping a bone with a knife. His surroundings are bare and institutional. On one side there is a tub full of bones, while on the other hangs a skeleton below which there are several cats, one of them clearly feeding. Another picture of a black man, *Old Chris*, contains a skeleton, a corpse and the live figure. Again there is a tub of bones, and an animal, this time a dog, sits beside the man.

Race, and along with that murder, magic, and the profane, are also to be unveiled, it seems. Two aspects of the pictures are particularly striking and they are both mentioned by Sievers – race and cannibalism. By their very power the pictures of Peyton and Old Chris make explicit what remains implicit in the pictures of women, while adding the otherness of the black. The suggestion

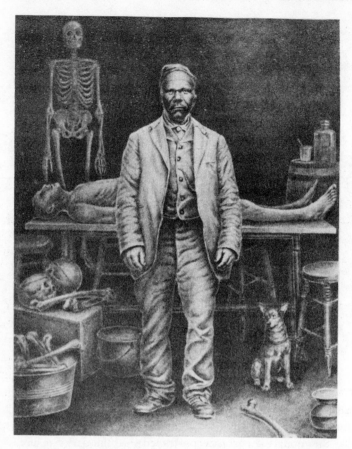

Plate 11 Old Chris.

of cannibalism, with its blurring of the boundaries between bodies as objects of knowledge and bodies as food, heightens our sense that anatomy is a transgression. This could be a sexual transgression, as is hinted at with the female corpses, it could be a more general violation felt in relation to all dead bodies, or it could be the transgression of cannibalism. Once you think about pulling the body apart in order to build up skeletons for study or to examine its constituent parts, you are close to the enormous transgression of Frankenstein.

We can confirm that large transgressions are involved by looking at the poems published to accompany these two pictures in *The X-Ray.* 'Peyton', by 'K', develops three relevant themes. First, it alludes to Peyton meditating on his own death as he works. Second, in describing what he actually does, the language of infernal magic is employed:

> While the cauldron bubbles and vapours smell,
> Tales of deeds that were dark and fell,
> As the darkest pit in deepest Hell.

Third, the bones are identified as those of people who murder or were murdered: 'the hands of a dainty infanticide . . . the bones of a suicide . . . the skull of a negro homicide'.[40] In 'To Old Chris', Brodnax, rather insistently, stresses the black man's own mortality – 'While you pursue your ghastly, ghoulish trade,/ Does no compunction ever come to you?'. Although the tone later softens as the dissecting students are identified as 'the ghouls', it is plain that Old Chris is excluded from medical knowledge; 'For science 'tis aimed, yet you get no part/ . . . you share not their art [i.e. medicine]'.[41] The poems make clear that the black men who prepare bones are allied to death, the profane and with evil deeds, and that they must stand apart from science and medicine in whose service they work.

The racial aspect of the pictures relates to what is best described as 'otherness'; the distancing of what is peripheral, marginal and incidental from a central norm, of illicit danger from safe legitimacy. Women are other to men, as blacks are to whites, as animals are to human beings, as death is to life – although different degrees and modes of otherness are here involved. All these forms of otherness are evoked by Brodnax. The idea of otherness is complicated, but certain themes are common: the treatment of the other as more like an object, something to be managed and possessed, and as dangerous, wild, threatening. At the same time, the other becomes an entity whose very separateness inspires curiosity, invites enquiring knowledge.[42] The other is to be veiled and unveiled.

This many-sided phenomenon was a central feature of nineteenth-century scientific disciplines: anthropologists sought to know other races, gynaecologists to penetrate the otherness of woman, anatomists to understand the relationship between life and death. In the same vein social commentators worked towards an understanding of the popular classes as a way of managing the intense sense of otherness such groups had inspired in the middle and upper classes.[43] The amalgam of desire for knowledge and attempts at management have been a recurrent theme in gender relations. Men strive to 'know' women in the biblical sense, just as the natural sciences continually aim to penetrate nature's mysteries. The other is simultaneously veiled, that is mysterious, threatening and separate, and to be unveiled, that is mastered by seeing and knowing. The process of unveiling is called science, and it depends on new modes of vision.

Brodnax, then, articulated in visual form a set of preoccupations which reveal much not only about the culture and society of which he was a part, but also about the nature of medical knowledge. The very fact that there were closely related antecedent images reveals that these preoccupations were not peculiar to him. The images of male anatomists and female corpses were given currency in their immediate historical context, while they simultaneously drew on centuries of imagery, myth and concepts. Medicine, like science, was based on the unveiling of nature. Woman, as the personification of nature, was the appropriate corpse for anatomy, which was not just literally male in that its exponents were men, but was symbolically male in that science was also the masculine practice of looking, analysing and interpreting. Hence the statue *Nature Unveiling Herself before Science*.

Veils are taken off after weddings, suggesting anticipated pleasures shortly to be satisfied. Veils also, as in Brodnax, evoke mystery while preserving nominal decency, specifically on the lower half of the body. Unveiling men makes no sense, possibly because neither mystery nor modesty are male preserves but are attributes of the other, which is always other to the masculine centre. This is so despite the fact that the strictly medical sense of unveiling – removing layers of bodily tissues – is itself gender neutral, and that other senses of unveiling have complex gender implications. Powerful though the associations are between femininity and (un)veiling, if this metaphor and the related images it generates are about otherness in general and all that this entails, then we must be receptive to their wider resonances. In *Old Chris*, Brodnax allowed the viewer to move from black, live human being, to corpse, to skeleton; a form of unveiling that brings with it its own kinds of otherness.

6

Science, Machines and Gender

There have been certain moments that stand out in retrospect because they gave rise to statements about the nature of rational or scientific power that were so compelling, forceful or frightening that they gripped the imagination of generations and provided a general reference point for subsequent debate. Easily the best known example of such a work is Mary Shelley's *Frankenstein* (1818), subsequently immortalized in virtually every literary and artistic genre.[1] In American culture the short stories of Edgar Allan Poe and Nathaniel Hawthorne have had a similar if less dramatic impact. The famous German silent film *Metropolis* (1926) should be seen in this context. It mobilized a number of familiar themes – tradition versus modernity, labour versus capital, men versus machines – around a sentimental story line, and equally important, it produced visual images of unusually compelling intensity. The scene where the inventor makes a robot in the likeness of a woman is certainly one of the most memorable moments in the history of film. In this chapter I want to show how Lang's film deployed ideas about the relationships between science and gender. The film is steeped in the polarities we have explored in earlier chapters, so it is best viewed from a broad historical perspective. In order to appreciate how *Metropolis* is related to the themes and traditions already discussed, we shall have to examine its mode of production and its content in some detail.

When *Metropolis* received its much publicized Berlin première early in 1927, the critics and public alike were hostile to it. Many commentators found the ending of the film banal and unsatisfying, although they generally praised the modern images of machines and buildings that continue to be a source of admiration.[2] *Metropolis* is a complicated and confused film. It drew, however, on some important themes relating to work, industrial organization and the nature of science that were particularly characteristic of European thought in the 1920s. Furthermore, it put these themes into play through a plot which hinges on the nature of femininity – especially its twin aspects, virginity and overt sexuality – and on the role of woman as the social and political bedrock of stable societies. This association of gender with analyses of science was, as we have seen, far from novel; it mobilized traditions which linked women with passion and superstition, and men with reason and knowledge, women with religion and sorcery, men with science and management, women with humanity, men with destruction, women with sexuality, men with the lust for power.

The story of *Metropolis* concerns a city-cum-industry run by Joh Fredersen in which the workers are reduced to a faceless mass of exploited bodies. A young woman, Maria, comforts them with reassurances that a saviour and mediator will come to deliver them from their anguish. Freder, the boss's son, sees Maria, falls in love with her and casts himself in the role of the people's deliverer and critic of his father. His father, however, learns that discontent is spreading among the workers and decides to enlist the help of Rotwang, the inventor, who has been working on a robot 'in the image of man, that never tires or makes a mistake'.[3] Fredersen discovers that the workers are meeting secretly in the old catacombs to hear Maria talk to them about prayer and patience. After taking Fredersen to the catacombs to see Maria in action for himself, Rotwang captures Maria, imprisons her in his house and makes, at the boss's request, a robot in her exact likeness. The robot is then programmed to incite the workers to revolt because Fredersen is looking for an excuse to use violence against them. Their uprising wreaks havoc and has the inadvertent effect of flooding the underground city where the workers live, thus putting in jeopardy the lives of their children. When they finally realize this, the workers, thinking she has destroyed their children, pursue Maria. In fact, they capture the robot, and burn it as a witch, thereby revealing its true nature – a machine not a person. Rotwang chases the real Maria onto the roof of the cathedral, from where he falls to his death after Freder goes to her rescue and fights him off. Maria, father and son are reconciled, and a workers' leader comes forward in the same spirit. It was, after all, Fredersen's son, aided by Maria, who had saved their children. The boss is symbolically united to the workers by a handshake at the end of the film.[4]

To understand the film, we need to know something of its conditions of production. Fritz Lang (1890–1976) was born in Austria and had trained as an architect and artist before turning to the film industry, in which he worked as an actor and scriptwriter, coming to prominence as a director in the 1920s. Lang thought of setting a film in a futuristic city during a visit to New York in 1924. His wife and close collaborator, Thea von Harbou (1888–1954) then wrote a novel upon which the film in turn was based.[5] The original film shown in Germany was much longer than the version currently available and apparently contained characters and events from the novel which are now missing. The version we know was made for the United States and was considerably altered. No copies of the original are known to exist. To speak of the film as 'Lang's' therefore constitutes a simplification; it was the work of many hands, but it is impossible to know exactly what the terms of the collaboration were or what the effect of the cuts was. In his later years as an exile in the United States, Lang was quick to criticize *Metropolis* and its romantic, simplistic ending.[6] Although all these points lead to interpretative problems, they do not undermine the possibility of an historical analysis of *Metropolis*, which need not depend on Lang's special status as the main creator of the film. When I mention Lang in this chapter I do so partly as a matter of linguistic convenience to avoid the necessity of saying 'the team that made *Metropolis*' and partly as a reflection of the critical literature most of which focuses on Lang.

It may be useful at this point to note the main respects in which the novel and the film (as it is known) diverge. In the

novel, Fredersen and Rotwang are locked in mutual hatred over
their love for Hel, Freder's mother, who had died when her son
was born. Fredersen 'stole' Hel from Rotwang. Von Harbou
situated Rotwang in an ancient magical tradition by explaining
the uniqueness of his house – a medieval island in a sea of
skyscrapers – in terms of an earlier occupant who had possessed
awesome occult powers. Similarly, she accounts for the anomalous
survival of a Gothic cathedral in a hyper-modern city through
the power of the groups of monks who still run it. Furthermore,
Fredersen has a mother from whom he is estranged because she
disapproves of his general conduct. His reconciliation with her
concludes the book and carries with it a pledge that he will
reform, rebuild and redeem Metropolis. In the novel, Rotwang's
death results from his belief that Maria, whom he sees in the
cathedral, is his beloved Hel; he cannot understand why she flees
from him – a mistake which is comprehensible only in the context
of a fight he has had earlier with Fredersen. When he regains
consciousness following this, he believes himself dead, and so
goes in search of his lost love. At the level of the plot, therefore,
the novel is fuller and more consistent than the film and contains
significantly different emphases. The use of florid religious
imagery is much more elaborate, the references to father–son
conflict more overt, and the symbolism generally more highly
developed. It is possible that the differences stem from a complex
combination of the cuts referred to above, the generic differences
between novel and film, and the challenge of transforming verbal
into visual images.

The difficulties in interpreting the film are of two main kinds.
The first stem from the peculiar historical circumstances of pre-
Nazi Germany, the use of films as instruments of Nazi propaganda
and the attempt to come to terms with fascism following the
Second World War. This issue is often reduced to a concern with
the question, 'Was Lang in general, and his work in *Metropolis*
in particular, marked by the same ideological tendencies which
led to the rise of fascism?' In other words, is it necessary to find
ways of dismissing them as morally and politically tainted? This
drive for moral clarity has led, for example, to a debate about
whether Rotwang is a precursor of the reviled Jewish figures of
later Nazi films – a point to which we shall return. The 'problem'
of Lang has been solved in a number of ways, one of which is

to attribute blame for any apparently unsound ideological tendencies in his films to the contributions of Thea von Harbou, who remained in Germany after Lang left, and was an active film-maker under Hitler.[7] Yet, to pose the question of Lang's political views in this way is to make assumptions about the second interpretative issue – the relationship between cultural products such as film and the historical setting in which they are made. Theoretically this is a particularly hard issue to deal with, and few attempts have been made to do so.[8]

To simplify, the issue is whether Lang was merely reflecting general, even unconscious tendencies in his own culture, the very ones that made Hitler's rise to power possible, or whether he was putting forward the views of a specific group with a coherent ideological perspective. Another possibility, although not one I support, that Lang's is a highly idiosyncratic vision, is little entertained because critics generally wish either to exonerate him from or implicate him in broader movements of the 1920s. I am not, of course, advocating a view of him or of the film as unique, since one of my purposes in analysing *Metropolis* here is to place it in a broad cultural context. But it is, I think, unsatisfactory to see him either as a passive reflector of his environment or as the mouthpiece of a particular group. For the moment a more general difficulty, reflecting the current state of scholarship, should be borne in mind. If we take it for granted that cultural artefacts are in some sense socially produced, then we need to search out and lay bare the various levels of mediation between economy, society and culture. For the case of Weimar Germany I have not been able to discover a literature that carries out such a job.

Of course, the standard cultural histories of the period make many assertions about these relationships, based on various theoretical suppositions and prejudices, but they fail to work out the links in any systematic way. For example, in his highly acclaimed work, *Weimar Culture*, Peter Gay locates *Metropolis* among works which portray 'the revenge of the father'. He finds it a film ' calculated mainly to sow confusion', a 'tasteless extravaganza' and 'a repulsive film'. He concludes his account of *Metropolis*, 'The revenge of the father and the omnipotence of the mother were twin aspects of the Weimar scene, both equally destructive to youth'.[9] Such an approach clearly cannot shed light on the highly specific fashion in which the film portrays the workplace and the labour process. We can juxtapose this portrayal with what is known about labour conditions, wage settlements and the introduction of industrial rationalization in the period. The links between these two levels, the material conditions and the representation, need to be systematically examined. I have, however, been unable to locate any rigorous attempts to look at how labour was represented in a variety of cultural settings (art, film, theatre, fiction, social theory) and to offer an overall interpretation of the way labour–capital relations were treated. What is said about this later on must therefore remain somewhat speculative.

The difficulties of interpreting a film produced in such a fraught context mean that we must be especially careful about attributing a moral position to its director. This is in part because such positions are rarely articulated unambiguously, and also because it is hard to know how the ordinary public understood the film at the time it was produced. The opinions of critics, while illuminating, are not necessarily representative. If we want to make assertions about *Metropolis* as an expression of the conscious and unconscious tendencies of its time, it helps to have some independent means of assessing what these tendencies were. My point is that these are frequently inferred by hindsight, starting from the subsequent ascendancy of fascism. This teleological approach is understandable, since our need to distance and purify ourselves from the Nazis is still very strong, as the persistent popularity of films about the Second World War containing stereotyped Germans testifies; yet it is also unhelpful.

Cultural histories of Weimar that mention *Metropolis* generally present it in terms of crises of belief and identity, highlighting the religious and Oedipal themes. The film certainly explored a number of easily recognizable Christian themes: Maria, the Virgin-mother; a son striving to save the world; a stern, almighty father; the virtues of patience and prayer; the necessity for suffering in order to overcome evil. These were even more heavily underscored in the novel, in which Fredersen is locked in conflict with the monks of the Gothic cathedral, who believe that doomsday has come when the city is in turmoil. Furthermore, Fredersen himself experiences the cataclysm as an occasion for repentance and he seeks to become the new redeemer of Metropolis. In the film, the use of crosses in the catacombs where Maria gives solace to the workers, of a halo of light around her head, of the Tower of Babel parable and even the frequent use of triangular motifs (the Trinity) further reveal an indebtedness to traditional religious language. Equally evident is the Oedipal theme. Freder rebels against and wishes to destroy his father. Indeed, in her novel Thea von Harbou wrote explicitly of Freder's parricidal drive. Historians have found the conflict between father and son revealing of the general cultural crisis of Weimar. Hence the ending of the film – in which father and son are reconciled, yet without any radical change in the power structure being on the cards – appears especially prescient of the rise of totalitarian power.

My concern here is with the deployment of science and technology within the film, and particularly with the ways these are related to magic and tradition on the one hand, and the dual nature of female sexuality on the other. Those who have emphasized science and technology often classify *Metropolis* as 'science fiction', a genre defined as 'a class of prose narrative which assumes an imaginary technological or scientific advance, or depends upon an imaginary and spectacular change in the human environment.'[10] At first sight the use of the robot supports the status of *Metropolis* as science fiction. Yet *Metropolis* was conceived as an expression, if a somewhat exaggerated one, of a city life already firmly rooted in American culture. The robot, in the sense of an artificially made human being, relates as much to ancient myth as it does to a projected future, and Lang's film, like von Harbou's novel, is striking for the persistence of historical reference. The clothes are not futuristic but contemporary or traditional, the language and value systems are those of the 1920s and its parent culture, the modes of transport those in common use. Even the machines, which might possibly evoke an idea of 'technological or scientific advance', exist as much as primitive deities as modern marvels. In short, to categorize *Metropolis* as science fiction draws our attention away from its use of modern science and technology in dynamic interplay with magic and tradition. The film lays bare the exceedingly fragile boundaries between good and bad science, good and bad beliefs, good and bad machines, and good and bad women.

Four topics of particular importance are raised in the film:

industry, science and technology, city life and modernism, and they all contain implications about gender. *Metropolis* is set in a city which is also a single industrial plant with one man in charge of everything. The workers service the machines, which require constant attention; thus, while both human labour and mechanical power are required to keep the Metropolis going, the former are subservient to the latter. The (male) worker must keep up with the machine, and this is unambiguously shown as the source of excessive fatigue over long shifts.

Two themes prominent in early twentieth-century debates about industrial organization are evoked in *Metropolis*: scientific management in its broadest sense and the role of corporations. As a movement, scientific management is commonly linked with the American engineer Frederick Winslow Taylor (1856–1915), whose work became widely known in America in 1910 as a result of a government inquiry, and whose *Principles of Scientific Management* (1911) had been translated into German in 1913. Taylorism built on earlier moves towards 'systematic manage-ment', which had stressed the importance of a system of management for directing and controlling production. Such streamlining of administration, through centralizing and standar-dizing managerial tasks to avoid wasted effort, is forcefully expressed in the depiction of Fredersen's austere, highly automated and efficient office. As developed by Taylor, the theory of scientific management was strongly committed to rationality and efficiency. It also entailed finding the best person for each task, breaking down jobs into their constituent tasks in order to analyse how each one could be undertaken in the most efficient manner and then training the workmen to use this (and only this) approach. Taylor and his followers maintained that their methods dramatically increased efficiency and so productivity. Something of the flavour of Taylor's system can be gleaned from his remark that '[the] work [of handling pig iron] is so crude and elementary in its nature that the writer firmly believes that it would be possible to train an intelligent gorilla so as to become a more efficient pig-iron handler than any man can be'.[11]

The implication – occasionally made explicit by Taylor, that less 'human' men make better workers – is clearly taken up and exaggerated in *Metropolis*, where the labourers move in a senseless mass, devoid of individuality. They are shown to be dominated and even enslaved by time, their bodies drawn beyond physiological efficiency – the goal of Taylorism – into stupor. The shifts in *Metropolis* last ten hours, and the clocks appropriately have a ten-hour face. Not only was working to fixed time schedules central to early industrialization, but scientific management extended this through the emphasis on the timed task, the importance of avoiding wasted effort, the need for production schedules and the setting of wage rates and bonus systems.[12]

Metropolis thus captured some aspects of scientific management – the subservience of people to the work process and the tyranny of time – and exaggerated them, as in a caricature, to heighten the viewer's sense of industrial inhumanity. Other central features of scientific management, however, find no expression in *Metropolis*. Two silences in particular stand out. First, the role of management and of technical expertise was central to Taylorism, which was unthinkable without both the enthusiastic co-operation of the managerial strata and the expertise of engineers. These groups of middle-class professionals are never seen in the film, yet in the social vision of scientific management they played a crucial part, for reasons which will become clear when the second silence has been identified. This concerns rewards for work. Taylor and his followers believed that fair wages were of the utmost importance and that higher productivity was directly in the workers' interest, because it would lead to higher wages. The reasoning behind this was perfectly plain – higher incomes undermined class solidarity, enhanced social mobility, and through the power to consume that better incomes offered, drew working people into a middle-class life-style. In theory at least the lure of moving into the professional and managerial classes would undermine any possible discontents.[13]

Of course, the discourse of scientific management itself was not free from tensions and inconsistencies. The goal of a classless, stable society fitted ill with the emphasis on the intense specialization of work that Taylorism required and with Taylor's own sense of the animality of manual workers. Significantly, *Metropolis* portrayed work as physically demanding rather than as requiring specialized skills, while the workers are never shown making products or having and spending money. In stark contrast to the rich, the workers are exhausted, walk like zombies, get killed in industrial accidents, work in hot, steamy conditions and thus lead miserable lives. In these respects they are closer to slaves than to the modern workers scientific management sought to create.

During the 1920s there was intense concern with the growth of large industrial complexes and monopolies as these assumed ever greater political and economic power. Metropolis was just such a body – a single giant unit, city-state and factory rolled into one. Corporatism constituted an ideology rooted in the transfer of power away 'from elected representatives or a career bureaucracy to the major organised forces of European society and economy'.[14] This shift has been associated with a weakening of parliamentary democracy, the growth of private power and an erosion of the distinction between the public and private sectors, and the development of centralized bargaining procedures in which labour leaders played a significant role. One historian has argued that Germany was moving clearly towards corporatism during the 1920s, a trend he identified with conservatism.[15]

Aspects of these themes are certainly explored by Lang. In *Metropolis* there is no political structure in which people can participate, hence any distinction between public and private – one of the traditional foundation stones of participatory democracy – is totally inapplicable. If we understand private power as suggesting both the ascendancy of particular interests and the dominance of individuals, then Fredersen represents such power. There is no hint of bargaining between major groups in the film, not least because labour has no voice, being reduced, literally, to a collection of faceless bodies. They require the managerial 'head' of Metropolis to direct them. The city-factory is thus a corporate entity in a particularly direct way, in that the film presents it as a single organism, requiring head, hand and heart to work together for it to survive. The ending may be thought to hold out the promise of a negotiated settlement, but this can be no more than conjecture, since the emphasis is sentimental, not practical. Furthermore, the workers are portrayed in distinctly unflattering terms; they are unable to distinguish the false from the true Maria; they can easily be roused to violence that is potentially injurious to their own families; they lust after revenge against (the robot) Maria; and they become instantly docile once their children are known to be safe. Certainly many of these points contribute towards an important point that the film makes. The work structures of Metropolis are shown to be sterile and destructive at all levels of the hierarchy because they lack human sentiment – presented as a distinctively feminine trait in contrast to the masculinized production system.

It could be argued that the portrait of labour and its control in *Metropolis* merely served to highlight the degradation of the whole system, and so sharpen a critique of modern industrialism. It is also likely that Lang took up certain themes that appealed to him dramatically, and developed them in an extreme form, partly for visual effect. There is no reason why he and his co-workers should have felt bound to produce a logically or politically consistent whole. We cannot, indeed should not, look to *Metropolis* for insights about corporatism and scientific management in Weimar Germany. But the film does reveal something of the nexus of tensions and problems which industrial development was seen to be spawning, particularly concerning the relationships between (male) workers and machines and the reduced human potential of industrial workers, seen as a loss of positive feminine attributes. In addition it suggests a number of specific social and cultural themes through which the anxiety over 'the modern' was focused.

Clearly, it would have been impossible for themes around modernity to be taken up in *Metropolis* without science and technology occupying a visible position. The film treated three modern themes in a way that owes less to contemporary events than to well-established literary and artistic motifs; fear of machines; the creation of artificial 'man'; and the 'mad' scientist. In order to pursue these more fully we will have to undertake a number of short detours. It will be easier to draw out the distinctiveness of *Metropolis* if we can establish some points of comparison. A variety of candidates exist that invite comparison with *Metropolis*, including Villiers de L'Isle-Adam's novel *L'Eve Future* (1886). This concerns the fabrication, by the inventor Thomas Edison, of an android that is an ideal woman. There are some evident similarities with Lang's film here.[16] No less relevant are Mary Shelley's *Frankenstein* (1818) and Nathaniel Hawthorne's *The Birth-mark* (1843), both of which will be discussed shortly.

These juxtapositions may seem curious and open to two specific objections; that both involve literary productions unsuitable for comparison with a film, and that they were produced in very different socio-cultural settings from *Metropolis*. In answer to the first objection it is appropriate to again point out that the film was itself first conceived as a novel, which we can locate with respect to literary traditions, and also that, as a silent film, its narrative structure, which relies heavily on the text shown on the screen, retains a marked literary character. To the second it may said that the general influence of *Frankenstein* is so extensive that its treatment of similar themes – making people, and power-seeking science – forces the comparison upon us. The same cannot be claimed, however, of Hawthorne's short story, written in the early 1840s. Certainly he was well aware of the Gothic tradition, but my reasons for choosing this work are somewhat different. It contains, in an exceptionally concentrated form, many of the themes I am considering here. It is not necessary to postulate Hawthorne's direct influence upon Lang for his writings to illuminate the general linkages between science, medicine and gender. Indeed, the example of Hawthorne reveals how very widely dispersed the language of power, control, domination, penetration and masculinity was.

The fear of machines is present in two distinct forms in *Metropolis*. We have already mentioned how the machines the workers service also dominate and control them; this is the first form that a fear of machines takes. Apparently machines keep the city going, although exactly how they do so remains unspecified. Their importance is none the less dramatically demonstrated when the workers wreck them in anger and flooding of their homes results. The film drew on a naïve faith in technology and simultaneously expressed a primitive fear of machines when these are transformed into monsters, named after non-Christian deities, who swallow up workers, just as primitive gods demanded the constant sacrifice of human victims.[17] Either way, the machines are rendered omnipotent – either because of modern technology or because of irrational belief – and therefore they are to be feared. It may be helpful to put this in the context of the 'cataclysmic' novel tradition, since, according to one commentator:

> novelists attributed the upheaval to class struggle, and that in turn was traced to the failure of industrial society to work out institutions that would protect the working man from enslavement

to the very technology that, in more utopian visions, was supposed
to free man from hunger and drudgery.[18]
This suggests the double character of machines in their capacity
to both liberate and enslave. There is another kind of duality in
relation to machines in the film. On the one hand, they are part
of its modern aesthetic, presenting visual challenges and delights
to Lang as they did to many artists of the period.[19] On the other
hand, they presented an ugly side, being demanding and vengeful,
the agents of death. Such ambivalence about machines was in no
way confined to the 1920s, although it may have been fuelled by
contemporary industrial developments and a general concern
about 'modernity'.[20]

The second form in which the fear of machines emerges in the
film is through the robot, a highly specific mechanical type that
is best considered in connection with how the film treats the
making of an artificial person. *Metropolis* draws on old traditions
concerning the artificial production of human beings. It is true
that this is achieved not directly from organic remains, as in
Frankenstein, nor by means of sculpture, as in the Pygmalion
myth, but via a robot and elaborate machinery. From the imagery
of the dissecting room and charnel house in Shelley's novel, we
have moved to that of the physics and chemistry laboratory. When
Rotwang the inventor creates the false Maria, it is flashing lights,
flasks and electrical phenomena which we see. Frankenstein also
used electricity to animate his creature, but here the similarities
end. Whereas his monster bears the visible marks of his unnatural
creation, Rotwang achieves a complete human likeness. There are
two quite different notions of alien presence here; the first is
alien because hideous, the second because evil, insidious and
undetectable. Where Frankenstein initially saw himself as a benign
father, Rotwang deliberately created an agent of destruction. The
larger projects that gave birth to the two creatures were also quite
different. Frankenstein was possessed by a desire to fathom the
secrets of (female) nature. Rotwang, too, may have had these
goals, but the viewer is not informed of them. Rather his boast
is that he has made 'a machine in the image of man, that never
tires or makes a mistake', the prototype for 'the workers of the
future – the machine men!'.[21] His work is thus explicitly linked
to the labour process, to automated production. Rotwang set
himself up as a Godlike figure, as of course Frankenstein also

did; both usurped the female procreative role. However, the former parodied God's creation of the human race by making machines in the image of man, whereas the latter did so by making a hideous distortion of man.

The question of the similarities between human beings and machines was not a new concern of the early twentieth century but went back to debates about 'man-machine' that became intense in the seventeenth century with Descartes' assertions that animals are automata. During the eighteenth century La Mettrie's *The Man Machine* (1747) caused a veritable sensation. Subsequently, many scientific and medical investigations explored the mechanistic aspects of human anatomy and physiology.[22] Yet these debates did not strike at the same deep-seated anxieties as *Metropolis*, in which the fear of automation and hence of total control over and manipulation of daily existence seems to be the animating concern:

> The technical superiority of the machine, by transforming mere efficiency into a human ideal, has set in motion a convergence between itself and man which tends, on the one hand to lift the robot to a sort of sub-human role, and on the other to assimilate man to the machine not only in the biological or psycho-physiological sense, but also in relation to his values and conduct. . . . The obsessive *leitmotiv*, . . . of human civilisation being threatened by a robot takeover, would seem thus to betray symbolically a widespread fear of the automatization of life.[23]

Metropolis added another dimension to this fear by making the robot a seductive woman. It thereby becomes insidious in a particularly threatening way, by luring men through desire. The machine appears feminine even before he makes it into 'Maria', since it has a distinctively womanly overall body shape. The result is two different forms of danger – technological and sexual – riveted together. The whole motif of the robot is portrayed in modern terms, visually speaking, in dramatic contrast to Rotwang himself.

Rotwang looks not like a modern scientist but like a hermit who knows about magic and alchemy; he wears a long gown, has a somewhat demented manner, owns old books, and lives in a medieval house nestled incongruously in the modern city and harbouring mysterious secrets. It is easy to see here how Rotwang recalls literary precedents such as Frankenstein and Faust and also

Aylmer in Hawthorne's *The Birth-mark*. It has been suggested
that the 'mad scientist' is a literary type in Gothic and Utopian
novels, and there do indeed appear to be a number of recurrent
themes that bear not only on *Metropolis* but also on the
relationships between science, medicine and gender. Five issues
in relation to the 'mad scientist' are of especial importance
here: masculinity; power, control and over-reaching; secrecy;
experimentalism; and science and magic. These issues can be
presented exceptionally vividly through a brief discussion of *The
Birth-mark*.

The story concerns a passionately enthusiastic natural philosopher, Aylmer, and his beautiful young wife, Georgiana, who has
a small mark on one of her cheeks. In her husband's opinion it
is an increasingly troubling blemish on her otherwise perfect
form. She eventually agrees to let him remove it, which, after
much arduous experimental work, he is able to do – at the cost
of her life. Here, then, is the classic tale of the over-reacher, and
the affinities with *Frankenstein* are obvious. The differences are
equally instructive. Although we can understand Shelley's tale in
terms of the masculine desire to dominate nature, Frankenstein
did not directly work on woman as Aylmer and Rotwang did.[24]
Hawthorne brings the gender question to the fore by making the
experimenter and subject husband and wife, and by explicitly
addressing the relationship between love of knowledge and love
of a person:

> [Aylmer] had devoted himself, however, too unreservedly to
> scientific studies, ever to be weaned from them by any second
> passion. His love for his young wife might prove the stronger of
> the two; but it could only be by intertwining itself with his love
> of science, and uniting the strength of the latter to its own.[25]

The passionate engagement with 'deep science' is characteristic of
the over-reacher, and as the novel version of *Metropolis* shows,
the relationship between Rotwang and Maria had an erotic
dimension, even if based on mistaken identity. In the film, the
way he stalks her in the catacombs and then abducts her suggests
sexually predatory behaviour. The fact that these scientists are
men is essential not only to the plot but to the sexual dynamic
that is integral to power over nature.

Rotwang, Aylmer and Frankenstein are all perfectly clear

about the power and control they seek. The equation between knowledge, power and danger is made openly. This theme is brought into particular prominence in *Metropolis* because the link with political authority is so direct – Rotwang is working for Fredersen, and Fredersen has total power in Metropolis. However, acquiring power over nature is not represented as a public matter; rather, it is repeatedly associated with secrecy. In *Frankenstein* much is made of his 'midnight labours', and the need for concealment dominated his whole mentality. Aylmer too worked only with a trusted helper and was horrified when his wife ventured into the laboratory. His entire enterprise is shown as a quest for nature's secrets, secrets which he finds it impossible to penetrate: 'our great creative Mother, while she amuses us with apparently working in the broadest sunshine, is yet severely careful to keep her own secrets . . . like a jealous patentee'.[26] It follows that those who wish for her secrets must be both cunning and secretive themselves. Rotwang is no exception to this pattern. He works in seclusion in a house easily turned into a prison for the real Maria, while an air of mystery hangs around him and his abode. The sense of secrecy is fed by the involvement of such over-reachers with difficult, dangerous, even transgressive experiments. The strong emphasis on an experimental approach comes from a number of sources – the perception of alchemy as a paradigm of overambitious knowledge, the association with magic, and the vividness with which experiment evokes the idea of prising secrets from nature. It also allows the 'mad scientist' to be portrayed as active, interventionist, as visibly moved by his passion for knowledge.

This passion for knowledge is never uncritically depicted. Possibly the association with magic serves to establish that something not quite legitimate is going on, indeed that it has profane qualities. The form of the profanity is, of course, important. The affront to nature and to God is generally clear. Such a search for knowledge is also profane because it is inappropriate to the human condition – a point Hawthorne repeatedly and eloquently made since it is Aylmer's abhorrence of his wife's 'fatal flaw of humanity' that drives him beyond the bounds of normal behaviour to a denial of the reality of disease and death.[27] 'He was confident in his science, and felt that he could draw a magic circle round her'; in other words, Aylmer wanted more of natural philosophy than it could reasonably give, he wanted magical control.[28] In Rotwang's case, too, we are encouraged to think of a mixture of science and magic – his appearance, his bizarre medieval house which included a modern laboratory, the symbols on the doors.

And yet, Rotwang displays a unique characteristic, certainly not shared by either Frankenstein or Aylmer – he is successful.[29] He actually achieved what he claimed he could, the robot did look like Maria, she did do as she was told. His knowledge was made palpably real. The problem, so far as the plot of *Metropolis* is concerned is that he served an evil master, for it was in Fredersen's interests that he made the robot, and it was Fredersen's plan gone awry that caused disaster. Perhaps this is to exaggerate the differences, for it is true that like other 'mad scientists' Rotwang is presented as obsessive, as possessed by a passionate love of, or lust for, power and knowledge that led to his downfall. Furthermore, the idea for the robot had clearly come to him long before Fredersen asked for his help. Rotwang is a complex figure who displayed prodigious intellectual powers, which even Fredersen respected and which were of infinite value in the modern Metropolis. Yet he also manifested the archaic powers of a sorcerer. In this respect he resembled the machines, at once suggestive of modern power and of primitive evil.

The exploration of modernity in *Metropolis* was undertaken as much through the idea of the city as through science and technology. If early twentieth-century thinkers wanted to voice reservations about the times in which they lived, the city offered an attractive vehicle for their doubts. The city could stand for a multitude of discontents, including, crime, decadence and immorality, as it had done for centuries. Yet, for equally long, the city had also represented positive values such as learning, civilization and enlightenment. In *Metropolis*, Lang highlighted modern, high-rise architecture, advanced transport systems and the vertical structure of the city as a representation of its social hierarchy. He was particularly keen in *Metropolis* to find novel cinematic ways of conveying the immense height of the buildings.[30]

What contemporary commentators found troublesome about city life, particularly in the United States, was the close proximity between different social, religious and ethnic groups. It was perceived as a location which threatened communities, for these could hardly hold together amidst the insistent mobility of urban life. Some who have written about Lang have pointed to distrust of the city as a characteristic of German conservative thought in the 1920s. Yet contemporaries found other meanings in modern city life apart from the threat of social disintegration, including a kind of exhilaration which went with being free from the oppressive intimacy of rural or small town life.[31] By contrast, Lang showed the Metropolis not as a place where groups mingle promiscuously but as one where they are rigidly segregated. The public areas are only for an elite whose composition is never specified and whose behaviour vividly evokes the decadent pleasure-seeking with which the Weimar period is so often associated.

However, there can be no doubt that the city stood for modern life, or that modernity was an important feature of the film. The modernity is conveyed in a number of ways, which do not always sit easily together. The self-indulgent merrymaking of the privileged elite was one way of suggesting it; others were the modern architecture, the industrial machinery, the transport systems and Fredersen's bare, functional office. These must be seen, however, in relation to the ancient catacombs, Rotwang's medieval house, the Gothic cathedral and the eighteenth-century costumes in which the gilded youth of Metropolis besport themselves. Thus the film does not present a simple futuristic or modernistic scenario, but sets up a dynamic between old and new. It is worth remembering how very controversial, socially and politically, simple functionalist architecture was at this time, and that the underlying issue was not only stylistic preference but an entire world-view.[32]

In so far as *Metropolis* rests on a world-view, it is organicism and not the cult of the modern that provides a unifying theme. 'Organicism' is not a straightforward concept, and many different claims have been advanced under its name. In relation to *Metropolis*, two strands of organicist thought are relevant, and they are summarized in the following propositions: 'the parts cannot be understood if considered in isolation from the whole' and 'the parts are dynamically interrelated or interdependent'.[33] Frequent allusions are made in the film to the need for an integrated harmony between different parts of the body: 'Between the brain that plans and the hands that build, there must be a mediator'; 'It is the heart that must bring about an understanding between them'. The film ends in fact with the following title: 'There can be no understanding between the hands and the brain unless the heart acts as mediator'.[34] These statements imply that a society must function as a whole system, just as an organism does, and that social unity is a prized value. Yet this is put forward in a context of intense exploitation and extreme division of labour, a fragmentation the organicist formulation does not seek to challenge. The concern with bringing together head and hands (both masculine) indicates a deep fear of splitting in the social order which will be mended not by ending the original divisions but by binding groups together in some unspecified way through the language of emotions and sentiment (both feminine). The organicist discourse in *Metropolis* works, then, at two levels: the first stresses harmonious relations among the elements of a social system, while the second registers divisions and hierarchy. The point about the hierarchy, however, is that each stratum depends on the others and therefore has no autonomous existence.

Visually, the distinction between the different levels is powerfully conveyed. The workers wear sombre clothes and live below ground where it is dark, while the elite live high up, travel in aeroplanes, wear pale clothes and experience the open air. The brain, the organ of calculation and hard thinking, is visually expressed in silent-film style by the exaggerated reactions and facial contortions of Fredersen and Freder. The workers, on the other hand, are purely physical; they are 'hands', and hands in another sense when they are shown moving dials on clocklike machines, their arms like the hands of a clock. Not only does the life of the mind not exist for them, but they are barely differentiated from one another. The ballet-like presentation of work, which shows highly abstract movements, heightens this sense that mechanical co-ordination between identical elements represents the sum total of life for the majority of the inhabitants of Metropolis who trudge to and from work in serried ranks. The congruence between organicism and silent-film technique extends to Maria, who as the 'heart' of the system, constantly presses her hands to her breast.

All the workers appear to be male, so that for the most part Maria is the only woman we see. The women workers/workers' wives become visible only when the masses rebel and then become alarmed about the fate of their children. The whole plot in fact rests on the potentially disruptive presence of Maria. Indeed, right at the beginning it is clear that, as a fount of feeling, she will not accept a regime based on heartless exploitation. Her good, pure femininity – she is both virgin and mother – is an essential part of the organicist vision, for it enables her to be the 'heart' of the city. It is equally important that the robot be her double – outwardly identical but inwardly her opposite. Femininity is thereby split into two; pure, good chastity and sensual, corrupt depravity. Gender comes to play a complex role in the film. The real business of life, whether it is labour or running Metropolis, is done by men, yet they lack some essential element to make them whole, and it is this ingredient which good femininity can contribute. So that although reason and sentiment could be seen as opposed to one another, they are also complementary.

But what of the destructive side of femininity? Full sensuality was presented as a form of unreason closely akin to mass fury and mass decadence, which are incompatible with male reason. Its fate was to be identified as witchcraft and suitably annihilated. The robot built by Rotwang, a master of knowledge, is portrayed as the antithesis of that knowledge. It should be pointed out that the paradox is sharpened by the robot looking unmistakably feminine, as we noted earlier, before it became 'Maria', suggesting that the destructive machine and the destructive side of female sexuality are identified with one another. Some commentators have dealt with this problem by suggesting that Rotwang is the black magician – as already mentioned, the precursor of the evil Jew of Nazi films. Equally, if not more plausibly, he could be seen in the traditions of hermits, alchemists, philosophers and anatomists, shown in paintings, such as those by Joseph Wright of Derby, as old men wearing robes, whose knowledge isolates them from others. The pentagram, shown on Rotwang's front door and in his laboratory, is, when inverted, a sign of witchcraft and inverted human nature. The term 'seal of Solomon' is also used, but this is in fact six-pointed, unlike the shapes shown in the film.[35]

To identify Rotwang with bad magic is to say that the power he had was wholly illegitimate and came from his attempts to do things which are beyond the proper province of the human being.

There is certainly some truth in this, yet his power was genuine in the sense that it really worked. He has a level of understanding which, it is implied, was unique and was highly valued by Fredersen. Rotwang cannot simply be a magician, then; he is also a scientist and inventor who grapples with the real world not the realms of fantasy. Indeed, if he were simply a wizard, the film would be far less interesting, not least because Fredersen's invitation to Rotwang to help him solve his political problems would seem less plausible. The alliance between political power and power over nature was forceful indeed, but legitimate power and knowledge could all too easily enter an unacceptable, illegitimate domain. The boundary between good and bad was perilously fragile.

Metropolis is an exploration of pure power. Fredersen has complete authority and control, just as Rotwang can command nature's forces. Yet both men find their power challenged because, the film implies, it was incomplete psychologically, lacking feminine sympathy. The plot resolved this by eliminating Rotwang and by giving Fredersen the capacity to empathize. His power – social, political, economic and technological – remained intact, but something was added to it to make it whole. This something was unambiguously identified as a feminine virtue, though some men, such as Freder, possessed it. The need for good femininity to fill the lacunae in male power was reinforced by the fact that Freder has no mother to mediate between him and his father, so Maria had to assume this role. She did so not directly but indirectly by creating tenderness in the son who then tried to pass it on to his father in order to bring his father to sympathize with the workers. The film thus works with a number of different kinds of power and the relationships between them; the power of the emotions (Maria and Freder), of the capacity to control nature (Rotwang), of absolute political authority (Fredersen), of wanton destruction (the robot, the masses and the monstrous machines).

Metropolis reveals much about the relationship between science and technology and other forms of power; or rather, science and technology offer Lang a verbal and visual language with which to speak about social relationships and political structures. The relationship between mental and manual labour is identical with that between rulers and ruled; the unifying force is the highly mechanized factory, which is also the state – an organic social system. The visual language is that of vertical hierarchy; the verbal image that of physiological systems. Femininity, triggering sexual attraction, is the dynamic element introducing change into the system through Freder being drawn to Maria, a woman of the people. In the end, only Maria can offer the quality, heart, which will reconcile head and hand and make the state truly organic. If the feminine disrupts, it also heals. Women do not represent a unitary power, but a force easily fragmented into opposites; nurturing chastity and disrupting sensuality.

In a similar fashion, scientific knowledge can split into genuine reason and illegitimate knowledge/magic, and technology potentially contains both the all-powerful, efficient machines and the monsters who claim the lives of men. When concepts split in this way they generate tensions – because the relationship between the two elements may be obscure and troublesome, and because each element can easily be transformed into the other, creating instability. Such unstable splits threaten to destroy the organic state; they require bridging. Likewise, there should be links between labour and capital. The bridges do not undermine the divisions they span but rather provide an illusion of cohesion.

Lang's film is best described as a caricature of modern life which exaggerates certain aspects to bring them to our attention. This method is most successful in relation to the workers. The denial of individuality, the fusion of man and machine, workers going to and from work in mindless synchrony, and the obsession with time and efficiency have been noted in critiques of capitalism since the time of the romantic writer and historian, Thomas Carlyle (1795–1881).[36] But it remains an open question what Lang and his co-workers really believed about these features of modern life. The film seems to have a conservative, palliative ending, in that master and workers are reconciled without anything being said about real material improvement. The conclusion constitutes a romantic promise, while the reality is that the organic system is preserved intact and, of course, remains hierarchical and exploitative. The use of organicist imagery, and the extended religious analogies surrounding Maria in particular, leave all the important political questions not even raised, let alone answered.

It would be wrong, however, to allow the banality of the ending to colour our reactions to the entire film. Commentators are virtually unanimous in finding the striking visual effects Lang deployed a brilliant success. This is not, I think, to 'reduce' discussion of the film to purely aesthetic terms but to acknowledge the source of its impact. Visual images play a crucial role in exploring and working with the themes discussed in this chapter. They express, often in historically specific ways, something of the power, authority and control that knowledge of nature offers. These complex visual languages speak to our imagination and are all the more important because they do so, since they readily combine with taken-for-granted assumptions about such issues as gender, just as *Metropolis* does. It is the very fact that the intertwining of science and gender was so generally accessible to cinema audiences that makes the film worthy of historical attention.

7

Medical Images of the Female Body

The female body has been extensively represented in public places; statues, monuments, decorative friezes and fountains all teem with women, who are, as often as not, standing for something else. Personification is a powerful instrument of ordering the universe, and in turn woman is a powerful instrument of personification in Western culture.[1] It is hardly possible to say briefly why woman has played this role, but four features of the personifying capacities of the female form stand out as especially pertinent to our present concerns. First, women have often been used to portray abstractions, such as virtues, and vices, and areas of knowledge. Their role in medical and scientific imagery is fully consistent with this. Second, personification is mythic, often literally, in that mythological characters are involved, but also metaphorically in that personification is a device which removes its subject from the immediacy of the present and into a distanced realm.[2] Distancing of this kind can achieve a number of effects, including universalizing subject-matter, providing imaginative space, defusing potential threats, and endowing issues with cultural dignity. We have noted several times how such a process of removal is involved in medical and scientific representations.

MOTHER NATURE CASTING (D) EVILS OUT OF HER CHILDREN.

Plate 12 The personification of nature as both a mother and a healer neatly illustrates the links between gender and medicine.

Third, the use of the female body to personify abstract qualities implies that it is a ready substratum onto which shared values and collective commitments can be projected, even if these have not been consciously articulated. Somehow, women's bodies permit cultural investment in them. Medical imagery treats them in precisely this way, so that they have often been taken as symbols and signs of national vigour, human vitality or morality. Fourth, personifications generally occupy public spaces. When we come to this feature, however, we notice a marked discrepancy between personifications in general, which usually pertain to the public domain, and medical/scientific visions in particular, which infrequently do so.

Such a bald statement distinguishing two radically different uses of the female form in terms of the public/private dichotomy certainly demands justification. Using terms like 'public' and 'private' serves the purposes not of description but of the analysis of belief systems and ideologies. They are ideal types which we can use to organize social-cum-cultural structures because their force has been, and remains central to, dominant ways of thought.[3] Personifications of women in art and sculpture contain a strong element of didacticism in the ways they make manifest virtues, vices, and a whole range of abstract qualities, the precise attributes of which the viewer is invited to consider. They are constructed to be carefully 'read', often for moral ends. This commitment on the part of painters and sculptors to informing, instructing and celebrating through personification led to many such works being located in public places, where anyone could look at them. Although some personifications of the female form do not fit this account, the fact that many do is significant when we come to contrast them with medical representations. If we take the idea of the public to include explicitly political activities, openness, that which pertains to people *en masse*, as a collectivity, and to stand for accountability and popular participation, the private position of medical imagery becomes clear.[4] Medicine in general is allied with privacy – a quality which is accentuated when we come to those parts of it that deal with sexual difference, especially when pictures are involved.

For the most part, medical texts and images are not and have not been freely available to the public. Pictures in particular are not displayed in galleries and museums open to all, nor are they printed in newspapers. Furthermore, some medical texts are not on open access, even in university libraries. It is true that this is often connected with specific subject areas (sex and/or violence), but the fact remains that public access is limited, and – in the case of television, where the coverage is rather more extensive – it is of recent date, is hotly debated and has been controversial ever since medical events began to be televised. The point I want to establish is that medicine, powerful as it may be, is not primarily in the public domain; on the contrary, terms like 'confidentiality', 'secrecy' and 'privacy' spring quickly to mind whenever anything remotely medical is discussed. The private position of medicine is sustained as much by professional structures characterized by closure as by general cultural norms.[5]

The relationship between medicine taken as a whole and the realm of public life is not at all straightforward. It requires, in the twentieth century at least, the sanction of the state and the co-operation of the populace. On the one hand, the official rhetoric of the medical profession stresses a concern with public health interpreted in its broadest sense, while on the other hand it is commonly understood that sectional interests are served by medicine, and that concern for the health of the people as a whole, one definition of public health, has never been a serious priority. At the same time as health education is promoted, people are denied full access to clinical data about themselves. For these reasons I suggest that both medicine and science bear ambivalent relationships to the public realm socially, culturally, professionally and ideologically.[6]

Although I am generally referring to contemporary examples in this final chapter, the problematic relationship to the public is by no means new. The models and prints I discussed earlier were not like public statues and monuments, for example, in that they were probably seen by the very few. Take the case of medical illustrations. William Hunter's atlas was printed in an enormous format, with lavish, expensive plates. Such publications were beyond the reach even of run-of-the-mill medical practitioners, let alone the general public. Technical limitations were certainly related to social ones, in that plates of the quality Hunter produced were of necessity costly. Modern printing techniques can make high-quality reproductions fairly generally accessible, yet this has not transformed medical publications into public property.

The wax anatomical models may well have been seen by more people than had access to illustrated medical works, but it is impossible to estimate the size of their audience, or to know whether they were made with public display in mind. I suspect that by and large this was not the major consideration. Of course, there were medically related exhibits that were open to the public during the eighteenth and nineteenth centuries.[7] Many of these would have to be included under the category of freak shows, for they displayed marvels and monstrosities of many different kinds. Anything in the cabinet-of-curiosities tradition has a particular epistemological status, because its purpose is to induce wonder, not to convey systematic scientific information. Indeed, many museums developed for the purposes of medical teaching and research were, and are, closed to the public.[8] We can explain these indicators of medical distance from the public arena both in terms of the professional manipulation of status, which was enhanced by, for example, dissociating medicine, a polite profession, from popular entertainment, by maintaining control over knowledge and giving it an aura of privilege, and also in terms of social conventions governing the display of the human body.

We now recognize the degree to which these conventions

are culturally determined. Eighteenth-century Europeans were accustomed to the sight of death, in both public and private settings, in a way that we are not.[9] We would be mistaken, however, to assume that earlier societies had either fewer or more restrictions governing the presentation of the body than we do. It is more a case of these being different; no matter how commonplace the sight of bodies was in circumstances we now regard as inappropriate, elaborate conventions existed regarding acceptable and unacceptable behaviour. For the historian, the ways such conventions change are deeply interesting even if difficult to interpret. Certainly the cultural codes concerning male and female bodies have undergone profound transformations, as have those related to medical practice. For example, we know that popular associations between butchers, barbers, surgeons, vivisectionists and even murderers have led medical practitioners to present themselves as distinctive; as rational, scientific, in alliance with polite culture, and clean, for instance, and to strive for enhancement of their social status – all processes which involved renegotiating body taboos. A telling instance of such a process is discussed by Ruth Richardson in relation to the passing of the Anatomy Act 1832, which permitted the use of unclaimed pauper bodies for medical purposes. This was an attempt to generate sufficient corpses for anatomy teaching by legal means. From the point of view of the medical profession, they were working towards dissociating themselves from the illicit, the profane and the unclean, as exemplified by grave-robbing, while from the point of view of the poor, the requisitioning of the bodies of paupers was an unacceptable violation.[10] Basic boundaries and tacit rules, then, vary within societies, according to class and religion, certainly, and also according to race and gender.

At the core of conventions regulating the human body, are the related distinctions between male and female, public and private. We have already noted how debates about midwifery rehearsed problems arising out of where and how acceptable boundaries are drawn between male and female practitioners in relation to the body of parturient woman. The concern about 'decency' was precisely about the precarious boundary between public and private. In the second half of the nineteenth century, arguments about the speculum took the same form. Was it decent for a male doctor to introduce an instrument into the body of an unmarried

Plate 13 The general concern about grave-robbing, and about the difficulty of determining the state of death with certainty, is intensified here by the portrayal of a female corpse.

woman? Clearly these issues arose and were responded to so passionately because gender distinctions, like those between public and private, also implicated the boundaries between clean and dirty, pure and defiled, healthy and pathological. Of course, all these terms operate at many different, although related levels, as is characteristic of the fundamental dichotomies in our culture. In addition, Mary Douglas has shown that these boundaries express the very heart of a society – its cosmology and its social structure.[11] Therefore, the precise means by which medicine negotiates them is a matter of the most general interest.

Although we may want to characterize medicine in general as bearing an ambivalent relationship to the public domain, this ambivalence is intensified when we examine the question of gender. For contemporary society we can illustrate these points by referring to the famous occasion when President Lyndon B. Johnson showed his operation scar to the public. While this could safely be treated as a joke to be added to existing stories about his lack of refinement, it was not the kind of behaviour expected of public figures. However, being a man, he had not exposed a dangerous or threatening part of the body. We learn from this episode that there are certain topics and sights of a medical nature that are not comfortably part of public life. But we also learn that the limits of acceptability are more loosely drawn for a man. It is totally unthinkable for an equally prominent woman to behave in such a way. Just such marked discrepancies between the ways we think about men's and about women's bodies reveal broader trends.

The idea that gender intensifies the private mode of medicine can be confirmed by numerous other experiences in daily life; the reticence which often surrounds the exact nature of operations, especially those performed on women, the hushed tone of voice many adopt when speaking about illness, hospitals and female complaints, the impossibility of getting access to one's own medical records, the inaccessibility of many medical books. Significantly, in the last case it is the pictures more than the text that are imagined to cause offence and make the books vulnerable to abuse. The issues here are not confined to the potential of medicine to cater for perverse sexual or violent pleasures. Rather, there are two quite general matters at stake: what is seen and how it is represented. Most medical publications depict conditions not normally seen by the general public. The sight of unfamiliar injuries, lesions and malformations can be deeply shocking. Equally, the photographs now so often used as illustrations in medical works create a dramatic impact by their unrelenting literalism, especially if they are in colour.

Thus it is not just the sight of forbidden parts or the profound suffering implied by the pathological conditions portrayed that is at issue, but their mode of representation. Colour photographs of healthy bodies do not have the same impact, nor do line drawings of medical subjects. This point is important because it shows that the issue is a particular combination of a form of representation with a specific class of subject-matter. A medical diagram illustrating the same information could in some cases convey the salient data as or even more effectively than an image striving for utter verisimilitude. Not all depictions have the same effect; a point which indicates that there may be a special matching

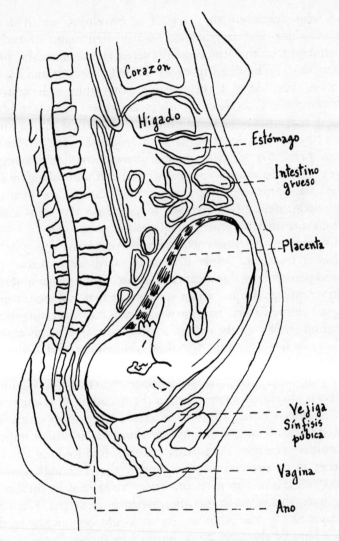

Corazón

Hígado

Estómago

Intestino grueso

Placenta

Vejiga

Sínfisis púbica

Vagina

Ano

Plate 14 This illustration is labelled 'Sagital section at the end of pregnancy. The little head is engaged in the pelvis.'

between the biomedical sciences and forms of visual literalism.

A delightful example may help make the case. In the 1950s a manual was produced for those assisting rural births in Mexico. It is illustrated with line drawings. These appear 'unprofessional' in the sense that they give the impression of being quick sketches, like a map drawn on the back of an envelope, which does not have the sharpness or crispness of a printed map. Everything is subordinated to the function of the image because the pictures have to work. They had to be clear, unambiguous and very easy to follow since they show, among other things, how to cope with obstetric emergencies.[12] I stress this because it is often claimed that insistent verisimilitude in medical illustrations is simply there to make the images more legible for students and practitioners. The Mexican manual shows how line drawings can convey the information perfectly well without being macabre. In fact, a variety of representational modes are available – acknowledgement of this serves to point up the significance of the widespread deployment of literalistic ones.

This chapter is concerned with more recent imagery for a number of reasons. While it may be hard for a reader of the 1980s to perceive the significance of eighteenth- or even nineteenth-century representations, when we look at material from our own time, we immediately bring a whole range of decoding skills to bear upon it. We easily recognize the most significant clues and can have a lively feeling for their resonances and complexity. Sometimes, it has to be admitted, it is harder to bring our own underlying assumptions to the surface, when the foreignness of the past is absent. However, when the decoding of contemporary items has been done, the way is opened for an examination of the workings of long-standing traditions, from which important continuities emerge. A further reason for looking at recent materials is to pre-empt the argument that although gender in general and women in particular were visualized in certain ways in the past, this is no longer the case in our current, rationalistic environment. Nothing, in my view, could be further from the truth. Many of the structures outlined in earlier chapters remain resolutely in place. The sexual ambiguity, the fantasies, the shades of violence, the collective investment in the nature of femininity still exist and are perhaps better understood when viewed from an historical perspective. Their cultural manifestations are, of course, quite distinctive.

Overt lyricizing, whether in verbal or visual form is harder to find now than it was in the eighteenth century. Yet the language of the biomedical sciences is no less suffused with covert assumptions and with imagery that require unpacking than it was in earlier times. Emily Martin's recent book *The Woman in the Body* makes this point brilliantly by analysing the different language women use of menstruation according to their class backgrounds, and also through a detailed comparison of medical writings on the female reproductive system with those on equivalent male functions. She found that the metaphors used of the female system conveyed radically distinct and generally negative assumptions about womanhood, in stark contrast to those used of the male system, which suggested success, power and generally positive qualities.[13]

We should not play down the differences between the late twentieth century and earlier times. In contemporary medical or scientific publishing, we would certainly be hard pressed to find equivalents of Hunter, Smellie or the wax models. They carried the values of their society, overtly and with pride, since they included among their implicit functions the enhancement of medical status through associating it with high culture in general and with art in particular.[14] Medical advertising for drugs in a variety of 'in house' publications offers a rough modern equivalent. Contemporary conventions in advertising are strongly naturalistic, hence adverts often consist of photographs or drawings, of supposedly believable scenes from everyday life. Sometimes metaphors are used, where the caption and picture match. For example, an advert for a drug claimed to be 'the peak of simplicity' was illustrated by a mountain![15] Although such advertisements may seem to be a bizarre form of evidence, they give us access to the same features of medicine that we have examined in earlier chapters between the eighteenth and early twentieth centuries – common assumptions about sex, gender, health and illness, social roles and the languages that mediate between these areas.[16] The examples I discuss were directed at general practitioners rather than at hospital specialists, and they presuppose stereotypes of various kinds that both construct and are constructed by medicine, as well as embodying everyday beliefs. Indeed, it is a precondition of their success as advertisements that they deploy commonplaces.

I have selected advertisements that appeared in *World Medicine*, a fortnightly magazine dealing with a wide range of medical and health issues, sent free to general practitioners and selected hospital doctors. It is filled with drug advertisements, for example, a 64-page issue contained forty (30 May 1981). These work on a number of different principles – they may just provide basic information, but most are elaborate pieces of iconography, sometimes covering more than one sheet. The visual language they deploy is naturally quite varied, and it would not be possible to do justice to its diversity here. But I do want to mention some general features of the advertisements which are especially pertinent to the themes of this book.

Gender is a central medical metaphor. We can discern this from the ways in which illnesses are visually tagged as 'male' or 'female'. Depression, anxiety, sleeplessness and migraine are likely to be associated with women, while disorders that can inhibit full movement and strenuous sporting activities are associated, metaphorically, with masculinity. These include asthma and hypertension. For example, Fisons, the makers of Intal, a drug used in asthma treatment, ran a series using well-known male sports personalities, which showed them leading active lives despite their illness. But in fact it did far more than this. There are many forms of activity, yet the advertisers chose ones that are stereotypically masculine – including rugby and cricket – thereby associating *both* the disease, *and* conspicuous fitness, with men.[17] We can see the same processes at work with hypertensive drugs, one of which is advertised using a photograph of two men in a glider with the caption, 'Keeping you on top of hypertension'.[18] This phrase is revealing because, although it might appear to be addressing patients, in fact it offers the dominant position to the (male) doctor; the text continues, 'on top of patient compliance with good tolerance'. Images and ideas of being 'on top' play on familiar, taken-for-granted assumptions about gender.[19] Such advertisements give expression to images of gender difference. The man rises above the trivia of daily life, he is daring, active, and at ease in the wider world. By contrast, women, as we will see, are domestic, harassed, limited, anxious; they inflict their miseries on their suffering families and fail to keep life in proportion.

It is, of course, not surprising that anxiety and depression are invariably advertised using pictures of women, although this hardly reflects a realistic assessment of the prevalence of these symptoms in the population as a whole.[20] The way that these draw upon long-standing feminine stereotypes is striking. One advertisement put it this way: 'Anxiety is a perfectly normal response to stress but there are times when it gets out of hand and becomes mentally and physically disabling. . . . When anxiety get out of proportion new Lexotan cuts it down to size.'[21] The accompanying pictures offer a dramatic illustration of the text. In the main one a (miniaturized) adult woman hides from a (giant) mouse behind an appropriately enlarged table leg. The smaller, 'after' picture, shows a woman's hand holding a toy mouse. The domestic setting (a kitchen), the housewife (the woman wears an apron) and the mouse work together to produce a powerful female type, whose biographical details readers can fill in. We use such images as occasions for constructing narratives about everyday life. It is, I suggest, reasonable to suppose that general practitioners reading the magazine do the same. Their acts of reading are miniature versions of the larger cultural dynamics in general and of these dynamics as they function in medicine in particular. The advertisements reinforce mental structures that practitioners have previously acquired from their education, clinical practice and social experience. At the same time, these pictures help to shape their mental worlds, through aspects of the imagery that powerfully convey cultural constructs. These features are often incidental to the information advertisements purport to communicate – indications, dosage, side-effects, precautions, contraindications, presentation and cost.

All societies, we may presume, have prevailing images of gender that are diverse and multifaceted. Some of these will have wider currency in a particular community than others, while all such images will be only selectively reinforced. An example may help clarify this point. We know that many businessmen are concerned about absenteeism among women employees and about the amount of time they supposedly spend in the ladies' room, despite the fact that surveys do not confirm their fears. Academic men seem not to worry about these matters, but by and large assume as a matter of course and not necessarily consciously that women are more lightweight intellectually. Both of these beliefs, which are, of course, connected through the metaphors of femininity they rest on, relate to deep-seated gender stereotypes possessing general currency. These can take different forms that are sustained and propagated by specific social groups. In relation to contemporary medicine, female mood swings have been used as the basis of a stereotype, while the association of women and,

say, gossip, is of no particular medical interest. The reason for
this is clear. Changes of mental disposition, whether they be
caused by anxiety, depression or the menstrual cycle, can be
presented as pathological, an attribution that is consistent
with current medical theories. Furthermore, mood changes are
pathological in a number of senses: they are recognized as
disruptive phenomena to be understood and then acted upon by
medical science; drugs exist to treat them; and social disturbances
are thought to be triggered by the physiological mechanisms
believed to cause them.

A particularly telling example of the neat locking together of
the theoretical, therapeutic and social aspects of pathology can
be found in an advertisement for Duphaston, used in the treatment
of premenstrual tension. The picture, which is not a photograph,
but a naturalistic drawing, shows a young woman in the
foreground, with her regulation family of husband, son and
daughter behind her playing with a kite. The main caption reads,
'"Thank you doctor for changing my family's life"'. The text, in
smaller print, contains a quotation: 'The lynchpin of the family
is the mother. When her life becomes a misery each month as
the disturbances of premenstrual syndrome recur, the consequences affect the whole family' – from an article by Katherina
Dalton in the *Journal of Maternal and Child Health*. Reference
is also made to the literature on clinical trials.[22] Pathology is seen
in terms of the disruption of family life, which is attributed to
the wife and mother. This disruption is further presented as
scientific fact. Therapeutic intervention, using the advertised drug,
is rooted in knowledge, clinical experience and the psychodynamics
of the family. This profoundly manipulative association between
women and the family has been a persistent theme in medicine,
particularly since the eighteenth century when the family was
initially conceptualized in naturalistic terms.[23]

Other visual devices equally convey the idea of feminine mood
shifts. One advertisement uses two masks made from photographs
of the model, who in her ivory sweater and pearls beams out
from the centre, flanked on one side by the anxious mask
(insufficient sleep) and the dopey one (impaired day-time performance). A 'before' and 'after' motif is being used here. The woman
in the centre shows the positive effects of the treatment advocated.
The two masks represent the woman before she became a united,

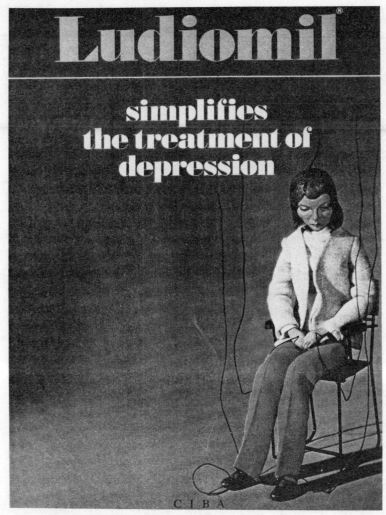

Plate 15 Before.

happy and healthy person, when she was split in two, each part suffering in its own way.[24] Masks suggest the capacity to change appearance, even identity, a capacity present in women, yet alleviated by medication. Another motif that is similarly used is the puppet. Here again there are 'before' and 'after' images. The first picture shows a female puppet in an office-type chair, head down, strings drooping. On the next page the reader is informed that the packs of anti-depressants are specially designed to be 'easy for the patient to remember or to check that *she* has taken

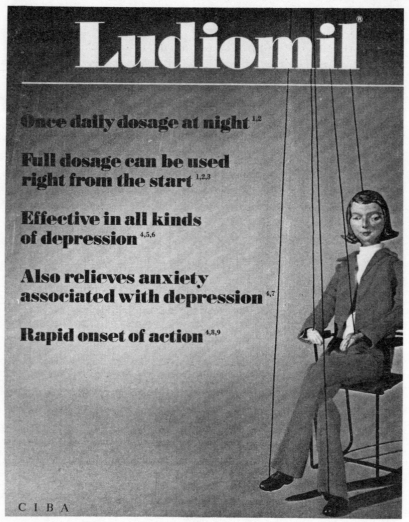

Ludiomil

Once daily dosage at night [1,2]

Full dosage can be used
right from the start [1,2,3]

Effective in all kinds
of depression [4,5,6]

Also relieves anxiety
associated with depression [4,7]

Rapid onset of action [4,8,9]

CIBA

Plate 16 After.

the tablet' (my emphasis). The next page contains the 'after'
picture; the same puppet, strings taut, is sitting up in the chair,
with hair curling up at the ends, a brighter jacket on and a smile
on her face. For such an advertisement to work, the notion that
women are puppet-like has to have some currency; presumably
it plays on an ambiguity between women being manipulated by
men in general and by drugs, and hence by medical men, in
particular. The idea that depression is something beyond the

woman's control, but which is pharmacologically responsive, is also conveyed. The puppeteer (an amalgam of doctor, drug and physiology) makes the strings tight or loose as *he* chooses. It is a nice piece of irony to find that a graph included in the advertisement is labelled as follows: 'Theoretically predicted blood-concentration patterns . . . in *man*' (my emphasis).[25]

None of these images should cause any surprise, since they play upon commonsense ideas that are practically banal. This does not render them less interesting to analyse. They depend on easy decoding. They draw together everyday and medical assumptions. They display persuasive power so long as we do not reflect on their underlying assumptions. However, these assumptions do need to be held up for inspection and analysis, precisely because it is so easy to take them for granted. But the exact forms this inspection and analysis should take require careful consideration.

Visual images are static entities that appear to stand outside the chaos of social life. They can be deconstructed so that the ways in which they have been produced become apparent and the nature of their relationship to social and cultural processes becomes explicit. None the less, we often attribute to images a degree of autonomy, even if we are critical of what the notion of 'autonomy' implies. It is impossible to sustain the view of asocial images in relation to medical advertisements, especially once the idea of medicine as a practice has been accepted. Although we customarily use the phrase 'theory and practice ' as if these were two separate things, to be understood using different approaches, a moment's consideration reveals that they are blended together. All medical practice, that is interactions between healers and clients/patients, takes place within conceptual frameworks of some kind which, to an extent, must be shared by both parties.[26] Since these frameworks encompass beliefs of many different kinds – epistemological, religious, social and so on – the nature of medical practice is perforce complex and cannot be reduced to a single dimension. I stress this because I want to return later to the question of medical power in relation to women, a topic which has been implicitly raised by many of my discussions. Such a perspective may also help us to ask questions about the kinds of social and cultural relationships that produce, and may be produced by, particular sorts of images. To test this out, I turn to a specific and recent example of the medical use of gender imagery, in this case in a literary context.

In the autumn of 1982, *World Medicine* published a conversation, previously broadcast on Radio 4, between Anthony Clare (psychiatrist) and Hugh Dudley (surgeon). The interview centred on Dudley's attitudes towards his work, surgery as a profession, and his life as a whole. In response to the question, 'What is the actual sensual fascination of surgery?', he replied as follows:

> You've almost answered the question. I think it does have a sensual fascination. It's doing something which has a defined output which you can see, which makes people grateful to you in a very direct way and, as a consequence, it is a fulfilling thing to do. Some surgeons would say it's like going to bed with a beautiful woman. You have a real climax over what you do. In addition, of course, it gives you great power because you are the life and death man for an individual person. Surgery is always associated with risk. People recognise that risk and you can see that they are subservient to you. You have the power of life and death over them in a very real way and if you restore life then you earn, in our society, their gratitude.[27]

I want to consider not Dudley as an individual, but the conditions that made his statements possible. In them the following elements are brought together – abdominal surgery, sexual pleasure, power and danger. It matters not the slightest what the biological sex actually is of the body under the knife, because sex here is the perfect metaphor for a particular admixture of power and pleasure. It is easy to see that literally centuries of Western culture lie behind such statements; they draw on ideas and associations made thousands of times before. These sentiments have deep roots. They are neither simply abstract ideas nor disembodied metaphors. They are produced and sustained by the practice of surgery itself, the culture surrounding it, the experience – both collective and individual – of being a surgeon on a daily basis. Furthermore, as Dudley makes clear, the very real gratitude of patients serves to nurture the element of power, both in the actual experience of surgeons and in their fantasies.

In thinking about power we have recourse to a range of metaphors, drawn from paradigmatic cases of power relations such as kinship, sexuality and war. Medicine is most obviously

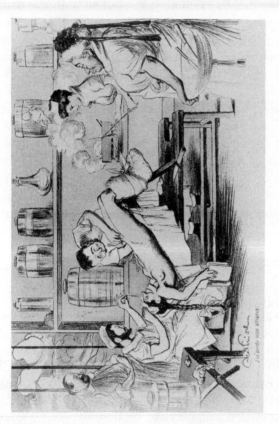

Plate 17 'I've lost my wedding ring!' The totally naked female patient, the enormous size of the incision in her abdomen and the knives serve to point up, humorously, the idea that surgeons incompetently, and almost nonchalantly, violate women's bodies.

allied with sexual power because of stereotypical associations between the professions and men and because medical practitioners hold special rights over the knowledge and treatment of sexual functions. All of these paradigmatic cases contain an element of power over the physical body. What remains distinctive about medicine is its capacity to naturalize human endeavours, and for this reason it is essential to examine it in tandem with the natural sciences, which conceptually speaking, possess the strongest naturalizing capacities. Language of the kind Dudley used displayed several facets of specifically medical power, while also revealing general characteristics shared by different types of power.

Some weeks later, the editor of *World Medicine* reprinted a poem by Gavin Ewart on the same theme. This was inspired by the expression of feelings about surgery similar to Dudley's by Richard Selzer, an American surgeon turned essayist. Ewart's poem, 'The Joys of Surgery' focuses, satirically, on the sexual pleasures of surgery. Again the surgeon's fantasies rather than the actual sex of the patient are at issue. The last six lines are of particular interest:

> while the pink peritoneum,
> lovely as an Art Museum,
> strikes you with desire and dumb
> till you very nearly come . . .
> God made this delightful chasm
> for your own elite orgasm.[28]

Ewart has added two themes to those present in Dudley's remarks, both pertinent to the central concerns of this book. He treats the body as giving rise to a visual delectation akin to art, and he draws attention to the deep, cavelike quality of the abdomen. The intertwining here between a particular form of knowledge-and-practice (surgery in particular/medicine in general), human imaginative capacities (metaphor, symbol, fantasy) and sexuality is intricate. Our analyses of power should be able to capture such intricacies.

Selzer himself was eloquent on the nature of medical, or rather surgical, power: 'the flesh splits with its own kind of moan. It is like the penetration of rape.' Despite his comments on the aggression implicit in Western medicine, Selzer is far from critical of the sexualizing of medical relationships. Indeed, one of his favourite words is 'love' – 'one enters the body in surgery, as in love, as though one were an exile returning at last to his hearth'.[29] Clearly, surgery is a male act. By using the notion of love, Selzer romanticizes and strives to soften the harshness of his vision. But it remains harsh; the high-flown, self-consciously literary approach in fact gives voice to the very aspects of medicine I have here explored. He presents himself above all as a dissector, both as surgeon and as writer, and appropriately enough, images of depth pervade his prose. His searches 'in the recesses of the body' have an evident sexual dimension, hence it is not surprising to find he espouses views about gender that are built on dense clusters of images:

> I love the solid heft of men as much as I adore the heated capaciousness of women – women in whose penetralia is found the repository of existence. . . . Women. . . are matter. . . . Man is albuminoid, proteinaceous, laked pearl; woman is yolky, ovoid, rich.[30]

Selzer adds a further element to the medical role – priestliness.[31] He thus conveys in his essays a number of overlapping impressions; that his vision is exclusive, because his profession works behind closed doors, that his calling is a sacred one, which allows him to be both priest and lover, and that he can see into the human condition by seeing into the body. Sexual difference is intrinsic to this vision, and it is built on gendered images of the body and of medical knowledge.

These complex intertwinings have implications for the ways we study the culture of science and medicine, and for the content of those investigations. It is possible to illustrate this point by returning to the question of power, a concept now freely used in all humanities and social science disciplines, by feminist scholars and by historians and sociologists of science and medicine from a variety of backgrounds and theoretical orientations. The attractions of the term are many, since it can as well describe abstract general processes as the acts of individuals and groups. It appears to give us a handle on reprehensible forms of dominance, and has thereby become loaded with moral, ethical and political values. Equally, it conveys excitement, and possibly even encourages us to identify with forms of domination. Enumerating specific examples of scientific and medical power helps to break down the term's totalizing implications. We can readily distinguish, for example, between the professional, ideological, economic and physical forms power takes in the biomedical sciences. And it is important to differentiate between scientific disciplines and medical specialities with respect to the types of power involved.[32] Similarly, historians of women can list institutions, in the broadest sense, that exercise power over women, including the family, the state, the Church and the legal system. Many would see medicine and natural knowledge as prime examples of such institutions.[33] The guiding model of power deployed here is sometimes drawn, with varying degrees of self-awareness, from property and labour relations, and accordingly it focuses on expropriation, exploitation, control and interests.

Sociological traditions, such as modernization theory, have also been influential and have encouraged scholars to examine professionalization, expertise and management as forms of power. Many recent perspectives on power have stimulated the posing of questions like 'Whose body is it anyway?', which invites answers couched in terms of rights and possession.[34] I argue that such a question is misconceived because it casts issues for which the body is the medium, in the language of property.[35] This is not to say that attempts to clarify the rights of citizens in general, and hence of patients, and of female ones more particularly, are untenable. Quite the contrary, within certain rather complex limits, I would want to support the commitment to self-determination implied by the question. My point is an entirely different one concerning the most productive form of analysis for understanding the relationships between gender and medicine, whether in a contemporary or a historical context.

In order to draw out some of the implications of using the language of property in relation to the human body, I shall turn briefly to the writings of John Locke (1632–1704), where these ideas were cemented together particularly forcefully.[36] In his *Second Treatise of Government* (first published 1690, but composed earlier), Locke uses three concepts – labour, property and the body – which he shows to be closely connected. His first mention of the concept of property in the *Second Treatise* comes not in relation to material possessions but the body – each persons most basic form of property. In the state of nature, Locke argued, a person acquires property (in the usual sense) by applying their labour (i.e. their bodily energies) to material objects; picking apples, planting fields and so on. For him, the human body cannot be appropriated by another person under any circumstances. More than this, being created by God, we have no right to injure or dispose of our own bodies, and therefore suicide, for example, is a violation of God's laws. If we take Locke's treatment of property in general, we note that legitimate property is an amalgam of two elements, the passive matter of nature and the active labour of human beings. The possession of property becomes the sign of responsible citizenship, it endows the owner with a mixture of personal, economic and political rights.

Western liberal democracies remain more or less committed to Lockean ideas. Certainly we recognize that property takes many different forms, requiring a variety of legal, political and conceptual responses. Many of Locke's key notions of property and the rights it confers have persisted. Is it either possible or appropriate to apply these to the human body? Locke gained certain advantages by treating the body as a form of property because it assisted his arguments in favour of responsible citizens and against patriarchalism and slavery. With respect to individuals, their bodies are their property in the sense that they alone actively determine how they are to be used. This right cannot legitimately be transferred to another person.

Yet there is a difficulty here, because the way in which the logic of Locke's general argument has been understood and used frequently omits to take account of the special value he wished to assign to God's creation. To express this specialness he presented the human body as sacred, which makes it unlike any other species of property. It remains a form of property, however, in that people have exclusive rights over their bodies, hence there is a dualism between person-as-owner and body-as-owned. There is perhaps a tension between body as sacred (i.e. as an integral part of personhood) and body as property (as in the custody of a person, and generating, through labour, property of the more conventional kind). Twentieth-century readers are likely to note that gender must inevitably become an issue at this point. For women the idea of body-as-owned is likely to prevail, in that they, for example, are 'given' in marriage, by one man to another.

Men are not 'given' in this sense, and hence are more likely to conceptualize themselves as person-as-owner, not only of themselves but of others.[37] Power, then, for Locke, is, through property, rooted in active human dominance over passive nature. Furthermore, the power deriving from property has commonly been understood to be both economic and political. When it came to power over human beings, both in the political and domestic settings, Locke himself consistently sought ways to limit it.

I conclude from this discussion of Locke that notions of property that work well for its inanimate forms are not necessarily adequate to understanding the relationships between human bodies (part of passive nature?) and the active subject. To model the analysis of power on forms of property relations is unfortunate. Yet this is just what many analyses of medical power over women have done. Often this has been sustained by crude views of interests and professionalization. The sway of this approach has been such that it is hard to imagine alternatives, precisely because it is so bound up with traditions of political thinking. Perhaps Locke himself offered some clues to alternative models of property. When he invoked the sacredness of one's own body as a gift of God, Locke appealed to the unbridgeable difference between inanimate matter and human beings, and allied the latter with divinity. Rather than turn to the language of politics and economics, if we want to understand the meanings of property in relation to human bodies and how these fit in with gender as a centrepiece of the biomedical sciences, we will do better to turn to the language of symbols, 'investment', gifts and identification in the domains of culture, religion and belief systems. I do not, of course, mean 'investment' in an economic sense. I use it to connote the way in which an object, an individual or a specific category of people are assigned and then carry important qualities – the innocence of children, the generosity of mothers, the protectiveness of fathers. Far from being trivial stereotypes, such investments express dense psychic and social concerns. Locke's appeal to the sacred is indeed instructive.

In earlier chapters I have endeavoured to show how we might begin a cultural analysis of the relationships between science, medicine and gender. This has not entailed dissolving all the boundaries around science and medicine, and treating them as indistinguishable from other cultural forms. Quite the contrary, it involves delineating the precise respects in which they are distinctive, in order to understand them as cultural phenomena. As part of this process, we need to distinguish between the mystification that institutions, disciplines or groups give themselves, which generally leads to a stress on their unique, non-contingent properties, and our ability as historians and critics to describe and analyse differences between cultural forms. *Sexual Visions* has considered a number of ways in which the biomedical sciences participated in the construction of authoritative visions of the differences between men and women from the eighteenth to the twentieth centuries. It was both their privileged epistemological status and their capacity to naturalize social relations which distinguished them from other domains. These qualities are better understood once we appreciate the central role that gender plays in science and medicine. To recognize the distinctiveness of the biomedical sciences in no way undermines the argument that they were perpetually, fully and inexorably a part of their culture. It is thus perfectly proper to analyse science and medicine as forms of culture.

Sexual Visions has been centrally concerned with imagery as an integral feature of all social interaction and as of especial importance for science and medicine because, contrary to what is frequently assumed, the human imagination is at their heart. I have shown how closely verbal and visual imagery worked together. This is only to be expected because the themes that I have been concerned with – gender, public/private, (un)veiling, nature/culture – were hardly bound to one medium of expression. Yet it has to be admitted that visual images, of women for example, are not just like verbal descriptions of them. The two types of imagery differ, although the precise ways in which they do so are hard to conceptualize. Vision has long held a privileged place in our intellectual traditions, and we have observed the special capacity to shock vested in some medical pictures. To this last claim it might be objected that the reaction of shock is an adventitious one, deriving, anachronistically, from our own prejudices. I have argued that this is not the case, but that reactions may be inferred from close readings of the artefacts themselves, from comparing them with one another, from juxtaposing texts and pictures and from their historical location.

The point about the distinctive power of visual images becomes much more interesting when we place it in the context of the epistemology of science and medicine. We have noted many times the special value placed on the sense of vision as the privileged route to knowledge by natural philosophers, medical practitioners and also by writers like Michelet. If the capacity for unimpeded vision has been at the core of the biomedical sciences, then we should be especially attentive to what were perceived as the obstacles in its way. It was for this reason that we examined ideas of veiling and unveiling, and noted how, once again, assumptions about and images of gender were constitutive. We are still a very long way from having an adequate account of the history of this epistemology, which developed in the early eighteenth century in the wake of sensationalism, and from tracing its labyrinthine effects.

Given that we are at an early stage in this project, *Sexual Visions* has focused on some specific aspects of it in an attempt to draw in a preliminary sketch map. To achieve this modest aim two related strategies have been followed. First, I have set out some of the methodological and interpretative issues raised by enquiring into the historical linkages between science, medicine and gender. Second, I have presented a series of case studies which, although they range widely chronologically and geographically, are informed by a respect for the complexity of the sources used. Such an enterprise is not undertaken responsibly if it simply sets out to find and document the 'oppression' of women by science and medicine. This is because it is not just women but gender that is at issue; a dynamic, socially constructed polarity. Nor is it oppression that is at issue but a whole array of cultural processes through which men's and women's bodies and roles are comprehended, managed and given meaning.

Accordingly, I have stressed the imaginative aspects of the biomedical sciences. I do not mean by 'imaginative' that which is fanciful, the extras after the 'real' business has been done. Rather, I wish to suggest the multiple ways in which science and medicine tell stories and produce images that convince both 'experts' and others, that act as sources for other social and cultural relationships, that satisfy people in the accounts they are able to give about matters that touch us most deeply – gender, sexuality and kinship.[38] It is indispensable for us to recognize that the force some of these images had, and have, can only be understood by appealing to their capacity to grip the imagination. To be sure, it is vital to show where, when and how they did so, but the no less essential first step is an awareness of the importance of imaginative dimensions of the biomedical sciences.

Such an awareness demands a serious consideration of visual images and of the power with which acts of seeing were endowed. This power is not of the kind to be expressed solely in a language of rights, property, interests or oppression. It is more like the power of myth.[39] For the approach advocated here to be valuable in history, some idea of mediation is essential, because it enables us to lay out the links between different levels, areas, processes and languages. It is also helpful to think in terms of collective investment and ask questions like: what did medical writers find of such overriding significance in (parts of) women's bodies at particular times, and why? Our answers will not take the form of castigation but of recognition – the recognition that gender, together with the biomedical sciences of which it was an integral part, expressed and informed cultural processes. The themes *Sexual Visions* has explored were part of a web which stretched back in time and so contained many mythic, traditional threads; the patterns none the less keep changing, shifting with historical circumstance. It is a continuing challenge to historians to describe and interpret such formidably intricate, elusive and significant processes.

Afterword

While completing *Sexual Visions*, I happened to pick up a book
I have long owned: *The Intelligent Woman's Guide to Atomic
Radiation*, by Margot Bennett, published as a Penguin Special in
1964. The blurb on the back cover announced: 'In the most real
sense women are more creative and less destructive than men'.
Here lay the reason behind the book's title; it 'is so intimately
concerned with life and inheritance'. The blurb continued, 'it is,
if you wish, a translation into plain English of ugly things that
are normally referred to in the foreign language of science'. The
remaining lines reiterate the clarity of the work's exposition,
addressing the reader as 'you'. Initially I thought that the contents
would at least offer supporting evidence for such sweeping
assumptions, perhaps even move towards an analysis of atomic
power in terms of gender. I was, of course, mistaken. Quite the
contrary: this web of gendered dichotomies constituted the
founding assumptions, not only of the author, but of the
publishers and presumably of at least a section of the readership.
It misses the point to suppose they can be provided with
'justification'. They are givens, of the kind I have analysed in the
foregoing chapters.

In order to draw out the main themes Bennett deployed, let

us set out these pairs in the same form as has been used earlier in the book:

women	*men*
creative	destructive
life and inheritance	threats to life and inheritance
plain English	foreign language of science
beauty (by implication)	ugliness
'you'	'them' (by implication)

These associations are familiar to us. The female side is life-giving and lovely, it is the realm of nature. By contrast, the male domain of science embodies a threat to life. But the blurb forces upon us another aspect of the polarity between masculinity and femininity – differences of language. The language for women is plain, direct and our own; that for men is doubly alien in that it is 'scientific' and hence abstruse, and 'foreign', that is, of the 'other'. Emotive, rich, yet slippery images of nature, science and gender are evoked.

Bennett's Introduction reveals just how tricky this whole cluster of ideas is. The author wants to make the most general possible claims about the significance of nuclear issues. She therefore uses 'man' and 'men' as if they meant simply 'human', although, having set up such a sharp contrast between men and women, the reader is never quite sure what is intended. She also locates the difference between the sexes specifically in the family, by claiming for all women 'a tenderness for children' irrespective of their reproductive experience. Women are thus to be understood in terms of 'the family'. Finally, in the Introduction, we come to Pandora's box: 'One thing is certain, radiation is with us for good; out of Pandora's box for ever. . . . Man can't afford to retreat; it is by discovery and invention, from fire and flint-axe onwards that he has survived'.[1] Pandora was, it should be remembered, both beautiful and stupid, and her husband, Epimetheus, the brother of Prometheus, was not able to prevent her opening the lid of her jar, to the eternal detriment of the whole human race.[2] The image of Pandora's box somewhat works against the manifest content of the text.

The Intelligent Woman's Guide to Atomic Radiation suggests

two distinct lines of thought that are central to the arguments I
have developed, although I have not previously stated them so
baldly. First, our ways of dealing with gender and natural
knowledge, having been built up in diverse forms over hundreds
of years, are complex, tortuous, productive, inventive and, it
must be admitted, confused. Being frank about the muddle can
be an important initial step in the process of tracing through
different lines of argument and the range of visual and verbal
images to achieve a form of clarity stemming from historical
analysis. Second, our response to the muddle should not stop at
this point. It is all too easy to see the tangles around gender,
science and medicine as simply evidence of 'sexism', of cultures
that denigrated women and denied them rights and value. Such
a judgement is both simplistic and facile. That the sexes were
conceptualized and treated as *different* is undeniable, and in
Sexual Visions I have attempted to explore some specific examples
of this perpetual engagement with natural difference. What we
need to maintain, however, is a sense of the difficulty of these
questions, of the urgency with which people respond to them,
of the elaborate struggles we engage in to find the appropriate
images and languages for them. I mention the Penguin Special in
order to make both these points, since it neatly exemplifies
centuries of accumulated 'confusion' as well as the greatness of
the quest to understand the relationships between gender and
systematic knowledge of the world of nature.

Notes

The references in these notes are abbreviated; the full citation may be found in the bibliography. Where a foreign-language edition is cited, any translations are my own.

Notes to chapter 1

1. Turgenev, *Fathers and Sons*, p. 155.
2. Webster, *The Great Instauration* shows how science and medicine in mid-seventeenth-century England mediated political and religious conflict.
3. Rosaldo and Lamphere (eds), *Woman, Culture and Society*, and MacCormack and Strathern (eds), *Nature, Culture and Gender*.
4. The classic statement of the social constructionist position is Berger and Luckmann, *The Social Construction of Reality*; on sexuality as socially constructed see Weeks, *Sexuality and Its Discontents*; Wright and Treacher (eds), *The Problem of Medical Knowledge* offers a selection of approaches for the biomedical sciences.
5. Williams, *Keywords*. Gender itself is not defined by Williams, but see the entries for 'Man' and 'Sex'.
6. Keller, *Reflections on Gender and Science*, and the work of Haraway, for instance, 'The biological enterprise' and 'Teddy bear patriarchy', are outstanding examples of how this can be done.

7. Barnes and Shapin (eds), *Natural Order*; Rousseau and Porter (eds), *Ferment of Knowledge*, chs 2 and 3; Cooter, *The Cultural Meaning of Popular Science*, esp. parts 1 and 2.

8. The journal *Representations* (February 1983 on) is an excellent example of the new preoccupation in the humanities with this concept.

9. The notion of 'realism' is discussed in more detail in Chapter 3.

10. Jarrett, *England in the Age of Hogarth*, is a good example of this, since he makes special claims for Hogarth's ability to understand his own age: 'Nobody saw these things more clearly than Hogarth and it was for this reason that Englishmen continued to gaze, for many years after his death, into the mirror which he had held up to them' (p. 11). There can be no clearer statement of the 'reflection' position.

11. The question of myth is discussed in Chapter 7. On myths in relation to the themes of this book, see Graves, *Greek Myths*; Warner, *Monuments and Maidens*; Kirk, *The Nature of Greek Myths*; and de Beauvoir, *The Second Sex*, part 3.

12. A good example is the Cambridge University Press series, 'Ideas in Context', which is strongly philosophical in orientation and is listed in the catalogue along with Political and Social Theory.

13. Weeks, *Sexuality and Its Discontents* and *Sex, Politics and Society* are examples of the new trend that also refer to other works in the field; see also Nead, *Myths of Sexuality*.

14. Shorter, *The Making of the Modern Family*; *A History of Women's Bodies*.

15. Weideger, *History's Mistress*; quotations from pp. 32 and 34.

16. Moscucci, 'The science of woman: British gynaecology 1849–1890'; Fee, 'The sexual politics of Victorian anthropology', in Hartman and Banner (eds), *Clio's Consciousness Raised*, pp. 86–102.

17. Sharpe, *Defamation and Sexual Slander in Early Modern England*; Rotberg and Rabb (eds), *Marriage and Fertility* – both provide samples of such work.

18. See the works cited in note 13 above; the foundational texts are Foucault, *The History of Sexuality*, vols 1 and 2.

19. Montesquieu, *Persian Letters*, letter 9, p. 49.

20. Foucault, see note 18; Donzelot, *The Policing of Families*; McLaren, *Reproductive Rituals* also emphasizes the role of popular belief.

21. Walters, *The Nude Male*; Clark, *The Nude*.

22. Gallagher and Laqueur (eds), *The Making of the Modern Body*, quotation from p. vii.

23. Mount, *The Subversive Family*; Barrett and Macintosh, *The Anti-Social Family*.

24. Scott, 'Gender: a useful category for historical analysis'.
25. Moscucci makes this point (see note 16), as of course, does de Beauvoir, *The Second Sex*.
26. De Beauvoir explores the question of otherness in the Introduction to Book 1 of *The Second Sex*. The sources for her conception of otherness include Hegel, Sartre and Levi-Strauss. See also Lloyd, *The Man of Reason*, chs 5 and 6.
27. Merchant, *The Death of Nature*; Easlea, *Fathering the Unthinkable*.
28. Ehrenreich and English, *For Her Own Good*; and in Hartman and Banner (eds), *Clio's Consciousness Raised*, the chapters by Wood, Smith-Rosenberg and Morantz.
29. Rose and Rose, *Science and Society*; Ehrenreich and English, *For Her Own Good*.
30. Young, *Darwin's Metaphor*, is a sustained attempt to show, in concrete historical terms, the fallacy of the use/abuse position.
31. Porter (ed.), *Patients and Practitioners*.
32. Attacks on 'quacks', 'quackery' and medicine perceived as heterodox are an excellent example of this; see Bynum and Porter (eds), *Medical Fringe and Medical Orthodoxy*, especially the paper by Loudon.
33. See, for example, *Journal of Interdisciplinary History* (1970 on).

Notes to chapter 2

An earlier version of this chapter was published in MacCormack and Strathern (eds), *Nature, Culture and Gender*, pp. 42–69. I am grateful to Cambridge University Press for permission to reuse material from it here. This book should be consulted on the current status of the debates on nature and culture, especially in anthropology.

1. The historical literature on women's work has been especially successful in revealing the diversity of women's activities. See, for example, Tilly and Scott, *Women, Work and Family*; Pinchbeck, *Women Workers and the Industrial Revolution*; and Prior (ed.), *Women in English Society*, especially the chapter by Prior.
2. The relationships between ideas about and experiences of gender have been explored by Davidoff and Hall, *Family Fortunes*, who also mention other work on the subject.
3. Michelet is discussed at length in Chapter 4; Mozart's opera and Bernardin de Saint-Pierre's novel will be considered later in this chapter. On the theme of distinct, co-existing meanings associated with gender, see Tomaselli, 'The Enlightenment debate on women'.
4. There are now well-developed philosophical debates on these

matters. A useful synthesis that considers themes close to this book is Lloyd, *The Man of Reason*.

5. Williams, *The Country and the City*; quotation from p. 9.
6. On work and gender, see Gamarnikow *et al.* (eds), *Gender, Class and Work*, which raises both historical and sociological questions. The specifically medical issues are discussed further in Chapter 3.
7. The literature on the Enlightenment is, of course, massive. Of relevance for our concerns in this chapter are Hankins, *Science and the Enlightenment*; Gay, *The Enlightenment: An Interpretation*. Also useful is Porter and Teich (eds), *The Enlightenment in National Context* because it comes at the issues from a different and unusual angle.
8. Sexuality in this period is now receiving more attention. Samples of recent approaches may be found in Boucé (ed.), *Sexuality in Eighteenth-Century England; Dix-huitième siècle* (special issue on sexuality in 1980); and Rousseau and Porter (eds), *Sexual Underworlds of the Enlightenment*.
9. Quotations are from Farrington, *The Philosophy of Francis Bacon*, pp. 62, 69 and 62 respectively – unfortunately these remarks are now so frequently quoted that they have become banal. Bacon's role in relation to science and gender is discussed by Merchant, *The Death of Nature*, esp. ch. 7; Keller, *Reflections on Gender and Science*, esp. chs 2 and 3; Lloyd, *The Man of Reason*, ch. 1; and Mellor, 'Frankenstein: a feminist critique of science', in Levine (ed.), *One Culture*, pp. 287–312. The larger importance of Bacon for subsequent generations of natural philosophers and political reformers is discussed by Webster, *The Great Instauration* – ch. 4, sect. 10, and ch. 5, sect. 1, touch on especially pertinent themes.
10. Descartes advocated the search for useful knowledge because human beings might 'thereby make [them]selves, as it were, masters and possessors of nature', *Discourse on Method*, p. 78.
11. Glacken, *Traces on the Rhodian Shore*; Thomas, *Man and the Natural World*; Jordanova and Porter (eds), *Images of the Earth*; Riley, *The Eighteenth-Century Campaign to Avoid Disease*.
12. On naturalistic approaches to sexuality, see the works cited in notes 8 and 13 to this chapter, since the idea of life-style was pivotal.
13. Questions of health and life-style are discussed in Lawrence, 'William Buchan: medicine laid open'; Jordanova, 'Earth science and environmental medicine', in Jordanova and Porter (eds), *Images of the Earth*, pp. 119–46, and 'The popularisation of medicine'; and Smith, 'Prescribing the rules of health', in Porter (ed.), *Patients and Practitioners*, pp. 249–82.
14. Although it appears to be a simple idea, 'habit' was in fact an

important philosophical and biological concept for many eighteenth-
and nineteenth-century thinkers. This was partly because all
associationist theories of mind took it as a basic term. But it was
extended by those who deployed it in a biological and medical
context to form a more general model of organic change. We see
this especially clearly in the transformism of Jean-Baptiste Lamarck
(1744–1829); see *Philosophie zoologique*, vol. 1, ch. 7. Its nineteenth-
century significance is summarized in Lalande, *Vocabulaire technique
et critique de la philosophie*, vol. 1, pp. 282–8.

15. For a more detailed discussion of these points, see Jordanova (ed.),
Languages of Nature, esp. pp. 51–158.

16. Cabanis, *Oeuvres philosophiques*, vol. 1, p. 275; a useful account
of Cabanis' life and work may be found in Staum, *Cabanis*.

17. Roussel, *Système physique et moral de la femme*, pp. 11–12; Roussel
is also discussed by Knibiehler, 'Les médecins et la "nature
feminine"'; by Bloch and Bloch, 'Women and the dialectics of
nature', in MacCormack and Strathern (eds), *Nature, Culture and
Gender*, pp. 25–41; and by Le Doeuff, 'Pierre Roussel's chiasmas'.

18. There is now an extensive literature on these aspects of Rousseau's
thought. Of particular value are Elshtain, *Public Man, Private
Woman*, pp. 147–70; Schwartz, *The Sexual Politics of Rousseau*;
and Weiss, 'Rousseau, anti-feminism and women's nature'.

19. On this idea in the biomedical sciences of the eighteenth century,
see Figlio, 'Theories of perception and the physiology of mind'.

20. Pomme, *Traité des affections vaporeuses des deux sexes*, pp. 578–82.
Luxury was a key term in eighteenth-century debates about social
roles from a naturalistic perspective. See, for example, Ross,
'Mandeville, Melon and Voltaire'; Sekora, *Luxury*, part 1.

21. Macquart, *Dictionnaire de la Conservation de l'Homme*, vol. 2,
p. 511.

22. Barthez, *Nouveaux elémens de la science de l'Homme*, vol. 2,
p. 298; on Barthez see Dulieu, 'P.J. Barthez'.

23. Cabanis, *Oeuvres philosophiques*, vol. 1, p. 278.

24. Macquart, *Dictionnaire de la conservation de l'homme*, vol. 2,
p. 110.

25. ibid., vol. 1, p. 77.

26. On wet-nursing and related issues in the period, see Lindemann,
'Love for hire'; Drake, 'The wet nurse in France'; Sussman, *Selling
Mothers' Milk*; Fildes, *Breasts, Bottles and Babies*.

27. On midwifery, see Donnison, *Midwives and Medical Men*; Gélis,
'Sages-femmes et accoucheurs'; and Gélis *et al.*, *Entrer dans la vie*;
Shorter, *A History of Women's Bodies*, esp. ch. 3; Versluysen,
'Midwives, medical men and "Poor women labouring of child"';

and items in notes 31 and 33 to this chapter, below.

28. Cadogan, *An Essay upon Nursing*, quotations from pp. 3, 4 and 24. Fildes states that there were at least eleven editions of this pamphlet in English and French between 1748 and 1792.
29. ibid., p. 7.
30. ibid., p. 11.
31. Wilson, 'William Hunter and the varieties of man-midwifery', in Bynum and Porter (eds), *William Hunter*, pp. 343–69; Forbes, 'The regulation of English midwives in the 18th and 19th centuries'; Jordanova, 'Policing public health' in Ogawa (ed.), *Public health*, pp. 12–32; and Petrelli, 'The regulation of French midwifery during the Ancien Régime'.
32. Crabbe, *Tales, 1812*, p. 45, lines 685–92.
33. Fores, *Man-Midwifery Dissected*; see also Porter, 'A touch of danger', in Rousseau and Porter (eds.), *Sexual Underworlds of the Enlightenment*, pp. 206–32, esp. pp. 215–22 and 229 for other examples along the same lines.
34. See the recent English edition of *Paul and Virginia*; and Charlton, *New Images of the Natural in France*; Robinson, 'Virginie's fatal modesty'.
35. Bernardin de Saint-Pierre, *Paul et Virginie*, pp. 70–1 and 67–8.
36. Mann, *The Operas of Mozart*, pp. 591–640, see also Hiatt, 'Queen of the Night', in Hook (ed.), *Fantasy and Symbol*, pp. 247–65. The words of the opera were probably written by a number of people, including the freemason and friend of Mozart, Schikeneder.
37. Chailley, *The Magic Flute, Masonic Opera*; Jacob, *The Radical Enlightenment*, explores freemasonry as a radical force in eighteenth-century Europe.
38. Mozart, *Magic Flute*, quotes from pp. 42, 51, 54, 59 and 62.
39. Chailley, *The Magic Flute*, p. 295.
40. Coser, 'The principle of patriarchy', p. 347.
41. On the idea of 'progress', see Pollard, *The Idea of Progress*, and Williams, *Keywords*, pp. 243–5; neither of these, it should be noted, analyse the idea for its gender implications, but see Tomaselli, 'The Enlightenment debate on women'.
42. Williams, *Keywords*, pp. 57–60, 87–93.
43. Babbage, *Reflections on the Decline of Science in England*; Brewster et al., *Debates on the Decline of Science*.
44. Mitchell, 'The passions according to Adam Smith and Pierre-Jean-Georges Cabanis'.
45. Lozte is quoted in Ploss et al., *Woman*, vol. 1, p. 129.
46. Durkheim, *Suicide*, p. 272.

47. See Chapter 6 on Fritz Lang's *Metropolis*.
48. Boas, *French Philosophies of the Romantic Era*, discusses the political, philosophical and psychological aspects of what I call 'the authoritarian response'; Laqueur argues that there was a new sense of hierarchy and of the incommensurability between the sexes in the late eighteenth and early nineteenth centuries, 'Orgasm, generation and the politics of reproductive biology', in Gallagher and Laqueur (eds), *The Making of the Modern Body*, pp. 1–41. Later evolutionary theories were certainly concerned with whether men or women were 'higher'.
49. De Beauvoir, *The Second Sex*, part 3.
50. Lovejoy, '"Nature" as an aesthetic norm'; Charlton, *New Images of the Natural*; Ehrard, *L'Idée de Nature*.
51. This wildness is best exemplified in the widespread preoccupation with women's madness, especially during the nineteenth century; Gilbert and Gubar, *The Madwoman in the Attic*; Showalter, *The Female Malady*; Shuttleworth, '"The surveillance of a sleepless eye"', in Levine (ed.), *One Culture*, pp. 313–35.

Notes to chapter 3

1. Fisher, 'Body image', in Sills (ed.), *International Encyclopedia of the Social Sciences*, vol. 3, pp. 113–16. Fisher points out, 'it has been suggested . . . that in Western culture men are supposed to transcend their bodies and to turn their energies toward the world. Women, on the other hand, are given approval for continuing and even increasing investments in their bodies' (pp. 115–16). See also Slochower, 'Psychoanalysis and art: their body language'.
2. Lanza *et al.*, *Le Cere Anatomiche della Specola*; other discussions of wax models are: Azzaroli, 'La Specola'; Deer, 'Italian anatomical waxes'; Haviland and Parish, 'A brief account of the use of wax models'; Premuda, 'The waxwork in medicine'; and Antoine, '"Les horreurs" anatomiques de Florence'. The standard reference work is Pyke, *A Biographical Dictionary of Wax Modellers*.
3. There are waxes in La Specola, Florence that closely resemble Bernini's Saint Theresa (the face) and figures on Michelangelo's Sistine Chapel ceiling; see Lanza *et al.*, *Le Cere*, pp. 208–9 and 37.
4. *Oxford English Dictionary*, vol. 8, p. 202; see also the supplement, vol. 3, pp. 1091–2.
5. Fried, *Realism, Writing, Disfiguration*, pp. 63–4.
6. Bryson, *Word and Image*, esp. ch. 1.
7. See Baudrillard, *Selected Writings*, esp. pp. 6–7 and 143–7 for a

different and much more elaborate use of the idea of hyperrealism. A usage closer to mine may be found in Eco, *Travels in Hyper-reality*, pp. 3–58.

8. Hunter, *Anatomia Uteri Humani Gravidi*, and *Introductory Lectures*, p. 70. I discuss this point in the context of Hunter's epistemology in 'Gender, generation and science', in Bynum and Porter (eds), *William Hunter and the Eighteenth Century Medical World*, pp. 385–412, esp. pp. 395–6.

9. Nochlin, *Realism*. In addition to Fried's work cited in note 5 to this chapter, see Wellek, 'Realism in literature', in Weiner (ed.), *Dictionary of the History of Ideas*, vol. 4, pp. 51–6.

10. *Oxford English Dictionary*, vol. 8, p. 202.

11. Nochlin, *Realism*, esp. pp. 40–5.

12. Stone, *The Family, Sex and Marriage*, plate 36 shows a group of young women examining a wax model. The caption reads: 'Sex education: exhibition of wax-work models of the reproductive system. Late eighteenth century', the only attribution given is 'Library of Congress'. See also Cole, 'History of anatomical museums'; Lawrence, 'Anatomy, museums and the Enlightenment'; Altick, *Shows of London*, esp. ch. 24. Pyke, *A Biographical Dictionary of Wax Modellers*, indicates the range of works in wax, the occasions for which they were produced and the sort of places where they were collected and/or exhibited.

13. On Greuze, see Brookner, *Greuze*; Bryson, *Word and Image*, ch. 5. The picture by Prud'hon/Meyer is in the Wallace Collection. The picture by Maurice Denis is reproduced in Wattenmarker, *Puvis de Chavannes and the Modern Tradition*, p. 131. Carrière's work, although popular in its day, is not now well known, but several examples may be found in National Museum of Wales, Cardiff; see Ingamels, *The Davies Collection of French Art*, plates 43 a and b, 44, 45 a and b. On Carrière, see also *Le Symbolisme en Europe*, p. 46, and Hamilton, *Painting and Sculpture in Europe 1880–1940*, pp. 77, 80, 141 and 159. I plan to undertake a study of Carrière in the context of late-nineteenth-century representations of motherhood.

14. This literature has recently been surveyed by Simonton, *Women's Education and Training in Late Eighteenth Century England*; see also Armstrong and Tennenhouse (eds), *The Ideology of Conduct*.

15. On advice books, see Curtis, 'A case study of Defoe's domestic conduct manuals'; Ehrenreich and English, *For Her Own Good*; Jordanova, 'The popularisation of medicine: Tissot on onanism'.

16. The idea of legibility in relation to art is interestingly used by Bryson in *Word and Image*; ch. 2 discusses physiognomy. On

phrenology, see Cooter, *The Cultural Meaning of Popular Science*, esp. part 1.

17. Elshtain, *Public Man, Private Woman*; Benn and Gaus (eds), *Public and Private in Social Life*; Lloyd, *The Man of Reason*, ch. 5.

18. The quotations are from Rousseau's *Emile* as cited by Wollstonecraft in her *Vindication*, p. 176 (I have used this version because it conveys the eighteenth-century flavour more vividly than a modern translation).

19. The quotation comes from the title of the chapter in which she denounces Rousseau; ibid., pp. 173–218.

20. Gélis *et al.*, *Entrer dans la vie*, especially the illustrations; Boucé (ed.), *Sexuality in Eighteenth-Century Britain*; and Rousseau and Porter (eds), *Sexual Underworlds of the Enlightenment*.

21. Haigh, *Xavier Bichat and the Medical Theory of the Eighteenth Century* both sketches in the mechanistic approach and examines the reactions against it that are often called 'vitalism'.

22. On the sensorium commune see Figlio, 'Theories of perception'.

23. Haigh, *Xavier Bichat*, ch. 4; Maulitz, *Morbid Appearances*; and Staum, *Cabanis* – all explore these questions and cite the literature in the field. Bichat's analytical approach is revealed both in the 'Physiological Table' and in the table of contents, called 'Analysis', of his *General Anatomy*, vol. 1, lxxxiv–lxxxviii, viii–xxxi; vol. 2, i–xxxii.

24. Lamarck certainly did this, using a sensationalist epistemology; Jordanova, *Lamarck*, offers an introductory account, but see also the discussion of him below.

25. On the Hunters as medical educators, see Lawrence, 'Anatomy, museums and the Enlightenment', esp. 7–8; 'In this method [i.e. William Hunter's], anatomy was not to be taught, as it had been, by instruction and demonstration on one or two cadavers, but by each student personally dissecting a whole corpse' (p. 7). Lawrence stresses that this method was generally adopted in the nineteenth century. On medical education see also Bynum and Porter (eds), *William Hunter and the Eighteenth Century Medical World*, part 2. The new passion for dissection is generally seen as the reason for the growth of grave-robbing in the eighteenth and early nineteenth centuries; see plate 9, and Richardson, *Death, Dissection and the Destitute*.

26. Haigh, *Xavier Bichat*, esp. ch. 7; Maulitz, *Morbid Appearances*; 'tissue' is defined in the *Oxford English Dictionary*, vol. 11, pp. 71–2.

27. Rudwick, *The Meaning of Fossils*; Porter, *The Making of Geology*.

28. The most important recent analysis of Lamarck is Corsi, *The Age*

of Lamarck. See also Burkhardt, *The Spirit of System*; Jordanova, *Lamarck*, and 'La psychologie naturaliste et le "problème des niveaux"'.

29. Lanza *et al.*, *Le Cere Anatomiche*, p. 209.
30. Veith, *Hysteria*, esp. ch. 8.
31. See Sena, *A Bibliography of Melancholy.*
32. Wornum, *Lectures on Painting by the Royal Academicians*, p. 106. The point about art and gender could be taken further; for example, in *The Rage of Edmund Burke*, Kramnick has observed how Burke's aesthetic language is gendered: 'The sublime is a package of masculine traits, the beautiful, feminine.' (p. 94) Furthermore, Burke associates each with a sex role – the sublime is embodied in the father, the beautiful in the mother (pp. 96–7). I am grateful to David Solkin for drawing my attention to these works.
33. See the discussion in Chapter 2, and especially note 10.
34. Richardson, *Death, Dissection and the Destitute*; Linebaugh, 'The Tyburn riot against the surgeons', in Hay *et al.*, *Albion's Fatal Tree*, pp. 65–117; Hogarth, 'The Stages of Cruelty' (1751), reproduced in Shesgreen (ed.), *Engravings by Hogarth*, plates 77–80. The third stage, 'Cruelty in Perfection', shows the corpse of a murdered pregnant woman, the mistress of the 'hero' of the series. Gender dynamics are thus integral to the moral of the plates. The link with medicine is made in the final plate, where the perpetrator of the murder is himself dissected. Shesgreen notes that a preliminary sketch for 'The Reward of Cruelty' contained 'intimations of cannibalism' in one motif. We shall return to this theme in Chapter 5.
35. The speculum is discussed in Moscucci, 'The science of woman', the concern about it can be seen in an anonymous pamphlet, *The Speculum and Its Moral Tendencies* of 1857.
36. Hunter, *Anatomia Uteri Humani Gravidi*, plate 4.
37. *Suite du recueil de planches, sur les sciences, les arts libéraux, et les arts méchaniques*; this volume is arranged alphabetically by subject, the plates on hermaphrodites are under 'Histoire naturelle, hermaphrodites', see supp. plate 1.
38. Jordanova, 'Gender, generation and science', esp. p. 390.
39. Smellie, *A Sett of Anatomical Tables*, plates 15 and 16. This issue has been touched on in Chapter 2.
40. Carter, *The Sadeian Woman*; Sade, *Juliette* (first published 1797) and *Justine* (first published 1791). I have discussed the lyrical versus the violating modes in another context; Jordanova, 'Naturalising the family', in Jordanova (ed.), *Languages of Nature*, pp. 86–116, esp. 109–11.

41. On Zummo, see Pyke, *A Biographical Dictionary of Wax Modellers*, pp. 162–3, 38–9, 87–8. Examples of *memento mori* in medical illustration are the plates in Gamelin, *Nouveau recueil d'ostéologie*.
42. Leslie and Chapman, *Madame Tussaud*. It is now well known that the Yorkshire Ripper, who murdered a large number of young women, frequented in his youth a waxwork museum that displayed models of the female abdomen.

Notes to chapter 4

1. The secondary literature on Michelet is extensive. In addition to works cited elsewhere, I have found the following helpful: Barthes, *Michelet*; Borie, 'Une gynécologie passionnée; in Aron (ed.), *Misérable et glorieuse. La femme du XIXᵉ siècle*, pp. 153–89; Calo, *La Creátion de la femme chez Michelet*; Pugh, *Michelet and His ideas on Social Reform*; Bann, *The Clothing of Clio*, ch. 2; Wilson, *To the Finland Station*.
2. For example, Orr, *Jules Michelet: Nature, History and Language*; Huss, 'Michelet and the uses of natural reference', in Jordanova (ed.), *Languages of Nature*, pp. 289–321; McCallum, 'Michelet's narrative practice'; Kaplan, *Michelet's Poetic Vision*.
3. The facts of Michelet's life are recounted in many places; for an authoritative account, see Viallaneix, *La Voie royale*.
4. Michelet, *The People*, p. ix; Zeldin, *France 1848–1945*, vol. 2, pp. 386–7.
5. For other works similar to Michelet's, see Thieme, *Bibliographie de la littérature française*, vol. 3, pp. 172–80; the entry on Michelet himself, vol. 2, pp. 314–20, includes reviews and hence indicates the range of reactions to his work.
6. Kaplan, *Michelet's Poetic Vision*, makes the mistake about feminism.
7. This is claimed at the front of the English edition by Charles Cocks, the translator.
8. Chadwick, *The Secularization of the European Mind in the Nineteenth Century*, pp. 154–6, 198–201; Charlton, *Secular Religions in France*, esp. pp. 148–50 and 184–9.
9. Michelet, *Journal*.
10. These details are given by Guérard in the Introduction to his translation of the work, first published in 1957; the quotation is from Warner, *Joan of Arc*, p. 238, who shows 'that a historical figure like Joan merges and to a certain extent disappears under the influence of other more prevalent and more charming images at different times. . . . Joan of Arc is a pre-eminent heroine because she belongs to the sphere of action, while so many feminine figures

and models are assigned and confined to the sphere of contemplation'
   (p. 28).
11. Michelet, *Joan of Arc*, p. vii.
12. ibid., p. 9.
13. ibid., p. 3.
14. These are discussed by Mellon in his edition of Guizot's, *Historical
    Essays and Lectures*, p. xlii; Bann, *The Clothing of Clio*, ch.
    2, and Seznec, 'Michelet in Germany: a journey in self-discovery'.
15. ibid., p. xxviii, xliii.
16. Johnson, 'Michelet à la mode'; Michelet, *Joan of Arc*, p. vi – both
    are typical.
17. Seznec, 'Michelet in Germany'. See also Evans, *Social Romanticism
    in France*, and Auerbach, *Mimesis*, pp. 473–5.
18. Praz, *The Romantic Agony*, pp. 32–3.
19. Pointon, 'Interior portraits: women, physiology and the male artist';
    pp. 8–9 discuss this issue.
20. Michelet, *The Bird*, p. 16.
21. Bernard, *An Introduction to the Study of Experimental Medicine*,
    quotations from pp. 22 and 14.
22. ibid., pp. xix, xvii, from the *éloge* by Paul Bert. On the theme of
    the hero, see Johns's excellent discussion in *Thomas Eakins: The
    Heroism of Modern Life*.
23. This is evident from his diary; for example, 'I had the happiness
    on Saturday to re-enter my wife's bed, to touch her for the first
    time since the birth, this dear bruised person' (14 July 1850, vol. 2).
    Another entry from 23 July suggests that he associated her giving
    birth with the possibility of losing her.
24. Medical writers like Pierre Roussel (1742–1802), Jean-Joseph Virey
    (1775–1846) and J.L. Moreau de la Sarthe (1771–1826), all authors
    of works on women, could be placed in this tradition. The general
    'Romantic' preoccupation with morbidity during the first half of
    the nineteenth century is marvellously evoked by Ariès, *The Hour
    of Our Death*, esp. part 4.
25. Michelet, *L'Amour*, p. 4.
26. Michelet, *La Femme*, pp. lxii, li.
27. ibid., e.g. pp. lii–iii, 28; Calo, *La Création de la femme chez
    Michelet*, p. 247.
28. Lipton has explored this issue in relation to Degas's pictures of
    women ironing; see her *Looking into Degas*, ch. 3.
29. Michelet, *La Femme*, pp. lvi–lix, quotation from p. lix.
30. Michelet, *L'Amour*, quotations from pp. 345 and 337 respectively.
31. ibid., p. 332.
32. These ideas were of course commonplace in nineteenth-century

Europe, a rewarding analysis may be found in Davidoff *et al.*, 'Landscape with figures; home and community in English society'.
33. Michelet's ideas on this subject are discussed in Delaney *et al.*, *The Curse*, pp. 210–11, and Barthes, *Michelet*, pp. 129–31, 135; for a general treatment of ideas about menstruation, although from an idiosyncratic viewpoint, see Shuttle and Redgrove, *The Wise Wound*.
34. Michelet, *L'Amour*, p. 56.
35. There has been widespread interest in the thesis that doctors took on a priestly role in relation to women during the nineteenth century; see, for example, McLaren, 'Some secular attitudes towards sexual behaviour in France: 1760–1860'.
36. Coleman, *Death Is a Social Disease*, esp. chs 6 and 8.
37. Sewell, *Work and Revolution in France*, pp. 223–32.
38. For example, Henry Murger, *Scènes de la vie de Bohème*, published in 1848, upon which Puccini's opera of 1896 was based. On the 'dangerous classes', see Chevalier, *Labouring Classes and Dangerous Classes*.
39. Michelet, *L'Amour*, p. 452; hence he did not think of male and female as fixed categories; see also p. 56 on the same theme.
40. Barthes, *Michelet*, p. 153.
41. Kaplan, *Michelet's Poetic Vision*, pp. 116–17.
42. See note 32 to this chapter, above; quotation from Michelet, *The People*, p. 5.
43. Michelet, *The People*, p. 168.
44. Michelet, *L'Amour*, pp. 54–5.
45. Appel, *The Cuvier–Geoffroy Debate*, ch. 7, esp. p. 192, and Jordanova, *Lamarck*, ch. 10.
46. On Pouchet, see the biography of him by Crellin in the *Dictionary of Scientific Biography*, vol. 11, 1975, pp. 109–10. His *L'Univers* was lavishly illustrated in its second French and subsequent editions and enjoyed considerable popularity, with twelve English editions between 1870 and 1895; Borie, 'Une gynécologie passionnée' discusses Michelet and Pouchet, pp. 164–70. Michelet, *L'Amour*, p. 15, pp. 447–8.
47. On the natural history books, see Huss, 'Michelet and the uses of natural reference', in Jordanova (ed.), *Languages of Nature*, pp. 289–321, who also shows the ways in which Michelet's prose was 'euphoric'.
48. For example, Michelet, *La Femme*, p. 30.
49. Examples of recent work along these lines are Levine (ed.), *One Culture*, and Jordanova (ed.), *Languages of Nature*.

Notes to chapter 5

1. *La Sculpture française*, p. 151.
2. Shirley Ardner has shown how in some cultures revealing their 'private parts' is the ultimate form of protest for women: 'Sexual insult and female militancy', in Ardner (ed.), *Perceiving Women*, pp. 29–53.
3. Steinberg, *The Sexuality of Christ*, pp. 147–8. In the chapter, entitled 'Swags of gossamer about the hips', Steinberg makes two additional remarks pertinent to the gender and unveiling question. First he notes Christian objections to 'transparent veils' as directed at 'the falsehood of fabrics that pretend otherwise', that is, which undress the body while denying the fact (p. 147). Second he suggests, 'perhaps we must rank the striptease with the drama, the dance, and the oratorio as another cultural form whose deep roots are religious' (p. 148). We are here concerned then with science as striptease. Of course, this approach has been pioneered by Morris Zapp; 'The classical tradition of striptease . . . which goes back to Salome's dance of the seven veils . . . offers a valid metaphor for the activity of reading. The dancer teases the audience, as the text teases its readers, with the promise of an ultimate revelation that is indefinitely postponed. . . . [N]o sooner has one secret been revealed than we lose interest in it and crave another. . . . The text unveils itself before us, but never allows itself to be possessed.' I am grateful to Professor Zapp for permission to quote his words here, and I am sure he would agree that we can extend his insights to the reading of the body, which is itself a text.
4. I am not, of course, suggesting that these preoccupations were new, but they did take some distinctive forms in the period I am concerned with. They differed in important ways from sumptuary laws, which were primarily designed to control luxury and hence expenditure and to regulate the economy through the clothing of different classes. What we find in the eighteenth century in particular is a fear about manly dressing in women; see L. Friedli, '"Passing Women"; a study of gender boundaries in the eighteenth century', in Rousseau and Porter (eds), *Sexual Underworlds of the Enlightenment*, pp. 234–60. Ironically, many women who tried to pass as men worked as medical practitioners. Women's dress during the French Revolution of 1789 raised similar issues; see George, 'The world historical defeat of the Républicaines-Révolutionnaires', esp. p. 422.
5. Warner, *Monuments and Maidens*, ch. 13.
6. *Oxford English Dictionary*, vol. 12, pp. 79–81, quotation from

p. 81. A similar range of meanings exists in French: Littré, *Dictionnaire de la langue française*, vol. 4, pp. 2522–4.

7. The exploration of ideas of veiling has been most extensively undertaken by literary critics; for example, Shaw, *The Lucid Veil*; Sedgwick, 'The character in the veil: imagery of the surface in the Gothic novel'; and Welsh, 'The allegory of truth in English fiction'. It is worth noting that in visual images 'naked truth' is rarely totally naked. An exception to this, reproduced in Welsh's article, is a late-nineteenth-century French image of a nude woman holding up a light, which has, significantly, no pubic hair (facing p. 17).

8. The quotations are from Lippincott, 'Charles Wilson Peale and his family of painters', p. 79, in *In This Academy*, pp. 75–97; on Peale, see also Appel, 'Science, popular culture and profit: Peale's Philadelphia Museum'; the 'Staircase Group' was painted in 1795, and is in the Philadelphia Museum of Art.

9. We can see the importance of religious meanings by examining definitions of revelation and apocalypse – *Oxford English Dictionary*, vol. 8, pp. 594–5, and vol. 1, p. 386. The associations with mystery are clear in the closely related idea of cloaking (ibid., vol. 2, p. 509); these were most elaborately developed in the Gothic novel. See the piece by Sedgwick (note 7), and Broadwell, 'The veil image in Ann Radcliffe's "The Italian"'.

10. For example, André (ed.), *Traité de physiognomonie. Texte latin anonyme*.

11. *Oxford English Dictionary*, vol. 12, p. 79.

12. I am aware that this argument is somewhat speculative. My aim is to draw attention to an unusually pervasive model of knowledge, which we are in the early stages of studying. Ginzburg in 'Morelli, Freud and Sherlock Holmes' has also argued for the long-term general significance of physiognomy, and although I do not concur with his conclusions, this is a stimulating attempt to draw out the larger issues.

13. On modesty as an important eighteenth-century idea, see Robinson, 'Virginie's fatal modesty', and on veiling in particular, Lechte, 'Woman and the veil – or Rousseau's fictive body'.

14. *La Sculpture française*, p. 390.

15. See the discussion below, pp. 115–16.

16. Goethe, *Faust*, part 1, pp. 44–5.

17. Webster, *From Paracelsus to Newton*, is an excellent recent introduction to these issues.

18. The very term 'quackery' implies a criticism of secret remedies and a concern for policing the boundaries of professional behaviour; see Bynum and Porter (eds), *Medical Fringe and Medical Orthodoxy*.

19. Alibert, 'Eloge historique de Pierre Roussel', p. 7.
20. Quotations are from Eliot, *The Lifted Veil*, pp. 19, 21 and 49. See also Beer, 'Myth and the single consciousness'; Waddell, 'Concepts of the inner world' and 'Experience and identification'.
21. Virey, 'Physiognomonie', pp. 191, 193.
22. Quotations from Graves, *The Greek Myths*, vol. 1, p. 145; see also Warner, *Monuments and Maidens*, ch. 10.
23. This point is wonderfully made in a number of paintings by Beryl Cook, reproduced in her *One Man Show*. See the following paintings: *Ivor Dickie* (a male stripper), *Motor Show* (an almost nude woman on a car), *Through the keyhole* (writhing bodies), *And This is the Butler* (naked woman looking through the keyhole).
24. Richardson, *Death, Dissection and the Destitute*.
25. Wolf-Heidegger and Cetto, *Die Anatomische Sektion*, plates 79, 231, 232.
26. On Vesalius, see Shiebinger, 'Skeletons in the closet', in Gallagher and Laqueur (eds), *The Making of the Modern Body*, pp. 42–82. Works which survey the field of anatomical illustration are Herrlinger, *History of Medical Illustration*; Thornton and Reeves, *Medical Book Illustration*.
27. Ariès, *The Hour of Our Death*, p. 610, see also pp. 409–46.
28. Wolf-Heidegger and Cetto, *Die Anatomische Sektion*, plate 285, discussion on pp. 335–6.
29. ibid., plates 231, 232, 235, 236, discussed on pp. 288–92.
30. *Oxford English Dictionary*, vol. 12, p. 80, and on 'tissue', vol. 11, pp. 71–2; discussion of pathological anatomy can be found in Maulitz, *Morbid Appearances*.
31. Wolf-Heidegger and Cetto, *Die Anatomische Sektion*, plate 88, discussion on pp. 182–3; Schupbach, 'A select iconography of animal experiment'. The role of gender in the anti-vivisection campaigns has been examined in Lansbury, 'Gynaecology, pornography, and the anti-vivisection movement'.
32. On Brodnax, see Wolf-Heidegger and Cetto, *Die Anatomische Sektion*, plates 286, 287 and 288, and pp. 336–7. Details of his biography may be found in *Encyclopedia of Virginia Biography*, vol. 4, pp. 30–1; *History of Virginia*, vol. 4 (Virginia Biography), pp. 108–10; and 'Obituary', *Southern Medicine and Surgery*, vol. 88, 1926, p. 744.
33. Wolf-Heidegger and Cetto, *Die Anatomische Sektion*, plate 89, discussion on p. 183.
34. For *Only a Dream*, see ibid., plate 287, and *Skull and Bones* (the student newspaper of the Medical College of Virginia), vol. 2, no. 15, pp. 1 and 4.

35. I have based this on published materials on Brodnax as well as on letters to and from him in the Special Collections Department, Tompkins-McCaw Library, Virginia Commonwealth University, and the Richmond Historical Society; see also note 32.
36. *The X-Ray*, 1926 (vol. 13 of the *Medical College of Virginia Yearbook*), p. 144.
37. Warner, *Monuments and Maidens*, pp. 321–4. Eakins's relationship with the Academy is also discussed by Lippincott, 'Thomas Eakins and the Academy', in *In this Academy*, pp. 162–87.
38. On Eakins, see Johns, *Eakins: Painter of Modern Life*, esp. chs 1, 3 and 4, and Fried, *Realism, Writing and Representation*; Gervaux and Eakins are compared in Rosenblum and Janson, *Art of the Nineteenth Century*, pp. 371–3.
39. *Bulletin of the Medical College of Virginia*, August 1927, p. 17.
40. *The X-Ray*, p. 104.
41. ibid., p. 72.
42. Gilman has pursued these themes in *Difference and Pathology: Stereotypes of Sexuality, Race and Madness*, where he both explores specific instances of stereotyping, especially in the nineteenth century, and at the same time attempts to account for the general phenomenon of stereotyping in terms of an object-relations psychoanalytic framework. From a different perspective de Beauvoir came at these same questions, as we noted in Chapter 2. On the relationships between race and gender, see Stepan, 'Race and gender: the role of analogy in science'.
43. On anthropology, see Stocking, *Race, Culture and Evolution*; on gynaecology, Moscucci, 'The science of woman'; on anatomy, Maulitz, *Morbid Appearances*; on social commentary, Coleman, *Death is a Social Disease*, esp. chs 4–9; and Chevalier, *Labouring Classes and Dangerous Classes*, esp. book 3, part 2. Naturally, not all these scholars have cast their analyses directly in terms of 'otherness'; none the less, as Gilman points out in *Difference and Pathology*, illness, sexuality and race are three basic categories through which the self–other relationship is defined (p. 23). Death is clearly linked to illness, gender to sexuality. And it is impossible to ignore class in this context, which was, like race, a basic category of social difference in the nineteenth century.

Notes to chapter 6

An earlier version of this chapter appeared as 'Fritz Lang's Metropolis: science, machines and gender', in *Issues in Radical Science*, (Radical Science no. 17), 1985, pp. 4–21. I am grateful to Free Association Books for permission to use the material here.

1. The literature on *Frankenstein* is extremely extensive. Items relevant to the themes of this chapter include Hindle's 'Introduction' to the Penguin edition; Brooks, 'Godlike science/unhallowed arts'; Poovey, 'My hideous progeny'; O'Flinn, 'Production and reproduction'; Mellor, '*Frankenstein*: a feminist critique of science', in Levine (ed.), *One Culture*, pp. 287–312; Mellor, 'Possessing nature', in Mellor (ed.), *Romanticism and Feminism*, pp. 220–32; and Musselwhite, *Partings Welded Together*, ch. 3.

2. Kaplan, *Fritz Lang: A Guide to References and Sources*. Kaplan gives a useful biographical overview, pp. 15–16. In addition to works cited later in the chapter, the following items on Lang and his context may be helpful: Bronner and Kellner (eds), *Passion and Rebellion: The Expressionist Heritage*; Eisner, *The Haunted Screen*; Willett, *The New Sobriety*. On Lang in particular, see Eisner, 'The German films of Fritz Lang', Elderfield, 'Metropolis', and Jenson, *The Cinema of Fritz Lang*.

3. Lang, *Metropolis*, p. 47T (i.e. title in the film).

4. ibid. This is a detailed description of the film, with quotations from the novel and the text of the titles.

5. Von Harbou, *Metropolis*, first published in 1927. She had already been a stage actress and was an established author by the time *Metropolis* was written; see Keiner, *Thea von Harbou*.

6. Lang's opinion on film endings was expressed in 'Happily ever after', for an interview where Lang criticized *Metropolis*; see Phillips, 'Fritz Lang on Metropolis'.

7. Kracauer, *From Caligari to Hitler*, is critical of von Harbou, see esp. p. 162.

8. The only serious attempt I know of to undertake such an analysis of *Metropolis* is Tulloch, 'Genetic structuralism and the cinema'.

9. Gay, *Weimar Culture*, pp. 148–9. See also Laqueur, *Weimar: A Cultural History*; Rhode, *Tower of Babel*, pp. 85–105; Monaco, *Cinema and Society*, pp. 118, 124, 128–9; Barlow, *German Expressionist Film*, pp. 118–33; and Kracauer, *From Caligari to Hitler*, pp. 162–4, for other attempts to link the film with the prevailing mood of Weimar Germany.

10. *Oxford Companion to English Literature*, p. 734; see also Atkins

(ed.), *Science Fiction Films*, and Jenkins (ed.), *Fritz Lang: The Image and the Look*, esp. p. 82.

11. Taylor, *Principles of Scientific Management*, p. 40. See also Litterer, 'Systematic management'; Nelson, 'Scientific management'; Maier, 'Between Taylorism and technocracy'; and Person, 'Scientific management'.

12. The classic statement remains Thompson, 'Time, work discipline and industrial capitalism'.

13. See note 11 to this chapter, above.

14. Maier, *Recasting Bourgeois Europe*, p. 9.

15. ibid., p. 13.

16. On Villiers, see Michelson, 'On the eve of the future', and Bernheimer, 'Huysmans: writing against (female) nature'. The latter deals with Villiers *en passant*, but the themes of the article as a whole are close to those of this book.

17. Names used in the film include Ganesha, Baal, Moloch, Mahomet, Golgoth, and Juggernaut. The origins of most of these may be traced in the *Oxford English Dictionary*.

18. Stoehr, *Hawthorne's Mad Scientists*, p. 269.

19. Banham, 'Machine aesthetic' and the article 'Machine aesthetic' in Bullock and Stallybrass (eds), *Fontana Dictionary of Modern Thought*, p. 361; this quotes van Doesburg's claim to have coined the phrase 'machine aesthetic' in 1921.

20. Berman, *All That is Solid Melts into Air*.

21. See note 3 to this chapter, above.

22. A useful survey of these developments is Vartanian, 'Man-machine from the Greeks to the computer'.

23. ibid., p. 146.

24. I am, of course, well aware that Frankenstein began work on a female companion for his monster, work that he later destroyed. None the less, the plot hinges on his relationship with the unnamed male being he created initially.

25. Hawthorne, *Selected Tales and Sketches*, p. 259.

26. ibid., p. 265.

27. ibid., p. 261.

28. ibid., p. 266.

29. Faust too was successful, but only with the help of Mephistopheles. Rotwang is *seen* to do it all himself, although it would be possible to interpret the film as implying that he had magical assistance.

30. Elderfield, 'Metropolis'.

31. Simmel, 'The metropolis and mental life', first published in 1903, esp. pp. 332–3.

32. A convenient way of appreciating the implications of new styles of

the period is through the Bauhaus; see the exhibition catalogue *Fifty Years Bauhaus*, especially the section on architecture, pp. 145–210. Fletcher's *A History of Architecture* contains some examples of factory design, pp. 1246, 1264–71 and 1290. Lang's aesthetic can also usefully be placed in the context of precisionist art; see *The Precisionist View in American Art*, esp. p. 19 (Spencer, 'City Walls'), pp. 28–37 (section on 'Urban Themes') and pp. 38–41 (pictures under the themes 'Reflections of an Industrial Society' and 'The Solid Geometry of Industry').

33. Phillips, 'Organicism in the late nineteenth and early twentieth centuries', p. 413; see also Saccaro-Battisti, 'Changing metaphors of political structures'.
34. Lang, *Metropolis*, pp. 60T and 130T.
35. On Rotwang as 'sub-Aryan', see Rhode, *Tower of Babel*, p. 97. Tulloch, 'Genetic structuralism and the cinema', p. 27 links Rotwang, anti-semitism and Solomon's seal. On Joseph Wright's figures, see Nicolson, *Joseph Wright of Derby*. The inverted pentagram is explained in J.C. Cooper, *An Illustrated Encyclopedia of Traditional Symbols*, p. 128.
36. Carlyle, *Past and Present*, first published in 1843.

Notes to chapter 7

1. Warner, *Monuments and Maidens*, is the most sustained analysis of this question. Another exploration of what women can 'stand for' is Sitter, 'Mother, Memory, Muse and Poetry After Pope'.
2. I am using 'myth' loosely, not to imply something which is false, but something which has a distinctive set of properties. In his *The Nature of Greek Myths*, Kirk provides a wonderfully incisive discussion of the confusion surrounding the term. He concludes that 'myth' has no single, essential quality, speaking rather of 'their characteristic density and complexity, their imaginative depth and their universal appeal' (p. 29), and he also stresses their narrative and social features: 'myths are on the one hand good stories, on the other hand bearers of important messages about life in general and life-within-society in particular' (pp. 28–9). On the history of the word 'myth', see Williams, *Keywords*, pp. 210–12.
3. Elshtain, *Public Man, Private Woman*, remains the outstanding account of how these polarities have developed in the history of political thinking. No claim is being made about how well public/ private ideas fit social life at any one moment. Whether we like it

or not, they have a vigorous life in our culture, in ways that are sometimes more, sometimes less apparent.

4. I am aware that even providing operational definitions of public and private is difficult. For my purposes, fairly simple, commonsense definitions are sufficient.

5. On medicine and the media, see Karpf, *Doctoring the Media*. The literature on professionalization is extensive; for a general analysis see Johnson, *Professions and Power*.

6. There has been little attempt by historians of science and medicine to address the relevance of the public–private distinction for their fields. For some attempts to do this in relation to public health, see Ogawa (ed.), *Public Health*, and Figlio, 'Unconscious factors of health and the public sphere', in Richards (ed.) *Crises of the Self*.

7. Lawrence, 'Anatomy, museums and the Enlightenment'; Altick, *Shows of London*; Cole, 'History of the anatomical museum'.

8. Hackett, 'A list of medical museums'.

9. This resulted from the existence of high rates of mortality and the absence of specialized occupations and institutions dealing with death, the dying and the dead. Shifts in sensibility in this respect are revealing; moving cemeteries out of town centres, or reactions against the sight of dead children, are valuable pointers to what had before seemed unexceptional. See Ariès, *The Hour of Our Death*; Whalley (ed.), *Mirrors of Mortality*; McManners, *Death and the Enlightenment*.

10. Richardson, *Death, Dissection and the Destitute*.

11. Douglas, *Purity and Danger* and *Natural Symbols*; the speculum debates are discussed in Moscucci, 'The science of woman'.

12. Eloesser *et al.*, *El Embarazo, el Parto y el Recien Nacido*.

13. Martin, *The Woman in the Body*.

14. We have already noted in Chapter 3 how the wax models were related to works of high art. At an individual level Hunter exemplifies the trend – he was an art collector and connoisseur, he took great pains with the illustrations to his work, his connections with the royal family enabled him to be among the first to see and appreciate the Windsor Leonardos, he was professor of anatomy at the Royal Academy; see Kemp, *Dr William Hunter at the Royal Academy of Arts*, and Brock (ed.), *William Hunter 1718–1783*.

15. *World Medicine*, date not known.

16. Advertisements have been used for similar purposes by Goffman, *Gender Advertisements*; Williamson, *Decoding Advertisements*; Massé and Rosenblum, 'Male and female created they them'; and Iversen, 'The new art history'.

17. *World Medicine*, 30 May 1981, p. 20; 31 October 1981, p. 88.

18. ibid., 15 October 1983, inside front cover.
19. Davis, 'Women on top', in her *Society and Culture in Early Modern France*, ch. 5.
20. Brown and Harris, in *The Social Origins of Depression*, have explored some of the main questions surrounding women and depression.
21. *World Medicine*, 27 November 1982, p. 2.
22. ibid., 15 October 1983, p. 10.
23. Jordanova, 'Naturalizing the family', in Jordanova (ed.), *Languages of Nature*, pp. 86–116.
24. *World Medicine*, 15 October 1983, p. 21.
25. ibid., date not known.
26. Porter (ed.), *Patients and Practitioners*, has initiated the exploration of these relationships.
27. 'A surgeon in the psychiatrist's chair', *World Medicine*, 2 October 1982, p. 32.
28. 'Joys of surgery', *World Medicine*, 27 November 1982, p. 72. Ewart's poem, 'The Joys of Surgery' was dedicated to Richard Selzer after the poet read a review of *Mortal Lessons* in the *Guardian*. The lines are reprinted here by kind permission of the author. The whole poem may be found in Ewart, *The Young Pobble's Guide to His Toes*, p. 135. (This book was published by Century Hutchinson, 1985.)
29. Selzer, *Mortal Lessons*, quotations from pp. 104 and 25. I believe that the passage on pp. 93–4 is the one that inspired Ewart's poem.
30. ibid., p. 19.
31. ibid., p. 94, and also the essay 'The surgeon as priest', pp. 24–36.
32. For a general work on power, see Lukes (ed.), *Power*.
33. Foucault has been the most influential recent exponent of this position and virtually all his books touch on it in one way or another; most important have been *Madness and Civilisation, The Order of Things, The Archaeology of Knowledge, The Birth of the Clinic* and vol. 1 of his *History of Sexuality*.
34. On modernization theory, see Smith, *The Concept of Social Change*; Ehrenreich and English, *For Her Own Good*, is an example of this approach applied crudely. On medicalization, in addition to Foucault's work, a useful volume which indicates how historians are using the term is Goubert (ed.), *La Médicalisation de la société française*.
35. For a general outline, see Friedmann, 'Property'.
36. My discussion here is based on Locke, *The Second Treatise*, in *Two Treatises of Government*, mainly chs 2, 4 and 5, and especially paragraphs 6 and 56.

37. Davidoff and Hall, *Family Fortunes*, esp. ch. 7, reveal some of the ways in which women were 'given', although this must never be understood in any absolute way. However complex such matters were in practice, the deep significance of common phrases that treated women as something to be given, as in the marriage service, should not be underestimated.
38. The outstanding analysis along these lines is Beer, *Darwin's Plots*.
39. See the discussion under note 2 to this chapter above.

Notes to Afterword

1. Bennett, *The Intelligent Woman's Guide*, p. 13.
2. Graves, *The Greek Myths*, vol. 1, pp. 144–5.

Bibliography

Alibert, J.L. (1803) 'Eloge historique de Pierre Roussel', in P. Roussel, *Système Physique et Moral de la Femme*, Paris, pp. 1–52.

Altick, R. (1978) *The Shows of London*, Cambridge, Mass.

André, J. (ed.) (1981) *Traité de physiognomonie. Texte latin anonyme*, Paris.

Anon (1857) *The Speculum: Its Moral Tendencies*, London.

Antoine, J.-P. (1980) '"Les horreurs" anatomiques de Florence', *L'Histoire*, 20: 96–8.

Appel, T. A. (1980) 'Science, popular culture and profit: Peale's Philadelphia Museum', *Journal of the Society for the Bibliography of Natural History*, 9: 619–34.

—— (1987) *The Cuvier–Geoffroy Debate. French Biology in the Decades Before Darwin*, New York and Oxford.

Ardner, S. (ed.) (1975) *Perceiving Women*, London.

Ariès, P. (1983) *The Hour of Our Death*. Harmondsworth.

—— (1985) *Images of Man and Death*, Cambridge, Mass.

Armstrong, N. and Tennenhouse, L. (1987) *The Ideology of Conduct: Essays in Literature and the History of Sexuality*, New York.

Aron, J.-P. (ed.) (1980) *Misérable et glorieuse. La femme du XIXᵉ siècle*, Paris.

Atkins, T.R. (ed.) (1976) *Science Fiction Films*, New York.

Auerbach, E. (1946) *Mimesis*, Berne.

Azzaroli, M.L. (1975) 'La Specola. The Zoological Museum of Florence

University', *Atti del 1° Congresso Internazionale sulla Ceroplastica nella Scienza e nell'Arte*, 5–31.

Babbage, C. (1830) *Reflections on the Decline of Science in England, and on some of its causes*, London.

Banham, R. (1955) 'Machine aesthetic', *Architectural Review*, 117: 225–8.

Bann, S. (1984) *The Clothing of Clio: A Study of the Representation of History in Nineteenth-Century Britain and France*, Cambridge.

Barlow, J.D. (1982) *German Expressionist Film*, Boston.

Barnes, B. and Shapin, S. (eds) (1979) *Natural Order: Historical Studies of Scientific Culture*, Beverly Hills and London.

Barrett, M. and McIntosh, M. (1982) *The Anti-Social Family*, London.

Barthes, R. (1954) *Michelet*, Paris.

Barthez, P.J. (1806) *Nouveaux élémens de la science de l'homme*, 2 vols, Paris.

Baudrillard, J. (1988) *Selected Writings*, Cambridge.

Bauhaus (1968) *Fifty Years Bauhaus*, London (exhibition catalogue).

Beer, G. (1975) 'Myth and the single consciousness: *Middlemarch* and *The Lifted Veil*', in I. Adam (ed.), *This Particular Web*, Toronto, pp. 91–115.

—— (1983) *Darwin's Plots: Evolutionary Narrative in Darwin, George Eliot and Nineteenth-Century Fiction*, London.

Bennett, M. (1964) *The Intelligent Woman's Guide to Atomic Radiation*, Harmondsworth.

Berger, P. and Luckmann, T. (1967) *The Social Construction of Reality*, Harmondsworth.

Berman, M. (1983) *All That is Solid Melts into Air: The Experience of Modernity*, London.

Bernard, C. (1865) *An Introduction to the Study of Experimental Medicine*, New York 1957.

Bernardin de Saint-Pierre, J.H. (1788) *Paul et Virginie*, Paris 1966.

—— (1982) *Paul and Virginia*, London (translated with an introduction by J. Donovan).

Bernheimer, C. (1986) 'Huysmans: writing against (female) nature', in S.R. Suleiman (ed.) *The Female Body in Western Culture*, Cambridge, Mass., pp. 373–86.

Bichat, X. (1800) *Recherches physiologiques sur la vie et la mort*, Paris 1981 (reprint of the 1855 edn).

—— (1801) *General Anatomy Applied to Physiology and the Practice of Medicine*, 2 vols, London 1824.

Boas, G. (1925) *French Philosophies of the Romantic Period*, Baltimore.

Boucé, P.-G. (ed.) (1982) *Sexuality in Eighteenth-Century Britain*, Manchester.

Brett, R.L. (1968) *George Crabbe*, revised edition, London.

Brewster, D., Moll, G., Sheepshanks, R. and F.R.S. (1975) *Debates on the Decline of Science*, New York.

Broadwell, E.P. (1975) 'The veil image in Ann Radcliffe's "The Italian"', *South Atlantic Bulletin*, 40: 76–87.

Brock, C.H. (ed.) (1983) *William Hunter 1718–1783: A Memoir by Samuel Foart Simmons and John Hunter*, Glasgow.

Bronner, S.E. and Kellner, D. (eds) (1983) *Passion and Rebellion: The Expressionist Heritage*, London.

Brookner, A. (1972) *Greuze: The Rise and Fall of an Eighteenth-Century Phenomenon*, London.

Brooks, P. (1978) 'Godlike science/unhallowed arts; language and monstrosity in Frankenstein', *New Literary History*, 9: 591–605.

Brown, G. and Harris, T. (1978) *The Social Origins of Depression: A Study of Psychiatric Disorder in Women*, London.

Bryson, N. (1981) *Word and Image: French Painting of the Ancien Regime*, Cambridge.

Bulletin of the Medical College of Virginia (1927) vol. 24, no. 6 (In Memoriam John Wilkes Brodnax).

Bullock, A. and Stallybrass, O. (eds) (1977) *Fontana History of Modern Thought*, London.

Burkhardt, R.W. (1977) *The Spirit of System: Lamarck and Evolutionary Biology*, Cambridge, Mass.

Bynum, W. and Porter, R. (eds) (1985) *William Hunter and the Eighteenth-Century Medical World*, Cambridge.

Bynum, W. and Porter, R. (eds) (1987) *Medical Fringe and Medical Orthodoxy*, London.

Cabanis, J. (1978) *Michelet, le prêtre et la femme*, Paris.

Cabanis, P.J.G. (1956) *Oeuvres philosophiques*, 2 vols, Paris.

Cadogan, W. (1748) *An Essay upon Nursing and the Management of Children from Their Birth to Three Years of Age*, London.

Calo, J. (1975) *La Création de la femme chez Michelet*, Paris.

Carlyle, T. (1843) *Past and Present*, London.

Carter, A. (1979) *The Sadeian Woman: An Exercise in Cultural History*, London.

Chadwick, O. (1975) *The Secularization of the European Mind*, Cambridge.

Chailley, J. (1972) *The Magic Flute, Masonic Opera: An Interpretation of the Libretto and the Music*, London.

Charlton, D.G. (1963) *Secular Religions in France 1815–1870*, London.
   (1984) *New Images of the Natural in France: A Study in European Cultural History 1750–1800*, Cambridge.

Chevalier, L. (1973) *Labouring Classes and Dangerous Classes in Paris during the first Half of the Nineteenth Century*, London.

Choulant, J.L. (1962) *History and Bibliography of Anatomic Illustration*,

New York and London.

Clark, K. (1956) *The Nude. A Study of Ideal Art*, London.

Cole, F.J. (1914) 'History of anatomical museums', in *A Miscellany Presented to J.M. Mackay*, Liverpool and London, pp. 302–17.

Coleman, W. (1982) *Death is a Social Disease; Public Health and Political Economy in Early Industrial France*, Madison, Wisconsin.

Cook, B. (1982) *One Man Show*, Harmondsworth.

Cooper, J.C. (1978) *An Illustrated Encyclopedia of Traditional Symbols*, London.

Cooter, R. (1984) *The Cultural Meaning of Popular Science: Phrenology and the Organization of Consent in Nineteenth-Century Britain*, Cambridge.

Corsi, P. (1988) *The Age of Lamarck*, Berkeley and Los Angeles.

Coser, R.L. (1978) 'The principle of patriarchy', *Signs. Journal of Women in Culture and Society*, 4: 337–48.

Crabbe, G. (1823) *The Works of the Rev. George Crabbe*, 8 vols, London.

(1967) *Tales, 1812 and Other Selected Poems*, Howard Mills (ed.) Cambridge.

Curtis, L. (1981) 'A case study of Defoe's domestic conduct manuals', *Studies in Eighteenth-Century Culture*, 10: 409–28.

Das, K. (1929) *Obstetric Forceps: Its History and Evolution*, Calcutta.

Davidoff, L., l'Esperance, J. and Newby, H. (1976) 'Landscape with figures: home and community in English society', in J. Mitchell and A. Oakley (eds) *The Rights and Wrongs of Women*, Harmondsworth.

Davidoff, L. and Hall, C. (1987) *Family Fortunes: Men and Women of the English Middle Class 1780–1850*, London.

Davis, N.Z. (1985) *Society and Culture in Early Modern France*, Stanford.

de Beauvoir, S. (1949) *The Second Sex*, Harmondsworth 1972.

Deer, L. (1977) 'Italian anatomical waxes in the Wellcome Collection: the missing link', *Rivista di Storia delle Scienze Mediche e Naturali*, 20: 281–98.

Delaney, J., Lupton, M.J. and Toth, E. (1977) *The Curse: A Cultural History of Menstruation*, New York.

Descartes, R. (1968) *Discourse on Method and the Meditations*, Harmondsworth.

Dictionary of Scientific Biography (1970–80) 16 vols, ed. C.C. Gillispie, New York.

Dix-huitième Siècle (1980) (Représentations de la vie sexuelle), no. 12.

Donnison, J. (1977) *Midwives and Medical Men: A History of Interprofessional Rivalries and Women's Rights*, London.

Donzelot, J. (1980) *The Policing of Families: Welfare versus the State*, London.

Douglas, M. (1970) *Purity and Danger: An Analysis of Concepts of Pollution and Taboo*, Harmondsworth.

(1973) *Natural Symbols. Explorations in Cosmology*, Harmondsworth.

Drake, T. (1940) 'The wet nurse in France in the eighteenth century', *Bulletin of the History of Medicine*, 8: 934–48.

Dulieu, L. (1971) 'P.-J. Barthez', *Revue d'Histoire des Sciences*, 24: 149–76.

Durey, M.J. (1976) 'Bodysnatchers and Benthamites: the implications of the Dead Body Bill for the London Schools of Anatomy, 1820–42', *The London Journal*, 2: 200–25.

Durkheim, E. (1897) *Suicide: A Study in Sociology*, London 1952.

Easlea, B. (1983) *Fathering the Unthinkable: Masculinity, Scientists and the Nuclear Arms Race*, London.

Eco, U. (1987) *Travels in Hyper-reality*, London.

Ehrard, J. (1963) *L'Idée de nature en France dans la première moitié du XVIIIᵉ siècle*, Paris.

Ehrenreich, B. and English, D. (1979) *For Her Own Good: 150 Years of the Experts' Advice to Women*, London.

Eisner, L.H. (1948) 'The German films of Fritz Lang: some impressions', *Penguin Film Review*, 6: 53–61.

(1973) *The Haunted Screen: Expressionism in the German Cinema and the Influence of Max Reinhardt*, London.

Elderfield, J. (1972) 'Metropolis', *Studio International*, 183: 196–9.

Eliot, G. (1878) *The Lifted Veil*, London 1985.

Eloesser, L., Galt, E. and Hemingway, I. (1963) *El Embarazo, El Parto y el Recien Nacido. Manual Para Parteras Rurales*, Mexico City.

Elshtain, J. (1981) *Public Man, Private Woman*, Oxford.

Evans, D.O. (1969) *Social Romanticism in France 1830–1848*, New York.

Farrington, B. (1964) *The Philosophy of Francis Bacon: An Essay on Its Development from 1603 to 1609 with New Translations of Fundamental Texts*, Liverpool.

Figlio, K. (1975) 'Theories of perception and the physiology of mind in the late eighteenth century', *History of Science*, 12: 177–212.

(1976) 'The metaphor of organisation: a historiographical perspective on the bio-medical sciences of the early nineteenth century', *History of Science*, 14: 17–53.

(1978) 'Chlorosis and chronic disease in nineteenth-century Britain: the social constitution of somatic illness in a capitalist society', *Social History*, 3: 167–97.

(forthcoming) 'Unconscious factors of health and the public sphere', in B. Richards (ed.) *Crises of the Self*, London.

Fildes, V. (1985) *Breasts, Bottles and Babies: A History of Infant Feeding*, Edinburgh.

Fisher, S. (1968) 'Body image', in D.L. Sills (ed.) *International Encyclopedia of Social Sciences*, 18 vols, New York, vol. 2, pp. 113–16.

Fletcher, B. (1975) *A History of Architecture*, 18th edn, London.

Forbes, T. (1971) 'The regulation of English midwives in the 18th and 19th centuries', *Medical History*, 15: 352–62.

Fores, S.W. (1793) *Man-Midwifery Dissected, or, the Obstetric Family Instructor*, London (written under the pseudonym John Blunt).

Foucault, M. (1967) *Madness and Civilisation. A History of Insanity in the Age of Reason*, London.

(1970) *The Order of Things: An Archaeology of the Human Sciences*, London.

(1972) *The Archaeology of Knowledge*, London.

(1973) *The Birth of the Clinic: An Archaeology of Medical Perception*, London.

(1979) *The History of Sexuality. Volume 1: An Introduction*, London.

(1985) *The Use of Pleasure (The History of Sexuality. Volume 2)*, New York.

French, R.D. (1975) *Antivivisection and Medical Science in Victorian Society*, Princeton and London.

Fried, M. (1987) *Realism, Writing, Disfiguration: On Thomas Eakins and Stephen Crane*, Chicago.

Friedmann, W.G. (1973) 'Property', in P. Weiner (ed.) *Dictionary of the History of Ideas*, vol. 4, New York, pp. 650–7.

Gallagher, C. and Laqueur, T. (eds) (1987) *The Making of the Modern Body: Sexuality and Society in the Nineteenth Century*, Berkeley, Calif.

Gamarnikow, E., Morgan, D.H.J., Purvis, J. and Taylorson, D.E. (eds) (1983) *Gender, Class and Work*, London.

Gamelin, J. (1979) *Nouveau receuil d'ostéologie et de myologie dessiné d'après la nature*, Toulouse.

Gay, P. (1966 and 1970) *The Enlightenment: An Interpretation*, 2 vols, New York.

(1974) *Weimar Culture: The Outsider as Insider*, Harmondsworth.

Gélis, J. (1977) 'Sages-femmes et accoucheurs: l'obstétrique populaire aux XVIIᵉ et XVIIIᵉ siècles', *Annales: économies, sociétés, civilisations*, 32: 927–57.

Gélis, J., Laget, M. and Morel, M.-F. (1978) *Entrer dans la vie. Naissances et enfances dans la France traditionelle*, Paris.

George, M. (1976) 'The world historical defeat of the Républicaines-

Révolutionnaires', *Science and Society*, 40: 410–37.

Gilbert, S. and Gubar, S. (1979) *The Madwoman in the Attic: The Woman Writer and the Nineteenth-Century Literary Imagination*, New Haven, Conn.

Gilman, S. (1985) *Difference and Pathology: Stereotypes of Sexuality, Race and Madness*, Ithaca, NY.

Ginzburg, C. (1980) 'Morelli, Freud and Sherlock Holmes: clues and scientific method', *History Workshop Journal*, no. 9: 5–36.

Glacken, C. (1967) *Traces on the Rhodian Shore: Nature and Culture in Western Thought from Ancient Times to the End of the Eighteenth Century*, Berkeley, Calif.

Goethe, J.W. (1988) *Faust*, parts 1 and 2, Birmingham.

Goubert, J.-P. (1982) *La Médicalisation de la société française*, Waterloo, Ontario.

Goffman, E. (1979), *Gender Advertisements*, London.

Graves, R. (1960) *The Greek Myths*, vol. 1, Harmondsworth.

Guérard, A. (1957) 'Introduction' to J. Michelet, *Joan of Arc*, Ann Arbor, Mich.

Guizot, F. (1972) *Historical Essays and Lectures*, ed. with an introduction by S. Mellon, Chicago.

Hackett, C.J. (1951) 'A list of medical museums of Great Britain (1949–50)', *British Medical Journal*, 16 June, pp. 1380–3.

Haigh, E. (1984) *Xavier Bichat and the Medical Theory of the Eighteenth Century*, (Supplement no. 4 to *Medical History*).

Hale, D.G. (1973) 'Analogy of the body politic', in P. Weiner (ed.) *Dictionary of the History of Ideas*, vol. 1, New York, pp. 67–70.

Hamilton, G.H. (1982) *Painting and Sculpture in Europe 1880–1940*, Harmondsworth.

Hankins, T.L. (1985) *Science and the Enlightenment*, Cambridge.

Haraway, D. (1979) 'The biological enterprise: sex, mind and profit from human engineering to sociobiology', *Radical History Review*, no. 20: 206–37.

(1984) 'Teddy bear patriarchy: taxidermy in the Garden of Eden, New York City, 1908–1936', *Social Text*, 4: 20–64.

Harbou, T. von (1927) *Metropolis*, New York 1963.

Hartman, M. and Banner, L. (eds) (1974) *Clio's Consciousness Raised: New perspectives on the History of Women*, New York.

Haviland, T.N. and Parish, L.C. (1970) 'A brief account of the use of wax models in the study of medicine', *Journal of the History of Medicine*, 25: 52–75.

Hawthorne, N. (1987) *Selected Tales and Sketches*, ed. M.J. Colacurcio, New York and Harmondsworth.

Hay, D., Linebaugh, P., Rule, J.G., Thompson, E.P. and Winslow,

C. *(1975) Albion's Fatal Tree; Crime and Society in Eighteenth Century England*, Harmondsworth.

Herrlinger, R. (1970) *History of Medical Illustration*, n.p.

Hiatt, L.R. (1979) 'Queen of the Night, mother-right, and secret male cults', in R.H. Hook (ed.) *Fantasy and Symbol in Anthropological Interpretation*, London, pp. 247–65.

Hufton, O. (1971) 'Women in revolution 1789–1796', *Past and Present*, no. 53: 90–108.

Hunter, W. (1774) *Anatomia Uteri Humani Gravidi*, Birmingham.

(1974) *Introductory Lectures Delivered by William Hunter to His Last Course of Anatomical Lectures at His Theatre in Windmill Street*, London.

Ingamels, J. (1967) *The Davies Collection of French Art*, Cardiff.

In This Academy. The Pennsylvania Academy of the Fine Arts, 1805–1976 (1976) Philadelphia (exhibition catalogue).

Iversen, M. (1983) 'The new art history', in F. Barker, Hulme, P., Iversen, M. and Loxley, D. (eds) *The Politics of Theory*, Colchester, pp. 212–19.

Jacob, M. (1981) *The Radical Enlightenment: Pantheists, Freemasons and Republicans*, London.

Jarrett, D. (1976) *England in the Age of Hogarth*, St Albans.

Jenkins, S. (ed.) (1981) *Fritz Lang: The Image and the Look*, London.

Jenson, P.M. (1969) *The Cinema of Fritz Lang*, London.

Joannides, P. (1970) 'Aspects of Fritz Lang', *Cinema* (Cambridge), August: 5–9.

Johns, E. (1983) *Thomas Eakins: The Heroism of Modern Life*, Princeton.

Johnson, D. (1977) 'Michelet à la mode', *Times Literary Supplement*, 6 May, pp. 542–3.

Johnson, T. (1972) *Professions and Power*, London.

Jordanova, L.J. (1981) 'La psychologie naturaliste et le "problème des niveaux": La notion du sentiment intérieur chez Lamarck', in *Lamarck et Son Temps. Lamarck et Notre Temps*, Paris, pp. 69–80.

(1984) *Lamarck*, Oxford.

(1986) (ed.), *Languages of Nature: Critical Essays on Science and Literature*, London.

(1987) 'The popularisation of medicine: Tissot on onanism', *Textual Practice*, 1: 68–79.

Jordanova, L.J. and Porter, R. (eds) (1979) *Images of the Earth: Essays in the History of the Environmental Sciences*, Chalfont St Giles, pp. 119–46.

Kaplan, E.A. (1981) *Fritz Lang: A Guide to References and Resources*, Boston.

Kaplan, E.K. (1977) *Michelet's Poetic Vision: A Romantic Philosophy of Nature, Man and Woman*, Amherst, Mass.

Karpf, A. (1988) *Doctoring the Media: Reporting of Health and Medicine*, London.

Keiner, R. (1984) *Thea von Harbou und der deutsche Film bis 1933*, Hildesheim.

Keller, E.F. (1985) *Reflections on Gender and Science*, New Haven, Conn.

Kemp, M. (ed.) (1975) *Dr William Hunter at the Royal Academy of Arts*, Glasgow.

Kirk, G.S. (1974) *The Nature of Greek Myths*, Harmondsworth.

Knibiehler, Y. (1976) 'Les médecins et la "nature feminine" au temps du code civil', *Annales: économies, sociétés, civilisations*, 31: 824–45.

Kracauer, S. (1947) *From Caligari to Hitler: A Psychological History of the German Film*, Princeton.

Kramnick, I. (1977) *The Rage of Edmund Burke. Portrait of an Ambivalent Conservative*, New York.

Lalande, A. (1928) *Vocabulaire Technique et Critique de la Philosophie*, 2 vols, Paris (revised edition).

Lamarck, J.-B. (1809) *Philosophie Zoologique*, New York 1960.

Lang, F. (1948) 'Happily ever after', *Penguin Film Review*, 5: 22–9.
  (1973) *Metropolis*, London (a detailed description of the film, with quotations from the novel, and the text of the titles).

Lansbury, C. (1985) 'Gynaecology, pornography and the anti-vivisection movement', *Victorian Studies*, 28: 413–37.

Lanza, B., Azzaroli Puccetti, M.L., Poggesi, M. and Martelli, A. (1979) *Le Cere Anatomiche della Specola*, Florence.

Laqueur, W. (1974) *Weimar: A Cultural History 1918–1933*, London.

Lawrence, C. (1975) 'William Buchan: medicine laid open', *Medical History*, 19: 20–35.
  (1987) 'Anatomy, museums and the Enlightenment', unpublished paper.

Lechte, J. (1985) 'Woman and the veil – or Rousseau's fictive body', *French Studies*, 39: 423–41.

Le Doeuff, M. (1981/2) 'Pierre Roussel's chiasmas: from imaginary knowledge to the learned imagination', *Ideology and Consciousness*, no. 9: 39–70.

Leslie, A. and Chapman, P. (1978) *Madame Tussaud. Waxworker Extraordinary*, London.

Levine, G. (ed.) (1987) *One Culture: Essays in Science and Literature*, Madison, Wisc.

Lindemann, M. (1981) 'Love for hire: the regulation of the wet-nursing business in eighteenth-century Hamburg', *Journal of Family History*, 6: 379–95.

Lipton, E. (1986) *Looking into Degas: Uneasy Images of Women and Modern Life*, Berkeley, Calif.

Litterer, J.A. (1961) 'Systematic management: the search for order and integration', *Business History Review*, 35: 461–76.

Littré, E. (1878–9) *Dictionnaire de la Langue Française*, 4 vols and supplement, Paris.

Lloyd, G. (1984) *The Man of Reason: 'Male' and 'Female' in Western Philosophy*, London.

Locke, J. (1965), *Two Treatises of Government*, New York.

Lovejoy, A.O. (1927) '"Nature" as an aesthetic norm', in *Essays in the History of Ideas*, New York, 1960, pp. 69–77.

Lukes, S. (ed.) (1986) *Power*, Oxford.

McCallum, P. (1985), 'Michelet's narrative practice: naturality, populism, and the intellectual', *Cultural Critique*, 1: 141–58.

McCann, R.D. and Perry, E.S. (1975) *The New Film Index: A Bibliography of Magazine Articles in English, 1930–1970*, New York.

MacCormack, C. and Strathern, M. (eds) (1980) *Nature, Culture and Gender*, Cambridge.

McLaren, A. (1973–4) 'Some secular attitudes towards sexual behaviour in France: 1760–1860', *French Historical Studies*, 8: 604–25.

(1984) *Reproductive Rituals: The Perception of Fertility in England from the Sixteenth to the Nineteenth Century*, London.

McManners, J. (1981) *Death and the Enlightenment. Changing Attitudes to Death among Christians and Unbelievers in Eighteenth-Century France*, Oxford.

Macquart, L.C.H. (1799) *Dictionnaire de la conservation de l'homme*, 2 vols, Paris.

Maier, C.S. (1970) 'Between Taylorism and technocracy: European ideologies and the vision of industrial productivity in the 1920s', *Journal of Contemporary History*, 5: 27–61.

(1975) *Recasting Bourgeois Europe: Stabilization in France, Germany and Italy in the Decade after World War I*, Princeton.

Mann, W. (1977) *The Operas of Mozart*, London.

Martin, E. (1987) *The Woman in the Body. A Cultural Analysis of Reproduction*, Boston, Mass.

Massé, M.A. and Rosenblum, K. (1988) 'Male and female created they them: the depiction of gender in the advertising of traditional women's and men's magazines', *Women's Studies International Forum*, 11: 127–44.

Maulitz, R. (1987) *Morbid Appearances: The Anatomy of Pathology in the Early Nineteenth Century*, Cambridge.

Mellon, S. (1972) 'Introduction', in F. Guizot, *Historical Essays and Lectures*, ed. S. Mellon, Chicago.

Mellor, A.K. (ed.) (1988) *Romanticism and Feminism*, Bloomington.

Merchant, C. (1982) *The Death of Nature: Women, Ecology and the Scientific Revolution*, London.

Michelet, J. (1860) *La Femme*, Paris.

—— (1861) *L'Amour*, 5th edn, Paris.

—— (1879) *The Bird*, London, 1981 (first English edition 1869, first French edition 1856).

—— (1957) *Joan of Arc*, trans. with an introduction by A. Guérard, Ann Arbor, Mich.

—— (1959–75) *Journal*, 4 vols, Paris.

—— (1973) *The People*, trans. with an introduction by J. McKay, Urbana.

Michelson, A. (1984) 'On the eve of the future: the reasonable facsimile and the philosophical toy', *October*, 29: 3–22.

Miller, K. (1985) *Doubles: Studies in Literary History*, Oxford.

Mitchell, H. (1979) 'The passions according to Adam Smith and Pierre-Jean-Georges Cabanis: two sciences of Man', *Bulletin of the Society for the Social History of Medicine*, no. 25: 20–7.

Monaco, P. (1976) *Cinema and Society: France and Germany during the Twenties*, New York, Oxford and Amsterdam.

Montesquieu, C. de S., Baron de la Brède et de (1721) *Persian Letters*, Harmondsworth 1973.

Morel, M.-F. (1977) 'Ville et campagne dans le discours médical sur la petite enfance au XVIIIᵉ siècle', *Annales: économies, sociétés, civilisations*, 32: 1007–24.

Moscucci, O. (1984) 'The science of woman: British gynaecology 1849–1890', D.Phil., University of Oxford.

Mount, F. (1982) *The Subversive Family: An Alternative History of Love and Marriage*, London.

Mozart, W.A. (1971) *Die Zauberflöte. Die Entführing aus dem Serail*, London.

Musselwhite, D. (1987) *Partings Welded Together: Politics and Desire in the Nineteenth Century Novel*, London.

Nead, L. (1988) *Myths of Sexuality: Representations of Women in Victorian Britain*, Oxford.

Nelson, D. (1974) 'Scientific management, systematic management, and labor, 1880–1915', *Business History Review*, 48: 479–500.

Nicolson, B. (1968) *Joseph Wright of Derby. Painter of Light*, 2 vols, London.

Nochlin, L. (1971) *Realism*, Harmondsworth.

(1986) 'Courbet's *L'origine du monde*: the origin without an original', *October*, no. 37: 77–86.

O'Flinn, P. (1983) 'Production and reproduction: the case of Frankenstein', *Literature and History*, 9: 194–213.

Ogawa, T. (ed.) (1981) *Public Health*, Tokyo.

Orr, L. (1976) *Jules Michelet: Nature, History and Language*, Ithaca, NY, and London.

Ortner, S.A. (1974) 'Is female to male as nature is to culture?', in M.Z. Rosaldo and L. Lamphere (eds) *Woman, Culture and Society*, Stanford, pp. 67–87.

Oxford Companion to English Literature, 4th edn, 1969.

Oxford English Dictionary and *Supplements* (1933 and 1972–86) 12 vols and 4 vols, Oxford.

Person, H.S. (1930) 'Scientific management', *Encyclopedia of the Social Sciences*, vols 13–14, pp. 603–8.

Petrelli, R. (1971) 'The regulation of French midwifery during the Ancien Régime', *Journal of the History of Medicine*, 26: 276–92.

Phillips, D.C. (1970) 'Organicism in the late nineteenth and early twentieth centuries', *Journal of the History of Ideas*, 31: 413–32.

Phillips, G.D. (1976) 'Fritz Lang on *Metropolis*', in T.R. Atkins (ed.) *Science Fiction Films*, New York, pp. 19–27.

Pinchbeck, I. (1930) *Women Workers and the Industrial Revolution 1750–1850*, London 1969.

Ploss, H.H., Bartels, M. and Bartels, P. (1885) *Woman: An Historical Gynaecological and Anthropological Compendium*, 3 vols, London 1935.

Pointon, M. (1986) 'Interior portraits: women, physiology and the male artist', *Feminist Review*, no. 22: 5–22.

Pollard, S. (1971) *The Idea of Progress. History and Sociology*, Harmondsworth.

Pomme, P. (1782) *Traité des affections vaporeuses des deux sexes*, Paris.

Poovey, M. (1980) 'My hideous progeny: Mary Shelley and the feminization of Romanticism', *Proceedings of the Modern Language Association*, 95: 332–47.

Porter, R. (1977) *The Making of Geology. Earth Science in Britain 1660–1815*, Cambridge.

Porter, R. (ed.) (1985) *Patients and Practitioners: Lay Perceptions of Medicine in Pre-Industrial Society*, Cambridge.

Porter, R. and Teich, M. (eds) (1981) *The Enlightenment in National Context*, Cambridge.

Pouchet, F.-A. (1863) *L'Univers*, Paris (2nd edn 1868).

Praz, M. (1970) *The Romantic Agony*, Oxford.

198   *Sexual visions*

The Precisionist View in American Art (1960) Minneapolis (exhibition catalogue).

Premuda, L. (1972) 'The waxwork in medicine', *Images*, no. 48: 17–24.

Prior, M. (ed.) (1985) *Women in English Society 1500–1800*, London.

Pugh, A.R. (1923) *Michelet and His Ideas on Social Reform*, New York.

Pyke, E.J. (1973) *A Biographical Dictionary of Wax Modellers*, Oxford; supplement, London 1981.

Rhode, E. (1966) *Tower of Babel: Speculations on the Cinema*, London.

Richardson, R. (1976) 'A dissection of the Anatomy Act', *Studies in Labour History*, no. 1: 1–13.

(1987) *Death, Dissection and the Destitute*, London.

Riley, J. (1987) *The Eighteenth-Century Campaign to Avoid Disease*, Basingstoke.

Roberts, H. (ed.) (1981) *Women, Health and Reproduction*, London.

Robinson, P. (1982) 'Virginie's fatal modesty: thoughts on Bernardin de Saint-Pierre and Rousseau', *British Journal for Eighteenth-Century Studies*, 5: 35–48.

Rosaldo, M.Z. and Lamphere, L. (eds) (1974) *Woman, Culture and Society*, Stanford.

Rose, H. and Rose, S. (1970) *Science and Society*, Harmondsworth.

Rosenblum, R. and Janson, H.W. (1984) *Art of the Nineteenth Century. Painting and Sculpture*, London.

Ross, E. (1976) 'Mandeville, Melon, and Voltaire: the origins of the luxury controversy in France', *Studies on Voltaire and the Eighteenth Century*, 155: 1897–912.

Rotberg, R.I. and Rabb, T.K. (eds) (1980) *Marriage and Fertility: Studies in Interdisciplinary History*, Princeton.

Rousseau, J.J. (1761) *Emile*, London 1974.

Rousseau, G.S. and Porter, R. (eds) (1980) *The Ferment of Knowledge: Studies in the Historiography of Eighteenth-Century Science*, Cambridge.

(1987) *Sexual Underworlds of the Enlightenment*, Manchester.

Roussel, P. (1784) *Système Physique et Moral de la Femme*, 2nd edn, Paris 1803.

Rudwick, M. (1972) *The Meaning of Fossils: Episodes in the History of Paleontology*, London.

Saccaro-Battisti, G. (1983) 'Changing metaphors of political structures', *Journal of the History of Ideas*, 44: 31–54.

Sade, D.A.F. de (1965) *Justine, Philosophy in the Bedroom and Other Writings*, New York.

(1976) *Juliette*, New York.

Schupbach, W. (1987) 'A select iconography of animal experiment', in

N. Rupke (ed.) *Vivisection in Historical Perspective*, London, pp. 340–60.

Schwartz, J. (1984) *The Sexual Politics of Jean-Jacques Rousseau*, Chicago.

Scott, J.W. (1986) 'Gender: a useful category for historical analysis', *American Historical Review*, 91: 1053–75.

La Sculpture Française au XIXe Siècle (1986) Paris (exhibition catalogue).

Sedgwick, E.K. (1981) 'The character in the veil: imagery of the surface in the Gothic novel', *Proceedings of the Modern Language Association*, 96: 255–70.

Sekora, J. (1977) *Luxury: The Concept in Western Thought. Eden to Smollett*, Baltimore.

Selzer, R. (1987) *Mortal Lessons: Notes on the Art of Surgery with a new preface*, New York.

Sena, J.F. (1970) *A Bibliography of Melancholy 1660–1800*, London.

Sewell, W.H. (1980) *Work and Revolution in France: The Language of Labor from the Old Régime to 1848*, Cambridge.

Seznec, J. (1977) 'Michelet in Germany: a journey in self-discovery', *History and Theory*, 16: 1–10.

Sharpe, J.A. (1980) *Defamation and Sexual Slander in Early Modern England: The Church Courts at York*, York.

Shaw, W.D. (1987) *The Lucid Veil: Poetic Truth in the Victorian Age*, London.

Shelley, M. (1986), *Frankenstein*, ed. M. Hindle, Harmondsworth.

Shesgreen, S. (ed.) (1973) *Engravings by Hogarth*, New York.

Shorter, E. (1976) *The Making of the Modern Family*, London.

(1983) *A History of Women's Bodies*, London.

Showalter, E. (1987) *The Female Malady: Women, Madness and English Culture 1830–1980*, London.

Shuttle, P. and Redgrove, P. (1978) *The Wise Wound: Menstruation and Everywoman*, London.

Simmel, G. (1903) 'The metropolis and mental life', in D. Levine (ed.) *Georg Simmel on Sociability and Social Forms*, Chicago 1971, pp. 324–39.

Simonton, D. (1988) 'Women's education and training in late eighteenth century England', PhD thesis, University of Essex.

Sitter, J.E. (1977) 'Mother, memory, muse and poetry after Pope', *English Literary History*, 44: 312–36.

Slochower, H. (1986) 'Psychoanalysis and art: their body language', *American Imago*, 43: 1–5.

Smellie, W. (1754) *A Sett of Anatomical Tables, with Explanations, and an Abridgement of the Practice of Midwifery, With a View to*

Illustrate a Treatise on that Subject, and Collection of Cases, London.

Smith, A.D. (1973) *The Concept of Social Change: A Critique of the Functionalist Theory of Social Change*, London.

Staum, M. (1980) *Cabanis: Enlightenment and Medical Philosophy in the French Revolution*, Princeton.

Steinberg, L. (1983) *The Sexuality of Christ in Renaissance Art and Modern Oblivion*, New York.

Stepan, N.L. (1986) 'Race and gender: the role of analogy in science', *Isis*, 77: 261–77.

Stoehr, T. (1978) *Hawthorne's Mad Scientists: Pseudoscience and Social Science in Nineteenth-Century Life and Letters*, Hamden, Conn.

Stone, L. (1977) *The Family, Sex and Marriage in England*, London.

Sussman, G. (1982) *Selling Mothers' Milk: The Wet-Nursing Business in France, 1715–1914*, Urbana.

Le Symbolisme En Europe (1975) Rotterdam and Paris (exhibition catalogue).

Taylor, F.W. (1911) *The Principles of Scientific Management*, New York and London.

—— (1913) *Die Grundsätze Wissenschaftlicher Betriebsführung*, Munich 1919.

Thieme, H.P. (1933) *Bibliographie de la Littérature Française de 1800 à 1930*, 3 vols, Paris.

Thomas, K. (1983) *Man and the Natural World: Changing Attitudes in England 1500–1800*, London.

Thompson, E.P. (1967) 'Time, work discipline and industrial capitalism', *Past and Present*, no. 38: 56–97.

Thompson, C.J.S. (1925) 'Anatomical mannikins', *Journal of Anatomy*, 59: 442–5.

Thornton, J.L. (1982) *Jan van Rymsdyk: Medical Artist of the Eighteenth Century*, Cambridge and New York.

Thornton, J.L. and Reeves, C. (1983) *Medical Book Illustration: A Short History*, Cambridge.

Tilly, L.A. and Scott, J.W. (1978) *Women, Work and Family*, New York.

Tomaselli, S. (1985) 'The Enlightenment debate on women', *History Workshop Journal*, no. 20: 101–24.

Tulloch, J. (1976) 'Genetic structuralism and the cinema: a look at Fritz Lang's *Metropolis*', *Australian Journal of Screen Theory*, 1: 3–50.

Turgenev, I. (1965) *Fathers and Sons*, Harmondsworth.

Vartanian, A. (1973) 'Man-machine from the Greeks to the computer', in P. Weiner (ed.) *Dictionary of the History of Ideas*, vol. 3, New York, pp. 131–46.

Veith, I. (1965) *Hysteria: The History of a Disease*, Chicago.

Versluysen, M. (1981) 'Midwives, medical men and "poor women labouring of child": lying-in hospitals in eighteenth-century London', in H. Roberts (ed.), *Women, Health and Reproduction*, London, pp. 18–49.

Viallaneix, P. (1971) *La Voie royale. Essai sur l'idée de peuple dans l'œuvre de Michelet*, Paris.

Villiers de l'Isle-Adam, P.-A. (1886) *L'Eve Future*, Paris 1960.

Virey, J.-J. (1820) 'Physiognomonie', *Dictionnaire des Sciences Médicales*, 42, Paris, pp. 188–228.

Waddell, M. (1986) 'Concepts of the inner world in George Eliot's work', *Journal of Child Psychotherapy*, 12: 109–24.

—— (1987) 'Experience and Identification in George Eliot's Novels', Occasional Papers no. 4, The Bridge Foundation for Psychotherapy and the Arts, Bristol.

Walters, M. (1978) *The Nude Male: A New Perspective*, Harmondsworth.

Warner, M. (1983) *Joan of Arc: The Image of Female Heroism*, Harmondsworth.

—— (1985) *Monuments and Maidens: The Allegory of the Female Form*, London.

Wattenmarker, R.J. (1975) *Puvis de Chavannes and the Modern Tradition*, Ontario (exhibition catalogue).

Webster, C. (1975) *The Great Instauration: Science, Medicine and Reform 1626–1660*, London.

—— (1982) *From Paracelsus to Newton; Magic and the Making of Modern Science*, Cambridge.

Weeks, J. (1981) *Sex, Politics and Society: The Regulation of Sexuality since 1800*, London.

—— (1985) *Sexuality and Its Discontents: Meanings, Myths and Modern Sexualities*, London.

Weideger, P. (1986) *History's Mistress: A New Interpretation of a 19th-Century Ethnographic Classic*, Harmondsworth.

Weiss, P. (1987) 'Rousseau, anti-feminism and women's nature', *Political Theory*, 15: 81–97.

Wellek, R. (1973) 'Realism in literature', in P. Weiner (ed.) *Dictionary of the History of Ideas*, New York, vol. 4, pp. 51–6.

Welsh, A. (1965) 'The allegory of truth in English fiction', *Victorian Studies*, 9: 7–28.

Whalley, J. (ed.) (1981) *Mirrors of Mortality: Studies in the Social History of Death*, London.

Willett, J. (1978) *The New Sobriety 1917–33: Art and Politics in the Weimar Period*, London.

Williams, R. (1983) *Keywords: A Vocabulary of Culture and Society*, revised and expanded edition, London.

Williams, R. (1975) *The Country and the City*, St Albans.

Williamson, J. (1978) *Decoding Advertisements: Ideology and Meaning in Advertising*, London.

Wilson, E. (1953), *To the Finland Station: A Study in the Writing and Acting of History*, New York.

Wolf-Heidegger, G. and Cetto, A.M. (1967) *Die Anatomische Sektion in Bildlicher Darstellung*, Basle and New York.

Wollstonecraft, M. (1792) *A Vindication of the Rights of Woman*, Harmondsworth 1975.

World Medicine (various dates) Sutton, Surrey.

Wornum, R. (ed.) (1848) *Lectures on Painting by the Royal Academicians: Barry, Opie and Fuseli*, London.

Wright, P. and Treacher, A. (eds) (1982) *The Problem of Medical Knowledge: Examining the Social Construction of Medicine*, Edinburgh.

Young, R. (1985) *Darwin's Metaphor: Nature's Place in Victorian Culture*, Cambridge.

Zeldin, T. (1973–7) *France 1848–1945*, 2 vols, Oxford.

Index